Precedent in the United States Supreme Court

IUS GENTIUM

COMPARATIVE PERSPECTIVES ON LAW AND JUSTICE

VOLUME 33

For further volumes:
http://www.springer.com/series/7888

Christopher J. Peters
Editor

Precedent in the United States Supreme Court

Springer

Editor
Christopher J. Peters
School of Law
University of Baltimore
Baltimore, MD, USA

ISSN 1534-6781 ISSN 2214-9902 (electronic)
ISBN 978-94-007-7950-1 ISBN 978-94-007-7951-8 (eBook)
DOI 10.1007/978-94-007-7951-8
Springer Dordrecht Heidelberg New York London

Library of Congress Control Number: 2013958448

Printed on acid-free paper

Springer is part of Springer Science+Business Media (www.springer.com)

Contents

Contributors

Larry Alexander School of Law, University of San Diego, San Diego, CA, USA

Neal Devins School of Law, College of William & Mary, Williamsburg, VA, USA

Deborah Hellman School of Law, University of Virginia, Charlottesville, VA, USA

Randy J. Kozel Law School, University of Notre Dame, Notre Dame, IN, USA

Chad M. Oldfather Law School, Marquette University, Milwaukee, WI, USA

Christopher J. Peters School of Law, University of Baltimore, Baltimore, MD, USA

Frederick Schauer School of Law, University of Virginia, Charlottesville, VA, USA

Colin Starger School of Law, University of Baltimore, Baltimore, MD, USA

Maxwell L. Stearns Francis King Carey School of Law, University of Maryland, Baltimore, MD, USA

Chapter 1
Introduction

Christopher J. Peters

The contributions to this volume address, from a variety of perspectives, the topic of the United States Supreme Court's faithfulness, or lack thereof, to its own prior decisions. That topic is perennially a "hot" one in American law and legal academia, and periodically in American politics as well. It is inevitable that whenever a new prospective Justice is nominated to serve on the Court, he or she will be grilled extensively by senators about his or her views on stare decisis.[1]

This sometimes-obsessive American focus on stare decisis owes much to the Court's controversial 1973 decision *Roe v. Wade*,[2] which recognized a constitutional right to abortion and, in so doing, triggered a political and legal reaction that continues to this day. At least since Ronald Reagan in 1980, Republican presidential candidates routinely have pledged, overtly or obliquely, to appoint Justices who will vote to overturn *Roe*, while their Democratic counterparts have promised to nominate Justices who will uphold that decision. Requirements of judicial ethics prohibit judges from announcing ahead of time how they are likely to rule in some future case, so questioning in Court nomination hearings often employs the general issue of stare decisis as a proxy for the specific question of whether the nominee will vote to affirm or to overrule *Roe* (and other politically progressive Court decisions from the 1960s and 1970s).

For its part, the contemporary Court has itself confronted the question of stare decisis in a number of cases challenging *Roe* and other progressive decisions. Sometimes the result has been respectful of precedent (and thus frustrating for political conservatives). For example, the Court famously (or infamously, depending on one's perspective) declined to overrule *Roe* in 1992's *Planned*

[1] From the Latin *stare decisis et non quieta movere* ("to stand by things decided, and not to disturb settled points").

[2] 410 U.S. 113 (1973).

C.J. Peters (✉)
School of Law, University of Baltimore, 1420 North Charles St., Baltimore, MD 21201, USA
e-mail: cpeters@ubalt.edu

C.J. Peters (ed.), *Precedent in the United States Supreme Court*, Ius Gentium: Comparative Perspectives on Law and Justice 33, DOI 10.1007/978-94-007-7951-8_1,

Parenthood v. Casey[3]—a decision much discussed in this volume—despite the recent accession to the Court of a majority of Republican-appointed Justices. And the Republican-dominated Court subsequently reaffirmed the contested 1966 decision *Miranda v. Arizona*,[4] which required that criminal defendants be informed of their Fifth Amendment "right to remain silent" in order for confessions to be admissible against them.[5]

But the recent Court has not always been so apparently deferential to the norm of stare decisis. In some other criminal-procedure contexts, the Court has overturned its own relatively recent pro-defendant rulings.[6] The Court also has overruled politically progressive decisions in areas such as religious freedom and, perhaps most controversially, campaign-finance legislation.[7] And, as I and others have documented (see Friedman 2010; Peters 2008), the current Roberts Court has been especially slippery about using "stealth overrulings" (or "underrulings") to gut precedents without formally rejecting them.

In the American legal academy, too, much recent discussion of stare decisis has its roots in *Roe*. The contemporary rise of originalism as a prominent methodology of constitutional interpretation can be traced, as an historical matter, to conservative scholars' reaction during the 1970s and 1980s to *Roe* and other seemingly nonoriginalist decisions; and with modern originalism has come a body of theory challenging the legitimacy of stare decisis in constitutional cases.[8] This challenge has spurred attempts by progressive defenders of these decisions to articulate justifications for precedent-following.[9]

Causally speaking, then, American debates about the Court's use of precedent largely stem from, and tend to be overshadowed by, the political dynamics of *Roe* and other contested progressive rulings. But it would be a mistake to assume that the topic is irredeemably infused with partisan politics, or that it has only parochial significance. Whether and to what extent the Court (a) does and (b) should adhere to its own prior decisions are questions that have broad

[3] Planned Parenthood of Se. Pa. v. Casey, 505 U.S. 833 (1992).

[4] 384 U.S. 436 (1966).

[5] See Dickerson v. United States, 530 U.S. 428 (2000).

[6] See, for example, Payne v. Tennessee, 501 U.S. 808 (1991) (overruling Booth v. Maryland, 482 U.S. 496 (1987), and South Carolina v. Gathers, 490 U.S. 805 (1989), to hold that juries may constitutionally consider victim-impact evidence). For an extensive discussion of *Payne*, see Colin Starger's contribution to this volume (Chap. 2).

[7] See Agostini v. Felton, 521 U.S. 203 (1997) (overruling Aguilar v. Felton, 473 U.S. 402 (1985), to hold that, with some restrictions, public schools may pay public schoolteachers to teach in private religious schools); Citizens United v. Federal Election Comm'n, 558 U.S. 310, 130 S. Ct. 876 (2010) (overruling overruling Austin v. Michigan Chamber of Commerce, 494 U.S. 652 (1990), and McConnell v. Federal Election Comm'n, 540 U.S. 93 (2003), to hold that legislative restrictions on election-related spending by corporations violate the First Amendment).

[8] On originalism as a reaction to *Roe* and other Warren Court and early Burger Court decisions, see my discussion in Chap. 10, Sect. 10.2.2. For a description of originalists' "special difficulty" with constitutional stare decisis more generally, see Sects. 10.1 and 10.2 of that chapter.

[9] Probably the most prominent example is the work of Michael Gerhardt (e.g., 2011).

implications for general jurisprudence and for democratic and constitutional theory, implications that potentially echo well beyond the confines of American law and politics.

From the perspective of general jurisprudence or legal philosophy, the Court's practices regarding stare decisis invoke persistent questions about the relationship between general legal rules on the one hand and, on the other, correct results in particular cases. Stare decisis purports to require that the Court adhere, at least presumptively, to prior decisions it now believes to be incorrect. But what justification might (could) the Court have for doing that—for reaching the wrong result just because some prior iteration of itself thought that result was the right one? The problem is a version of the familiar tension between, as Justice Louis Brandeis influentially put it, the value of law that is "settled" and the value of law that is "settled right."[10]

Larry Alexander, in Chap. 3 of this volume, associates this problem with circumstances involving "legal transitions," that is, attempts to replace suboptimal legal rules or systems of rules with more-optimal ones. Such problems of transition are endemic in primarily common-law traditions like those in Britain, the United States, and other former British colonies, in which a significant driver of legal development is case-by-case decisionmaking by courts. But these questions are hardly unique to common-law systems. Indeed, the underlying clash between general rules and particularized justice extends well beyond contexts that can accurately be said to involve legal transitions. A version of it crops up, not just when some authoritative body like the Supreme Court must determine whether to formally and overtly overrule one of its precedents, but anytime a judge or other legal official must decide—perhaps surreptitiously—whether to obey or enforce a valid legal rule or command she believes to be wrong. In this respect, the problem of precedent is closely related to the profound mystery of legal authority, of whether (and when, and why) those subject to the law ever have reason to obey it when they think it will produce injustice.[11]

As a matter of constitutional and democratic theory, the Court's practices of precedent touch on fundamental issues of separation of powers and democratic legitimacy. American-style judicial review famously presents what Alexander Bickel (1986, 16) called the "counter-majoritarian difficulty": It begs the question why an elite group of nonelected, life-tenured Justices, supposedly acting in the name of long-dead constitutional Framers, should be given the power to override the products of the majoritarian political process. Many, perhaps most, plausible answers to this question depend at least in part on the idea that the Court will act in

---

[10] Burnet v. Coronado Oil & Gas Co., 285 U.S. 393, 406 (1932) (Brandeis, J., dissenting) ("Stare decisis is usually the wise policy, because in most matters it is more important that the applicable rule of law be settled than that it be settled right."). Brandeis's famous aphorism is referenced by several contributors to this volume (see Colin Starger's Chap. 2 and Randy Kozel's Chap. 9), and his influential *Coronado Oil* dissent is discussed at length by Starger (see Chap. 2, Sect. 2.2).

[11] For a general discussion of this problem, see Peters (2011, 1–12, 33–67).

a way that might be called *principled*[12]—that it will not decide based solely or primarily on the personal moral or political views of a majority of the Justices. From one point of view, a willingness by the Court to adhere to past decisions, despite the current view of most Justices that those decisions are wrong, is consistent with, even constitutive of, this element of principle, while a willingness to overturn such decisions is corrosive of it.[13] To others, however, the Court's failure to interpret the Constitution correctly in the first place represents the crisis of principle, one that can be resolved only by overruling the offending precedent to correct the error.[14] Add to this the fact that the Court's constitutional decisions, unlike its rulings in other legal contexts, cannot be reversed by ordinary legislation and thus will stand—erroneous or not—forever, unless the Constitution is amended (an exceedingly difficult process and thus an exceedingly rare occurrence) or the Court itself overturns them.

These important issues of legal philosophy and democratic theory transcend the nakedly political underpinnings of American debates about stare decisis, enlarging the sphere of their relevance to encompass other legal systems and cultures. Participants in any legal system that allocates substantial authority to the process of case-by-case court decisionmaking should care about whether, when, and why those courts ought to remain faithful to their prior resolutions of similar issues. Even a purely code-driven civil-law culture (a vanishing breed, if ever it existed at all) has adopted a position in normative debates about the propriety of stare decisis—a position denying any judicial obligation to adhere to past decisions. Certainly the normative dynamics of stare decisis are salient in common-law or hybrid systems that rely on courts to do much of the heavy legal lifting.

Moreover, with the international proliferation of bills of rights and constitutional judicial review that echo the American versions in many respects, more and more legal cultures will need to engage with norms of constitutional adjudication, including those governing the durability of judicial constitutional decisions. The U.S. Supreme Court, and the legal and academic professionals who follow it, have been grappling with these issues now for some two centuries. It hardly seems jingoistic to suggest that the participants in other, newer constitutional systems might benefit from the experiences and answers the Court and its observers have to offer, even if the primary benefit turns out to be one of negative example.

My hope as editor of this volume, then, is that it will prove interesting, perhaps even useful, to audiences both in the United States and from other legal systems. (This is the notion behind the book's publication as part of the *Ius Gentium* series.) The volume arose from a live symposium held at the University of Baltimore School of Law in March 2012. Each participant in that symposium has expanded his or her remarks into a chapter in this book, and Randy Kozel, who did not

---

[12] See, for example, Wechsler (1959).

[13] This sort of reasoning was a central element of the controversial justification of precedent-following offered by several Justices in *Planned Parenthood v. Casey*. See 505 U.S. at 864–69 (plurality opinion of Justices Kennedy, O'Connor, and Souter).

[14] This is the position taken by many constitutional originalists (see my discussion in Chap. 10). It also seems to describe the view expressed by Larry Alexander in Chap. 3.

participate in the symposium, also has added a chapter (Chap. 9). In selecting the contributors, I looked first for scholars who I knew would write something original and provocative and write it well. I looked also for a diversity of viewpoints, methodological approaches, and levels of seniority among the contributors. In most cases the authors came first, their particular topics later: I allowed each author to choose what exactly he or she would write about, providing only general guidance where it was requested. I hoped for a series of essays that would fit well together yet stand each on its own as a meaningful contribution to our understanding of the Court's relationship to precedent. I think that is what I got, although of course the reader will have to judge for herself.

The essays begin with Colin Starger's entry in Chap. 2, which sets the stage for what follows by exploring the Court's own "precedent about precedent"—the development of its doctrine regarding whether and when it will adhere to its prior constitutional decisions.[15] Starger explains that, somewhat surprisingly, the Court did not claim to have any doctrine of stare decisis at all for its first twelve or thirteen decades—more than half its history. Prior to the early twentieth century, the Court referred to stare decisis as simply a maxim of good judicial practice rather than something on the order of a presumptively binding legal rule. Using graphical "opinion maps," Starger traces the Court's modern doctrinal approach to constitutional stare decisis back to Justice Brandeis's often-cited dissenting opinion in the 1932 *Burnet v. Coronado Oil* case,[16] in which Brandeis meticulously catalogued previous instances of constitutional overrulings, thus transforming stare decisis from a commonsense question of wise practice to a doctrine-driven matter of legal rules. Starger then illustrates how competing judicial attitudes toward constitutional stare decisis—a "weak" tradition, allowing for overruling solely or primarily on grounds of disagreement with the reasoning of the precedent case, and a "strong" tradition, purporting to require some good independent reason for overruling—each derive rhetorical force from Brandeis's *Coronado Oil* opinion. And while most observers look to the plurality opinion in 1992's *Planned Parenthood v. Casey* as the

[15] This phrasing of Starger's—"precedent about precedent"—may itself become a fixture of the Court's stare decisis doctrine. In April 2013, Starger posted an abstract of what is now his Chap. 2 on SSRN (www.ssrn.com), an online scholarship database popular with American law professors. In his abstract, Starger referenced *Payne v. Tennessee*—a centerpiece of his analysis—and asked, "does the Court's contemporary 'precedent about precedent' have genuine precedential value?" Two months later, in June 2013, near the close of its Term, the Supreme Court decided *Alleyne v. United States*, 133 S. Ct. 2151, which overruled a 2002 decision in holding that a fact that increases a defendant's mandatory minimum sentence is an element of the crime that must be proven to a jury. In dissent, Justice Samuel Alito cited *Payne* several times and closed his opinion with the following sentence: "The Court's decision creates a precedent about precedent that may have greater precedential effect than the dubious decisions on which it relies." 133 S. Ct. at 2173 (Alito, J., dissenting). (Justice Sonia Sotomayor liked this "precedent about precedent" trope so much—though she didn't think much of Alito's deployment of it—that she repeated it in her *Alleyne* concurrence when replying to Alito's arguments. 133 S. Ct. at 2166 (Sotomayor, J., concurring).) It's hard to avoid the comforting conclusion that (at least some) Supreme Court Justices really do pay attention to (at least some) legal scholarship after all.

[16] 285 U.S. at 405 (Brandeis, J., dissenting).

definitive contemporary exploration of stare decisis by the Justices themselves, Starger identifies opposing opinions in a lesser-known case decided a year earlier, *Payne v. Tennessee*,[17] as the source of many of the arguments wielded by adherents of both the weak and the strong traditions on the recent and current Court.

Starger concludes with the suggestion that the function of the Court's "precedent about precedent" is more rhetorical than constraining. Justices—sometimes even the same Justice in different cases—seem to adopt the weak or strong approaches to stare decisis in an unprincipled, results-driven manner. Starger does not find this particularly troubling: He thinks consistency in even a single Justice's stare decisis jurisprudence is too much to expect, given the need to balance continuity with change on a case-by-case basis. This (admittedly tentative) position is questionable; to acknowledge that the force of precedent should vary with context is not to endorse a general approach to stare decisis that morphs to suit a Justice's preferred substantive results.

Nonetheless, in surveying the Court's own professed doctrine of constitutional stare decisis—and exposing the soft spots and fissures in that doctrine—Starger's analysis lays a useful foundation for both the normatively and the descriptively focused chapters that comprise the remainder of the book. Chapters 3 and 4 directly confront some of the major normative issues. In Chap. 3, Larry Alexander mounts a forceful (though somewhat qualified) normative attack on stare decisis in constitutional cases. Alexander begins with the (admittedly debatable) premise that a Justice ought not disobey the Constitution itself solely on the ground that she believes implementing the Constitution will produce a morally incorrect or suboptimal result. Assuming this is so, he asks, how could it then be the case that a Justice should obey prior Court decisions that in effect disobey the Constitution by incorrectly interpreting it? One common answer is that the Court's interpretations of the (written) Constitution are, or can become, themselves part of the (legally binding) Constitution, by virtue of widespread and sustained public acceptance of those interpretations. If this is so, then by obeying an earlier Court decision that meets the relevant criteria of public acceptance—however erroneous it may be as an interpretation of the previously existing Constitution—a subsequent Court is in fact obeying the Constitution as it now exists. Alexander is skeptical of this answer, however, because it seems to rely on public acceptance of an erroneous Court interpretation *with knowledge that the interpretation is erroneous*, a criterion Alexander thinks rarely will be satisfied.

A second common answer is that overruling (some) erroneous constitutional precedents would upset the expectations of those who have reasonably relied on those precedents, with possibly disastrous results. (Alexander posits the example of the *Legal Tender Cases*, which held in 1871, arguably incorrectly, that the Constitution permits the government to issue paper money.[18] Imagine a Court decision overturning that precedent more than 100 years later.) Alexander doubts that obeying an erroneous precedent to avoid disastrous consequences is different

[17] 501 U.S. 808 (1991).

[18] 79 U.S. 457 (1871).

in kind from disobeying the Constitution itself to avoid an unjust or otherwise "infelicitous" result. And he argues that even if the fact of reliance on an erroneous precedent makes a sufficient moral difference, the Court could minimize or eliminate the harm to reliance interests by simply delaying the implementation of its overruling decision for long enough to allow the system to adjust (e.g., by weaning itself off paper money) or, more likely, to allow for a formal constitutional amendment pursuant to Article V to ratify the otherwise erroneous precedent. Only if the uncertainty caused even by a delayed overruling would be sufficiently catastrophic, Alexander suggests, does the Court have good reason to adhere to an erroneous precedent.

Alexander then turns his attention to the arguments against overruling made by the plurality in *Planned Parenthood v. Casey*, focusing in particular on the two most controversial of those arguments. "[P]eople have organized intimate relationships and made choices that define their views of themselves and their places in society, in reliance on the availability of abortion," the *Casey* plurality asserted,[19] and overruling *Roe* would harm these reliance interests. But Alexander does not think this sort of "reliance" should be taken seriously, particularly when pitted against the importance of interpreting the Constitution correctly. Nor does he agree with the *Casey* plurality's suggestion that harm to the Court's own authority, which might flow from the public's perception of too-frequent overrulings, is sufficiently weighty to overcome the harm caused be erroneous constitutional interpretations.[20]

Alexander's arguments might be challenged on a number of points. It is not self-evident, for example, that erroneous Court interpretations of the Constitution must be understood by the public to be erroneous (and be accepted anyway) in order to become authoritative. Perhaps the public (or the body of legal officials—whichever group within American society has the authority to determine what counts as law) has implicitly authorized the Court to render authoritative constitutional decisions even if those decisions are, as an interpretive matter, incorrect, so long as the decisions meet certain other criteria—substantive acceptability to a large majority of the public over time, for example. If this is the case, then subsequent Courts would have reason to obey erroneous prior interpretations that meet the public-acceptance test, even if the public did not recognize those interpretations as erroneous.

Alexander also downplays the possible significance, to normative evaluations of stare decisis, of uncertainty and disagreement about constitutional interpretation. It is this line of argument that Deborah Hellman takes up in Chap. 4. Hellman contends, against conventional wisdom in legal-philosophy circles, that judges have *epistemic* reasons to adhere to precedent—reasons to follow a precedent on the basis that doing so is more likely than not doing so to generate a correct decision. Most theorists have rejected epistemic justifications of stare decisis on one or both of two grounds. The first has to do with the conceptual mechanics of epistemic authority. Suppose a judge believes that the correct result in the case she must decide is *X*. But suppose she is faced with an on-point precedent that clearly dictates a different

[19] 505 U.S. at 856.

[20] See 505 U.S. at 861–69.

result, *Y*. And suppose she believes that the judge that decided the on-point precedent is a better (more accurate) decisionmaker than she is. (Imagine an inexperienced jurist faced with a precedent decided by Holmes or Cardozo.) The judge may then have reason to change her mind and reach result *Y* rather than result *X* in her case. The reason would be that someone she recognizes as an epistemic authority—the *éminence grise* who decided the precedent case—has declared *Y* to be the correct result. In this scenario, precedent has made a difference—but in a persuasive way, not in an authoritative one. The judge has reached a result consistent with the precedent, not because she believes she must follow the precedent despite her disagreement with it, but because (thanks to her respect for the wisdom of the precedential judge) she no longer disagrees with it. The judge has not really *obeyed* the precedent at all; and thus the principle of stare decisis itself is doing no real work.

Hellman argues, however, that a judge may have epistemic reasons to *act* in obedience to a precedent, even if she lacks reason (at least decisive reason) to *believe* the precedent is correct. The legal system of which the judge is a part may conclude that judges are more likely, on the whole, to make correct decisions by following precedent than by relying solely on their own judgment, and it may establish a rule or other norm of precedent-following as a result. An individual judge may then have reasons (of professional ethics or separation of powers) to follow the rule dictated by her legal system and thus obey a precedent with which she disagrees in substance. Indeed a judge's recognition of her own fallibility may give her reason to obey a precedent with which she disagrees, even absent a systemic rule requiring her to do so. These kinds of reason would be *epistemic* reasons, in the sense that they are based on the premise that judges are more likely to reach correct results by following precedent than by not doing so.

Hellman also takes issue with the second common objection to epistemic justifications of stare decisis, which is in essence a normative one. Even if epistemic reasons to follow precedent can exist as a conceptual matter (the objection goes), there is no good cause to think that precedents actually *are* more likely to be correct than the unfettered judgment of the individual judge. After all, precedential cases were themselves decided by (fallible human) judges; and often they were decided many years ago, under moral assumptions (about gender roles, for instance, or racial hierarchy) that now seem benighted. Why should the present-day judge subordinate her own best judgment to that of some earlier, morally backward court?

Hellman's answer to this challenge is ingenious and largely original. The primary epistemic value of precedent, she suggests, lies not in the supposed epistemic authority of the precedential decisions themselves, but rather in the checking function served by the *process* of engaging with precedent. A presumptive norm of precedent-following counterbalances the natural human tendency toward overconfidence by requiring judges to take opposing arguments (those of the precedential courts) seriously and to articulate good reasons for their disagreement with those arguments. Judges are more likely to generate correct results under a norm of stare decisis, not because the precedents themselves are likely to be correct, but because the exercise of grappling with the precedents is likely to enhance the quality of judges' decision-making. More conventionally (and more tentatively), Hellman also suggests that the precedents themselves *are* relatively likely to be correct—not because the judges that decided them are smarter than subsequent judges, but rather because precedents tend to be the products of a gradual, collective, Burkean, common-law process of testing and refinement over time.

Hellman thus offers the framework of a response to Alexander's skepticism about stare decisis. Alexander looks in vain for a convincing reason to prefer wrongly-decided precedents over correct interpretations of the Constitution. But Hellman points out that which constitutional interpretations are correct and which are not, like most issues judges face, is almost always a matter of uncertainty and contestation. Deference to precedent might be a reasonable response, at a systemic level and perhaps on an individual level, to these persistent facts of uncertainty and disagreement.

Hellman's defense of stare decisis is hardly unassailable, of course. On the conceptual level, the strength and, ultimately, the existence of an epistemic reason to follow precedent is vulnerable to the very problem of disagreement that grounds that reason in the first place. A judge who disagrees strongly with the merits of a precedent has, on that basis, grounds to doubt the epistemic value of the precedent; strong enough disagreement might justify (or seem to justify) rejecting the precedent altogether. (This problem affects epistemic justifications of authority more generally, and indeed I deploy it in Chap. 10 as part of my attack on what I call "Moral Guidance" accounts of constitutional authority.)[21]

On the normative level, it isn't clear how squarely Hellman's defense fits the unusual context of constitutional decisionmaking by the Supreme Court. Supreme Court Justices tend to arrive on the Court with reasonably well-formed notions about the law, and the constitutional cases they decide tend to carry a strong political valence. Against this backdrop, is it realistic to think that the requirement of engaging with precedent often will trigger the kind of judicial self-reflection and second-guessing that can materially improve the Court's decisionmaking? Or are Justices more likely to pay rhetorical lip service to stare decisis while actually deciding cases on ideological grounds, as Starger suggests in Chap. 2 (echoed by Neal Devins in Chap. 6 and Frederick Schauer in Chap. 7)? Nor is it obvious that Hellman's quasi-Burkean "many minds" argument for the merits of precedent carries the same force when applied to the relatively small sample size of the Court's constitutional case law.

While neither Alexander's nor Hellman's arguments is airtight, however—as if any position on this nuanced and contentious question could be—their chapters helpfully join, and frame, the overarching normative debate about the propriety of stare decisis in the Court's practice. In Chap. 5, Maxwell Stearns brings to that debate a straightforward descriptive insight: The easier it is to *create* a precedent, the easier it will be to *overrule* that precedent. Stearns takes issue with the conventional wisdom among many American public-law scholars that the Court's justiciability doctrines—"standing" requirements and similar limitations on who may bring a constitutional challenge and when the challenge may be brought—are

[21] See Chap. 10, Sect. 10.7.3.

indefensible impediments to the creation of valuable constitutional precedents. Justiciability requirements limit litigants' ability to "time" constitutional challenges to coincide with sympathetic membership on the Court or other favorable conditions. Stearns points out, however, that if these litigation-timing impediments were relaxed, the resulting precedents would become less valuable, as they would themselves be more vulnerable to subsequent carefully timed challenges aimed at overruling them. Litigants bringing constitutional claims would get favorable rulings at a lower cost, but those rulings would in effect be worth less. Stearns thus suggests that justiciability barriers may actually be a good thing for litigants seeking valuable constitutional precedents. And he goes a step further, proposing that the Court itself should be more reluctant to overrule precedents that were, for justiciability reasons, more difficult to obtain.

Stearns might be stretching an "is" into an "ought" with this final suggestion. The fact that the durability of precedent depends to some extent on the sturdiness of justiciability barriers as a *descriptive* matter does not seem to imply any particular approach to stare decisis as a *normative* matter. Stearns's analysis certainly might give us (normative) reason to oppose the relaxation of justiciability doctrines: If we want Court decisions to be relatively durable, we ought to continue making it difficult to "time" those decisions to the happenstance of an ideologically favorable Court. (Of course, some litigants might prefer the inverse tradeoff: an easier-to-obtain decision that also is shorter-lived.) But it's far from clear that Stearns's analysis identifies a (normative) reason for the Court itself to respect precedent. After all, the Court's treating the difficulty of obtaining a precedent as a reason not to overrule it would seem to produce a windfall for the litigants who obtained that precedent: They would be getting the benefit of both the (new) justiciability barriers to the Court's reconsideration of the precedent and the (original) justiciability barriers to getting the precedent in the first place. Shouldn't the former be enough?

Indeed, one might reasonably derive a very different normative message from Stearns's penetrating descriptive analysis. If justiciability requirements make it hard to obtain a Court decision—including a decision overruling a prior decision—what then is the necessity of additional barriers to overruling? Perhaps the practical obstacles to overruling (including the difficulty, given justiciability doctrines, of timing a challenge to coincide with an ideologically sympathetic Court) are sufficient to foster consistency, predictability, and other rule-of-law values without a supplementary norm of stare decisis.[22]

---

[22] Of course, a cynic might respond that a Court (or individual Justice) that is inclined to ignore stare decisis to achieve results it desires will also be inclined to ignore justiciability barriers to those results. Such a Court or Justice would find ways around justiciability requirements in order to decide cases involving challenges to disfavored prior decisions, and then would find ways around stare decisis norms in order to overturn those decisions. Justiciability doctrines would not be sufficient to protect rule-of-law values against this kind of results-driven behavior; but neither would a stare decisis norm. It may nonetheless be the case, however, that other practical obstacles to overruling—including the fact of relatively infrequent turnover in the Court's membership—would continue to serve the rule-of-law values even in the face of purely results-driven behavior by members of the Court.

Stearns's analysis thus provides a useful segue to the chapters that follow. His empirical focus on the process of constitutional litigation writ large presages both Neal Devins's essay in Chap. 6, which examines the relationship between ideological coherence on the Court and respect for stare decisis, and Frederick Schauer's contribution in Chap. 7, which suggests that the realities of adjudication inevitably obscure the Court's actual practices regarding stare decisis. And by placing stare decisis within a larger context that also features other prominent adjudicative norms, Stearns foreshadows the themes of Chaps. 8, 9, and 10, each of which engages the relationship between the Court's approach to stare decisis and its methodologies of constitutional interpretation.

In Chap. 6, Devins uses the insights of social psychology and the evidence of history to support the somewhat intuitive propositions that "coherent" Supreme Courts—those featuring a majority of Justices who agree on crucial issues—are far more likely to overrule precedents, and to aggressively attempt to create broad precedents, than are "incoherent" Courts. Devins explains the social-psychology dynamics that contribute to the formation (or absence) of coherent Court majorities. He then surveys three historical periods to illustrate the divergent behavior of coherent versus incoherent Courts. The post-1936 New Deal Court (1937–1953), Devins shows us, was highly coherent on most issues (thanks to a flurry of appointments by Franklin Delano Roosevelt) and thus ambitious in both overturning precedent and establishing broad holdings intended to bind future Courts. The Warren Court (1953–1968) was mostly incoherent and cautious before 1962, dominated (at least in national-security cases) by the centrist Justices Felix Frankfurter and John Marshall Harlan II, but became coherent thereafter with the appointments of Justices Arthur Goldberg (replaced a few years later by Abe Fortas) and Thurgood Marshall, generating most of its still-influential decisions during that period. In contrast, the Rehnquist Court (1986–2005) was incoherent on most issues, controlled (like the early Warren Court) by two centrist swing Justices (Sandra Day O'Connor and Anthony Kennedy). This incoherence helps explain the Rehnquist Court's failure, previously discussed, to overrule *Roe* and *Miranda*, and its relatively minimalist rulings on religious freedom, affirmative action, and other controversial topics. Finally, Devins offers a preliminary assessment of the Roberts Court (2005–present) as similarly incoherent and thus for the most part similarly cautious and modest.

On its surface, Devins's study suggests that stare decisis exerts very little actual normative constraint on the Court. If the Justices really felt constrained by precedent, after all, their patterns of overruling would not seem to depend so heavily on extraneous factors such as substantive ideological coherence among the Court's membership. Digging a little deeper, however, reveals some interesting nuance in the descriptive conclusions one might draw from Devins's essay. Incoherent Courts seldom directly overrule precedent; but, as Devins notes, they sometimes engage in "stealth overrulings," that is, decisions that contradict the logic or reasoning of a precedent or severely restrict its scope without formally overruling that precedent.[23]

[23] Devins cites Friedman (2010) and Peters (2008), which (as mentioned above) both explore this phenomenon of "stealth overruling" or "underruling."

This suggests at least that stare decisis exerts a sort of *in terrorem* influence on the Justices, causing them to be wary of being *seen* to overrule precedents (if perhaps not of actually overruling them). And Devins's analysis reveals an intriguing *ex ante* attitude toward the effects of precedent on the part of both coherent and incoherent Courts. Coherent Courts attempt to establish broadly binding precedents; incoherent Courts avoid doing so by rendering minimalist decisions. A Court that believed stare decisis to be unconstraining would hardly consider the potential precedential effects of its own rulings on future Courts.

One comes away from Devins's essay, then, with a sense that most Justices' (or at least the typical Justice's) normative attitudes toward precedent are complex and ambivalent. Frederick Schauer's contribution in Chap. 7 is unlikely to dispel this impression. Schauer is interested in whether we can reliably know, as a descriptive matter, just what the Justices' normative attitudes toward precedent really are. Considerable political-science research over the past two decades suggests that the Court is driven primarily by results-oriented ideology, by social-psychology dynamics (like those explained by Devins), or by some similar mélange of "attitudinal" factors, and virtually not at all by allegiance to stare decisis. Schauer points out, however, that these studies all share a fundamental weakness: They examine only the cases the Court actually decides, which, it turns out, are unlikely to be cases in which a stare decisis norm might matter. If it were true that the Court actually adhered to stare decisis (and if this adherence were generally known), then cases challenging precedents would rarely come before the Court: Thanks to the "selection effect," disputants would not think it worthwhile to bring such presumptively hopeless cases in the first place, or (more rarely) they would bring them unsuccessfully and not appeal them, or (more rarely still) they would appeal them but not seek ultimate review by the Court. The cases that made it to the Court, then, would almost exclusively be close cases—cases in which there is no on-point precedent, or in which the applicable precedents cut in opposite directions. And these are precisely the kinds of cases in which a stare decisis norm, if it existed, would have the least effect (and thus would not be revealed in empirical studies).

Schauer thus concludes that if there is a meaningful stare decisis norm on the Court, it would not show up in empirical research; or, to put it another way, the political-science consensus that there is no such norm cannot be trusted. And Schauer notes a further complexity: The selection effect he discusses itself relies on the existence of information about the Court's attitudes toward stare decisis. If the selection effect is to winnow away cases governed by on-point precedents, then litigants, their lawyers, and lower-court judges must believe that the Court is in fact unlikely to overturn those precedents. But, since empirical research seems incapable of revealing whether the Court actually respects stare decisis, these participants (and thus the selection effect) are operating without good information about the likely consequences of their decisions. The phenomenon Schauer portrays approaches the status of paradox: The selection effect renders it impossible to know whether the Court adheres to stare decisis, but that same selection effect depends for its operation on a widespread belief that the Court adheres to stare decisis.

Schauer concludes by suggesting a way around the near-paradox: The Court could deliberately signal its respect for stare decisis, by (for example) frequently accepting cases that challenge precedents with which a majority of the Court is known to disagree and then affirming those precedents. Schauer asserts, however, that the Court has not done this and seems unlikely to—a conspicuous failure that, like the celebrated dog that didn't bark, itself strongly implies that the Court doesn't really respect stare decisis after all.

Schauer's argument from the selection effect is a powerful rejoinder to the too-easy conclusions of many academics (mostly, but not exclusively, political scientists) that the Court's invocation of stare decisis is nothing but a smokescreen for results-oriented decisionmaking. I suspect, though, that there is more (and more-accurate) information available about the Court's actual practices regarding stare decisis than Schauer acknowledges, if not of the type or the level of certainty that the political-science research implies. The Court does sometimes overrule its prior decisions (even relatively recent ones), and it does sometimes affirmatively decline to overrule its decisions, as in *Casey*. These overt acts of overruling or not overruling provide some direct evidence of the Court's views about stare decisis. Their existence, moreover, means that the selection effect does not weed out every case controlled by an on-point precedent. And yet there are many precedents that are rarely or never challenged: decisions that are longstanding and well-established, even if they remain controversial in certain quarters (1966's *Griswold v. Connecticut*,[24] recognizing a constitutional right to use contraceptives, comes to mind), and (at the other end of the spectrum) recent decisions with no intervening change in the Court's ideological makeup (such as 2010's *Citizens United*).[25] The conjunction of these phenomena suggests that lawyers, litigants, and lower-court judges share a general professional sense that the Court will respect some sorts of precedents and may be willing to rethink others. Like many things about the law, the constraining effects of precedent may flow less from formally stated norms than from informal conventions and understandings.

Schauer, Devins, and Stearns each grapple in different ways with empirical questions about the Court's relationship to stare decisis. The book's final three chapters reassert a normative focus, one that encompasses perhaps the most vigorous debate about precedent in current American legal scholarship: its compatibility with certain approaches to constitutional interpretation, in particular originalism. Participants in this debate usually assume that interpretive methodology trumps stare decisis, so that one's views about constitutional stare decisis must follow from one's views about constitutional interpretation rather than the other way around. In Chap. 8, Chad Oldfather cleverly subverts this typical assumption by imagining a world in which stare decisis norms apply *to* interpretive methodologies—that is, in which the Court is required to give precedential effect, not merely to the result of a

[24] 381 U.S. 479 (1965).

[25] I put aside precedents that, like *Brown v. Board of Education*, 347 U.S. 483 (1954), are so universally accepted today as correct that no one, or at most a lunatic fringe, would want to challenge them.

prior constitutional decision, but also to whatever method of interpretation the prior Court used to reach that decision.

This is not in fact the world in which the actual Court operates, and Oldfather's thought experiment suggests a good reason why. A regime of "methodological stare decisis," Oldfather explains, would commit the Court to following the same interpretive approach in some very broad swath of cases—perhaps every single case involving constitutional interpretation (that is, every constitutional case) or, only slightly less broadly, every case involving the interpretation of some subset of constitutional provisions that can meaningfully be distinguished from some other subset (e.g., structural vs. rights provisions). Of course there are institutional impediments to such a broad methodological commitment, most prominently persistent disagreement within the Court itself (and sometimes within individual Justices) about which methodology is the best or correct one. And there are serious structural impediments as well, as Oldfather points out. Committing to a single interpretive methodology, once and for all, as the result of a single case would place enormous pressure on the Court to get it right in that case, something the Court is extraordinarily unlikely to do. Normally we expect courts deciding issues of first impression to consider carefully the likely impact of their decisions on future similar cases, but the set of "future similar cases" in the context of constitutional interpretation will be much too large for this task to be feasible. The Court, then, is very likely to get the methodological choice wrong, or at least to be perceived by future Courts as having gotten it wrong, which will put substantial pressure on these future Courts to overrule the methodological precedent—thus undermining the supposed rule-of-law values thought to justify stare decisis.

The absence of a norm of stare decisis with respect to interpretive methodologies, Oldfather thus concludes, is not surprising and probably is a good thing. (Oldfather draws a contrast with the application of stare decisis to other aspects of constitutional methodology often referred to as "decision rules"—doctrinal heuristics for applying the Constitution to particular cases, such as the familiar "tiers of scrutiny" in equal-protection and due-process jurisprudence. Because these decision rules can be cabined within the boundaries of particular constitutional provisions, Oldfather explains, they do not pose the structural problem of radically unpredictable consequences that interpretive stare decisis would present.)

We might wonder whether Oldfather is being a bit too pessimistic about the feasibility of a clause-driven approach to interpretive methodology—an approach by which the Court would settle on fixed interpretive methodologies, but could choose different methodologies for different constitutional provisions (e.g., originalism for the Due Process Clause, living-constitutionalism for the Free Speech Clause, and so on). Clause-bound interpretative stare decisis might not pose significantly greater foreseeability problems than tiers of scrutiny and other provision-specific decision rules. Of course, many Justices (such as Justices Thomas and Scalia on the current Court) probably would deny the propriety of divvying up interpretive methodologies among different parts of the Constitution; originalists, at least, tend also to be universalists.

In any event, if Oldfather is right about the unworkability of a unitary approach to interpretive methodology, then his conclusions dovetail with those of Randy Kozel in Chap. 9 to suggest that the Court will not soon endorse either an overarching interpretive philosophy or a comprehensive approach to stare decisis. Kozel argues that the questions of interpretive methodology and stare decisis are unavoidably bound together: One's preferred interpretive method will affect one's conclusions about whether and when to follow precedent. Some aspects of the precedent question clearly are independent of interpretive method, such as the benefits of continuity (on the one hand) and the costs of incoherence in the law (on the other). Kozel asserts, however, that other aspects of the question depend for their resolution on a choice of interpretive method. Many originalists, for example, see nonoriginalist interpretation as, in essence, disobedience to the Constitution, and as such they contend that incorrect precedents must be overruled regardless of the rule-of-law costs of doing so. Other originalists distinguish among nonoriginalist precedents, accepting that some (those that err on the side of giving democratic government too much power, for example, or those that have attained supermajoritarian approval) need not or should not be overruled despite their incorrectness. And of course many nonoriginalists—such as those who take a common-law approach to the development of constitutional law—consider (some) Court decisions to be part of the meaning of the Constitution itself, even if those decisions are inconsistent with the original meaning of the document. The question of the costs of following precedent thus often turns, Kozel argues, on the question of which interpretive methodology one adopts.

As Kozel notes, an important consequence of this interdependence between interpretive methodology and stare decisis is the impossibility of a coherent approach to stare decisis on a methodologically pluralistic Court. Justices disagree amongst themselves about proper approaches to constitutional interpretation, and some individual Justices even claim to reject allegiance to any particular interpretive methodology at all. This fact of interpretive pluralism, which seems likely to remain the rule into the indefinite future, probably explains why the Court focuses almost entirely on interpretation-independent considerations (such as reliance, workability, and the Court's reputation for principle) when it discusses stare decisis in decisions like *Casey*.

Kozel thus suggests that the Court will not settle on a comprehensive approach to stare decisis unless its members agree on a unitary approach to constitutional interpretation. And Oldfather offers reasons why the Court is unlikely to commit to a unitary interpretive approach. The upshot is a sense of pessimism (if that isn't too strong a word) that the Court will ever adopt coherent approaches to either constitutional interpretation or constitutional stare decisis.

My own contribution in Chap. 10 continues the general project begun by Kozel of drawing normative connections between constitutional interpretation and stare decisis. I don't agree with Kozel on every point: I am not convinced, for instance, that an assessment of the costs of stare decisis, properly understood, depends in part on the interpretive methodology one favors. Those originalists who equate nonoriginalist interpretation with constitutional disobedience (termed "structural" originalists by

Kozel) reject allegiance to nonoriginalist precedent in all or nearly all circumstances, not because anything in their methodology requires them to do so, but rather because they have made a judgment that constitutional obedience is imperative no matter what its costs. This is a judgment about a duty to obey constitutional law, not about how constitutional meaning should be identified. For their part, "living constitutionalists" who think that some nonoriginalist precedents nonetheless comprise part of constitutional meaning do not favor allegiance to "incorrect" constitutional decision as a result; they simply disagree with originalists regarding what a "correct" decision is. One's theory of interpretation *qua* theory of interpretation cannot tell us, without more, how that theorist should feel about stare decisis.

I think Kozel is quite right, however, to suggest that we look beneath both interpretive methodologies and approaches to stare decisis for their normative underpinnings. I take up this task in Chap. 10, arguing that interpretive methodologies and approaches to stare decisis both must stand or fall as implications of some foundational theory of constitutional authority—of why the Constitution deserves our obedience in the first place. I begin by deconstructing the claim made by some originalists (the "structural" originalists described by Kozel) that their preferred methodology is especially incompatible with constitutional stare decisis. This "special difficulty with precedent," I contend, can be explained (if at all) only by reference to an account of the Constitution's binding authority. I then assess four existing accounts of constitutional authority to determine whether any of them implies both originalism and a distrust of stare decisis. While three such accounts—which I term, respectively, the Values Imposition, Consent, and Moral Guidance accounts—can in theory support originalism and motivate a rejection of stare decisis, I argue that none of these accounts is both normatively and descriptively plausible. A fourth account, Dispute Resolution, appears more plausible, but I contend that it implies neither strong originalism nor a rejection of stare decisis. I conclude that neither thoroughgoing originalism nor a strong distrust of precedent is supported by a plausible account of constitutional authority.

To put the point slightly differently: I argue in Chap. 10 that a convincing theory of why the Constitution binds us implies at least an openness to the possibility that the Court should itself be bound, if only presumptively, by its prior decisions. Constitutional authority permits constitutional stare decisis (and, not incidentally, rejects robust originalism in constitutional interpretation). These conclusions will be controversial, and I'm certain my arguments have many weaknesses. A disadvantage—or perhaps an advantage—of editing a volume to which one also contributes an essay is the practical impossibility of critically assessing one's own chapter. I won't even attempt the task, leaving it instead to the reader, whom I hope will benefit from this collection of essays as a whole despite the undoubted flaws in my contribution to it.

* * *

The efforts and encouragement of many people made this volume possible, and I am grateful to all of them. A succession of three Deans at the University of Baltimore School of Law—Philip Closius, Michael Higginbotham, and Ronald Weich—provided material and monetary support in various forms for the book and the live symposium from which it arose. The members of several faculty committees approved summer stipends that were used in part to prepare this book. Of course the book would not exist without the outstanding efforts of its contributing authors, most of whom also spoke at the symposium. My UB colleagues Kimberly Brown, Nienke Grossman, and Michael Meyerson generously agreed to moderate panels at that symposium, and Laurie Schnitzer did much of the heavy logistical lifting for the event. Participants in a faculty workshop at UB, particularly José Anderson, John Bessler, Kim Brown, Gregory Dolin, Garrett Epps, and Colin Starger, offered helpful comments on my chapter; John Bessler and Mortimer Sellers deserve my thanks for organizing the workshop. At a Constitutional Law Colloquium at the Loyola University School of Law in Chicago, I received invaluable feedback and advice on my then-nascent chapter from Ian Bartrum, Randy Kozel, Lee Strang, and Rebecca Zietlow. I also am grateful to the aforementioned Tim Sellers for agreeing to include the book in the *Ius Gentium* series that he edits for Springer, and to Neil Olivier and Diana Nijenhuijzen at Springer for their editorial guidance. Perhaps the most crucial contribution to this book was that of Emily Kolas (UB Class of 2013), who almost singlehandedly citechecked and formatted the text, much of it after her graduation and while she was studying for the Bar. And as always, I am profoundly thankful for the love and support of my wife, Trish Webster, and of our families.

References

Bickel AM (1986) The least dangerous branch: the Supreme Court at the bar of politics, 2nd edn. Yale University Press, New Haven

Friedman B (2010) The wages of stealth overruling (with particular attention to *Miranda v. Arizona*). Georgetown Law J 99(1):1–63

Gerhardt M (2011) The power of precedent. Oxford University Press, New York, rev

Peters CJ (2008) Under-the-table overruling. Wayne Law Rev 54(3):1067–1104

Peters CJ (2011) A matter of dispute: morality, democracy, and law. Oxford University Press, New York

Wechsler H (1959) Toward neutral principles of constitutional law. Harv Law Rev 73(1):1–35

Chapter 2
The Dialectic of Stare Decisis Doctrine

Colin Starger

Abstract This chapter examines the Supreme Court's "precedent about precedent"—its doctrine regarding whether and when the Court may overturn its own prior constitutional decisions. Due largely to the influence of Justice Louis Brandeis in the early twentieth century, the role of stare decisis in the Court's constitutional cases transformed from that of a vague common-law maxim to the status of contested doctrine. Using graphical "opinion maps" to trace the evolution of the Court's case law on stare decisis, the author illustrates the division of stare decisis doctrine into two competing traditions: a "weak" tradition that allows overruling based on the supposedly faulty reasoning of a prior decision; and a "strong" tradition that demands some independent, non-merits-based justification for overruling. The author demonstrates that individual Justices frequently have aligned themselves with both traditions across different cases, and suggests that the force of the Court's "precedent about precedent" is more rhetorical than constraining.

2.1 Introduction

In the United States Supreme Court, the concept of stare decisis operates as both metadoctrine and doctrine. On the one hand, stare decisis functions as a generally applicable presumption in favor of adherence to precedent. This presumption is metadoctrinal because it provides a generic argument against overruling that applies independently of the substantive context of any given case. On the other hand, when the Court considers overruling a particularly controversial precedent, it usually weighs the constraining force of stare decisis by invoking factors and tests announced

C. Starger (✉)
School of Law, University of Baltimore, 1420 North Charles St.,
Baltimore, MD 21201, USA
e-mail: cstarger@ubalt.edu

C.J. Peters (ed.), *Precedent in the United States Supreme Court*, Ius Gentium: Comparative Perspectives on Law and Justice 33, DOI 10.1007/978-94-007-7951-8_2,

in its own prior case law. In other words, the Court has precedent about when to follow its precedent. This "precedent about precedent" seems doctrinal in the conventional sense—it is the Court's doctrine of stare decisis.

The development of a stand-alone stare decisis doctrine in the Supreme Court was hardly inevitable. The Constitution does not mention precedent at all and thus provides no textual guidance about when stare decisis should be respected. Perhaps predictably, the Court historically decided overruling questions on a case-by-case basis without any reference to "precedent about precedent." Prior to the early twentieth century, if Court opinions discussed stare decisis at all, they typically referred to the concept as a "maxim" or "principle" that abstractly weighed in favor of following past decisions.[1] Though the maxim commanded respect, its authority and meaning were derived from common-law tradition rather than from prior Court pronouncements.

Not so today. Consider the Court's controversial 2010 *Citizens United* decision.[2] In *Citizens United*, a sharply divided Court struck down a federal law barring certain corporate electioneering expenditures on the ground that the law violated the First Amendment. While most remember *Citizens United* as opening the door to unlimited political spending by "super PACs," the case also featured a fierce debate about the majority's overruling of two existing First Amendment cases.[3] Writing for the majority, Justice Kennedy cited the Court's 2009 decision in *Montejo v. Louisiana* for the proposition that the "relevant factors in deciding whether to adhere to the principle of *stare decisis* include the antiquity of the precedent, the reliance interests at stake, and … whether the decision was well reasoned."[4] In dissent, Justice Stevens countered that whether a precedent was "well reasoned" was a "merits argument" not entitled to "weight in the *stare decisis* calculus."[5] Quoting 1992's *Planned Parenthood v. Casey,* Stevens insisted that "[a] decision to overrule should rest on some special reason over and above the belief that a prior case was wrongly decided."[6]

Critically, this argument between Kennedy and Stevens in *Citizens United* assumed a doctrinal form. The authority of *Montejo* was pitted against that of *Casey* to support conflicting positions on whether stare decisis requires adherence to

---

[1] See, for example, Pennsylvania v. Coxe, 4 U.S. 170, 192 (1800) (argument of counsel) ("*Stare decisis*, is a maxim to be held forever sacred, on questions of property."); Cook v. Moffat, 46 U.S. 295, 309 ("So far … as the present case is concerned, the court do not think it necessary or prudent to depart from the safe maxim of *stare decisis*."); Bienville Water Supply Co. v. City of Mobile, 186 U.S. 212, 217 (1902) ("[W]e may, on the principle of *stare decisis*, rightfully examine and consider the decision in the former case as affecting the consideration of this.") (all emphases in originals).

[2] Citizens United v. Federal Election Comm'n, 558 U.S. 310, 130 S. Ct. 876 (2010).

[3] See *Citizens United*, 130 S. Ct. at 913 (overruling Austin v. Michigan Chamber of Commerce, 494 U.S. 652 (1990), and McConnell v. Federal Election Comm'n, 540 U.S. 93 (2003)).

[4] *Citizens United*, 130 S. Ct. at 912 (quoting Montejo v. Louisiana, 129 S. Ct. 2079, 2088–89 (2009)) (emphasis in original).

[5] *Citizens United*, 130 S. Ct. at 939 (Stevens, J., dissenting) (emphasis in original).

[6] *Id.* at 938 (quoting Planned Parenthood of Southeastern Pa. v. Casey, 505 U.S. 833, 864 (1992)).

precedent despite disagreement with prior reasoning. As it happens, the cited opinions in *Montejo* and *Casey* themselves cite back to earlier cases to support their competing interpretations about the appropriate test for overruling precedent. The clash in *Citizens United* over stare decisis thus reflects an ongoing dialectic in Court discourse that is distinct from any First Amendment controversy. Instead of a generic maxim associated with common-law tradition, the concept of stare decisis appears to have become a contested doctrine.

How did this happen? How did stare decisis transform from a common-law maxim into a doctrinal dialectic? The goal of this chapter is to answer this essentially historical question and then analyze its implications for our current understanding of precedent on the Supreme Court. After undertaking a historical analysis that charts the evolution of stare decisis on the Court from maxim to contested doctrine, the chapter seeks to shed light on how much stare decisis doctrine actually constrains decisionmaking or affects outcomes in directly substantive territories of the Court's constitutional jurisprudence. Put another way, this chapter maps the dialectic of stare decisis doctrine in order to assess whether the Court's "precedent about precedent" has any genuine precedential value.

The chapter proceeds in three sections. Section 2.2 begins the inquiry by reviewing the early era of the Court's precedent jurisprudence, which extends from the Founding up until Justice Brandeis's landmark dissent in 1932's *Burnet v. Coronado Oil & Gas Co.*[7] This section demonstrates that, prior to Brandeis's dissent, abstract stare decisis discussions played almost no doctrinal or analytical role in Court debates about overruling precedent. However, Brandeis forever changed this discourse. His *Coronado Oil* dissent catalogued the Court's actual overruling practices in such a powerful manner that his attendant stare decisis analysis immediately assumed canonical authority. After Brandeis, debates about overruling appealed to Court doctrine on stare decisis.

Section 2.3 analyzes the evolution of the Court's stare decisis discourse from *Coronado Oil* until *Citizens United.* Through the use of graphical "opinion maps," this section illustrates how modern stare decisis doctrine became a dialectic. The dialectic pits competing lines of opinions against each other. The competing opinion lines diverge on whether stare decisis requires adherence to precedent in the face of disagreement with prior reasoning. Although both lines ultimately trace back to Brandeis's *Coronado Oil* dissent, this section demonstrates how the contemporary conflict emerged from a key debate between Chief Justice William Rehnquist and Justice Thurgood Marshall in 1991's *Payne v. Tennessee*. The *Payne* debate serves as the blueprint for the Court's modern dialectic of stare decisis doctrine.

With the history thus mapped, Sect. 2.4 takes a critical look at the competing claims in the contemporary stare decisis dialectic. By analyzing in context the arguments pressed by both sides, this final section considers whether the Court's stare decisis doctrine has any genuine precedential value. It concludes that even though the doctrine's actual constraint on Supreme Court decisionmaking is minimal, it retains real political and rhetorical significance.

[7] 285 U.S. 393, 405 (1932) (Brandeis, J., dissenting).

2.2 Early-Era Stare Decisis Jurisprudence and the Impact of Brandeis

Article III of the Constitution vests the "judicial Power of the United States" in the Supreme Court and in inferior courts established by Congress. Beyond describing the subjects of the power's jurisdiction, Article III does not articulate principles governing the proper exercise of this judicial power. Similarly, although Article VI establishes the Constitution as the supreme law of the land, and although various Amendments guarantee important substantive and procedural rights, no constitutional provision explains how to interpret or apply this supreme law and its guaranteed rights. The Constitution, in short, specifies no rules of judicial adjudication.

This absence of constitutionally mandated adjudicatory rules has never posed a problem for the Supreme Court. From the start, the Court was able to go about interpreting the Constitution with little difficulty. This is because the Constitution did not displace all the law that came before it; the new republic inherited the common law and its associated traditions. Just as common-law doctrines regarding property and contract persisted, so too continued common-law traditions governing interpretation of doctrine.

Of course, the Court never formally announced all the adjudicatory rules or metadoctrinal principles it adopted from the common law. Rather, the rules and principles guiding Court deliberations were organically revealed in its published opinions starting in 1791. Careful analysis of these opinions indicates that the common-law maxim *stare decisis et non quieta movere* ("to stand by things decided, and not to disturb settled points") played a role in Court adjudication from the Founding. However, this analysis also shows that early-era stare decisis discourse differed significantly from modern stare decisis doctrine.

2.2.1 The Early Era

For purposes of this inquiry, the early era of the Court's stare decisis jurisprudence extends from 1791 until 1916. The era begins in the year the Court issued its first written opinion and ends when Louis Brandeis became an Associate Justice.[8] During this 125-year period, the phrase "stare decisis" appeared in only 40 published decisions.[9] Closer examination reveals that stare decisis was invoked in 22 majority opinions, 15 dissenting opinions, one concurring opinion, and five reported

[8] See West v. Barnes, 2 U.S. 401 (1791) (first published opinion by the Court), and Hutchinson Ice Cream Co. v. Iowa, 242 U.S. 153 (1916) (first Brandeis opinion for the Court).

[9] This number is based on a simple keyword search for "stare decisis" in Westlaw's comprehensive Supreme Court database. This search produces 45 separate decisions published before 1916. However, I eliminated five of these decisions because the phrase did not appear in an actual opinion or summary of counsel's argument.

arguments of counsel.[10] The vast majority of these early stare decisis references involved no analysis of the concept. Instead, invocation of the maxim usually served a simple rhetorical function in arguments about following precedent. A brief survey of these early decisions uncovers the typical usage.

The very first reported reference to stare decisis in the *United States Reports* is actually both typical and atypical. In 1800's *Pennsylvania v. Coxe*, the Court considered an action seeking to force the Secretary of the Land Office to issue patents to the Holland Company for lands that had been warranted to the company by act of the Pennsylvania General Assembly.[11] In his argument, counsel for the Holland Company stated: "*Stare decisis*, is a maxim to be held forever sacred, on questions of property; and, in the present instance, applies with particular force, as the rule was given by the state herself, through the medium of her officers."[12]

This reference is typical in its use of stare decisis to support a generic appeal to follow existing law and also in its suggestion that precedent applies with special force on questions of property. However, the reference is atypical because it urges adherence not to a Supreme Court precedent, but rather to an act of the Pennsylvania legislature. Early-era appeals to stare decisis normally concerned fidelity to Court precedent alone. Stare decisis was not usually understood to require the Court to follow law set down by inferior or foreign courts, much less by a state legislature.

Although the earliest references to stare decisis in the *United States Reports* surfaced in arguments of counsel, the concept soon found rhetorical use in majority and dissenting opinions alike. Thus, in 1831's *Ex parte Crane*, Justice Henry Baldwin dissented from the majority's conclusion that the Supreme Court had a previously unrecognized *mandamus* power.[13] After surveying the "embryo system of American jurisprudence," Baldwin concluded that "this court is called on to assert a power, which in the 42 years of its existence it has never exercised," and so announced, "I must follow my own judgment, and dissent in the threshold: *obsta principiis—stare decisis*."[14]

Where Baldwin deployed stare decisis to summarize his argument about absence of precedent, others used the phrase to summarily justify fidelity to existing precedent. 1847's *Cook v. Moffat* supplies a representative example. In that case, the Court affirmed a line of decisions regarding discharge of contracts under state insolvent laws.[15] Justice Grier concluded his majority opinion by observing:

> [I]n order to meet the views of the learned counsel for the plaintiff in error, we should be compelled to overrule every case heretofore decided .... But ... [¶] [s]o far, at least, as the

---

[10] These numbers are based upon an examination of the decisions discussed in note 9 above. Although modern Supreme Court reports do not separately summarize the arguments of counsel, this practice is evident in early-era reporting as late as 1870. See Legal Tender Cases, 79 U.S. 457, 459–528 (1870) (devoting 69 pages to reporting arguments of counsel).

[11] See Pennsylvania v. Coxe, 4 U.S. 170 (1800).

[12] *Id.* at 192 (emphasis in original).

[13] See generally Ex parte Crane, 30 U.S. 190 (1831).

[14] See *id.* at 221, 222 (Baldwin, J., dissenting).

[15] Cook v. Moffat, 46 U.S. 295 (1847).

present case is concerned, the court do not think it necessary or prudent to depart from the safe maxim of *stare decisis*.[16]

Not all early-era discussions of stare decisis advocated following the maxim in such a conclusory fashion. Indeed, some opinions that argued for overruling precedent featured more-extensive analysis about the Court's obligation to its own prior decisions. The oldest exemplar of this genre is Chief Justice Roger Taney's majority opinion in 1850's *The Genesee Chief*. The case held that federal admiralty jurisdiction extended to certain navigable lakes and rivers, which effectively overruled an 1825 decision called *The Thomas Jefferson*.[17] Acknowledging this change in the law, Taney first explained that *The Thomas Jefferson* "did not decide any question of property, or lay down any rule by which the right of property should be determined."[18] He then argued that when Court precedent concerns property rights, "*stare decisis* is the safe and established rule of judicial policy, and should always be adhered to."[19] However, since *The Thomas Jefferson* concerned jurisdiction only, and because the Court was "convinced that the former decision was founded in error [that would] produce serious public as well as private inconvenience and loss," Taney concluded that the case should be overruled.[20]

Chief Justice Taney's suggestion that stare decisis had less force in jurisdictional questions was implicitly contested in a fascinating case decided just 3 years later: 1853's *Marshall v. Baltimore & Ohio Railroad Co.*[21] The plaintiff in the case, a shady character named Marshall, had allegedly contracted with the Baltimore and Ohio Railroad Company to peddle influence in the Virginia legislature in order to obtain passage of a law favorable to the corporation. The law passed, but the corporation refused to pay. Marshall then audaciously sued the railway company in federal court. After losing below, Marshall appealed to the Supreme Court, where he faced numerous objections—including the very existence of federal diversity jurisdiction.[22] Marshall, a citizen of Virginia, claimed diversity existed because the corporation was a "citizen" of Maryland.

On the jurisdictional question, the Court held for Marshall. Citing *Louisville Railroad v. Letson*, an 1844 decision that recognized corporate citizenship for diversity purposes, Justice Robert Grier's majority opinion explained:

> [*Letson*] has, for the space of ten years, been received by the bar as a final settlement of the [jurisdictional] questions which have so frequently arisen under this clause of the Constitution.... There are no cases, where an adherence to the maxim of "*stare decisis*" is

[16] *Id.* at 309 (emphasis in original).

[17] See The Genesee Chief, 53 U.S. 443, 458–59 (1851) (overruling The Thomas Jefferson, 23 U.S. 428 (1825)).

[18] *The Genesee Chief*, 53 U.S. at 458.

[19] *Id.* (emphasis in original).

[20] *Id.* at 459.

[21] 57 U.S. 314 (1853).

[22] Diversity jurisdiction refers to federal courts' exercise of authority over cases involving parties who are citizens of different states and an amount in controversy greater than a statutory minimum. See 28 U.S.C. § 1332.

> so absolutely necessary to the peace of society, as those which affect retroactively the jurisdiction of courts. For this reason alone, *even if the court were now of opinion that the principles affirmed in the case … were not founded on right reason*, we should not be justified in overruling them.[23]

Here Grier articulated a very robust vision of stare decisis. He insisted that 10 years of reliance on *Letson* rendered the correctness of the precedent's reasoning wholly irrelevant, effectively insulating the decision from overruling.

Although the majority ultimately ruled against Marshall, holding his contract void on public policy grounds, Grier's jurisdictional and stare decisis analyses did not go unchallenged. Indeed, Justice Peter Daniel vociferously dissented. Refusing to comment on "the settlement of the discreditable controversy," Daniel wryly suggested that the parties "settle their dispute by some standard which is cognate to the transaction in which they have been engaged."[24] He then frontally attacked the Court doctrine that recognized corporations as citizens. After detailing his critique, Daniel expressed his incredulity at the majority's appeal to stare decisis. He argued that the doctrine creating "this new class of citizen corporations" was "strictly a new creation, an alien and an intruder" that could "trace its being no farther back than" *Letson*.[25] Daniel then opined:

> [Stare decisis] is doubtless a wholesome rule of decision when derived from legitimate and competent authority… but, like every other rule, must be fruitful of ill when it shall be wrested to the suppression of reason or duty, or to the arbitrary maintenance of injustice, of palpable error, or of absurdity.[26]

Seeing *Letson*'s doctrine as absurd, unjust, and devoid of constitutional reason, Daniel argued the precedent should not be saved by the principle of stare decisis. By appealing to the lack of soundness of a precedent's reasoning in deciding to overrule, Daniel thus voiced a weak view of stare decisis.

The debate in *Marshall* between Justices Grier and Daniel marks the first time in Supreme Court discourse that majority and dissent explicitly clashed over the interpretation and application of stare decisis. Remarkably enough, this conflict over the rights of corporations and the role of stare decisis preceded *Citizens United* by 157 years. Just as in *Citizens United*, the competing Justices in *Marshall* staked out opposite positions on whether stare decisis requires adherence to precedent despite disagreement with prior reasoning. However, unlike Kennedy and Stevens in *Citizens United*, neither Grier nor Daniel appealed to prior Court precedent to support his view of stare decisis. This failure to cite stare decisis precedent seems a real missed opportunity for Justice Daniel in particular: Daniel could have invoked Chief Justice Taney's then-recent analysis in *The Genesee Chief* for the proposition that Court precedents about jurisdiction have little stare decisis value. Citing *The*

---

[23] 57 U.S. at 325–26 (citing Louisville, C. & C. R. Co. v. Letson, 43 U.S. 497 (1844)) (latter emphasis added).

[24] *Marshall*, 57 U.S. at 338 (Daniel, J., dissenting).

[25] *Id.* at 343.

[26] *Id.*

Genesee Chief might well have lent more authority to Daniel's argument in favor of overruling *Letson*.[27]

Of course, hindsight is always 20-20. Critiquing Daniel's failure to cite *The Genesee Chief* now is probably unfair given the discursive norms of the time. Indeed, out of the 40 published opinions referencing stare decisis in the early era, only one relied on prior authority to justify an abstract argument about overruling precedent. This single exception to the rule—Justice Edward White's dissent in 1903s *Kean v. Calumet Canal & Improvement Co.*—is thus entirely unrepresentative of the era.[28] Far more representative are the opinions discussed and analyzed above: *Pennsylvania v. Coxe*, *Ex Parte Crane*, *The Genesee Chief*, and *Marshall v. Baltimore & Ohio Railroad Co*. Whether these cases mention stare decisis briefly or discuss the concept in some detail, they all show that stare decisis was originally understood as a common-law maxim rather than the subject of Court doctrine. Prior to the twentieth century, Supreme Court Justices simply did not frame arguments about the propriety of overruling precedent by reference to prior Court decisions.

2.2.2 The Influence of Brandeis

Louis Brandeis changed all that. In a series of dissenting opinions culminating in 1932's *Burnet v. Coronado Oil & Gas Co.*, Justice Brandeis developed an analysis of stare decisis based upon a rigorous empirical study of the Court's actual overruling practices. Brandeis so carefully mined and categorized the Court's own "precedent about precedent" in his opinions that his attendant framework for the proper application of stare decisis itself assumed canonical authority. In both content and form, Brandeis's *Coronado Oil* dissent established new discursive standards that effectively gave birth to the Court's modern stare decisis doctrine. Given its importance to the Court's current jurisprudence, a careful reading of *Coronado Oil* is in order.

The substantive context giving rise to Brandeis's famous dissent concerned the federal government's attempts to levy taxes against the Coronado Oil & Gas Company. This private corporation derived all of its income from oil fields that it leased from the State of Oklahoma; it claimed exemption from federal income taxation on the theory that its lease made it an instrumentality of the State. Five Justices agreed with the corporation. In his opinion for the majority, Justice James McReynolds singled out a 1922 precedent called *Gillespie v. Oklahoma* and argued that "the present claim of exemption cannot be distinguished from the one presented

[27] Of course, Grier might have responded that *The Genesee Chief* concerned the expansion of federal jurisdiction rather than its contraction. The merits of this distinction are irrelevant; the point is that Grier and Daniel did not debate it.

[28] See Kean v. Calumet Canal & Improvement Co., 190 U.S. 452, 505–07 (1903) (White, J., dissenting). Compared to Brandeis's subsequent use of "precedent about precedent," Justice White's argument for overruling was neither successful nor influential in Court discourse.

in [*Gillespie*]."[29] Because the "opinion in *Gillespie* ... has often been referred to as the expression of an accepted principle," McReynolds concluded that the Court should "adhere to the rule there approved."[30] Though he did not use the phrase, McReynolds clearly took refuge in the principle of stare decisis.

In dissent, Justice Brandeis minced no words, starting with his opening lines: "Under the rule of *Gillespie v. Oklahoma*, vast private incomes are being given immunity from state and federal taxation.... [T]hat case was wrongly decided and should now be frankly overruled."[31] From this direct framing of the issue, Brandeis launched immediately into his stare decisis analysis. His first sentence is oft-repeated: "Stare decisis is not, like the rule of *res judicata*, universal inexorable command."[32] Brandeis then concisely articulated the general arguments for and against the application of stare decisis. He began:

> Stare decisis is usually the wise policy, because in most matters it is more important that the applicable rule of law be settled than that it be settled right.... This is commonly true even where the error is a matter of serious concern, provided correction can be had by legislation.[33]

According to Brandeis, then, stability in the law was the overriding justification for the presumption in favor of following precedent. He saw stability in judicial decisionmaking as so critical that the burden to correct "bad" precedents should ordinarily fall on legislatures. However, that was not the whole story:

> But in cases involving the Federal Constitution, where correction through legislative action is practically impossible, this court has often overruled its earlier decisions. The court bows to the lessons of experience and the force of better reasoning, recognizing that the process of trial and error, so fruitful in the physical sciences, is appropriate also in the judicial function.[34]

To Brandeis, the effectively unreviewable nature of the Court's constitutional decisionmaking demanded an exception to the general presumption in favor of stare decisis. He therefore concluded that the Court should not hesitate to overrule precedents that contradict experience or good reason.

While sharp and succinctly put, Brandeis's abstract analysis is not what gives the opinion its real rhetorical force. Rather, his footnotes are what jump off the page and

---

[29] Burnet v. Coronado Oil & Gas Co., 285 U.S. 393, 398 (1932) (citing Gillespie v. Oklahoma, 257 U.S. 501 (1922)).

[30] *Coronado Oil*, 285 U.S. at 398–99.

[31] *Id.* at 405 (Brandeis, J., dissenting).

[32] *Id. Res judicata* ("a thing adjudicated") refers to the doctrine also known as "claim preclusion," which bars the same parties from litigating a second lawsuit on the same claim. Brandeis actually cribbed his "universal inexorable command" phrase from a dissent he had penned 8 years earlier in *Washington v. W.C. Dawson & Co.*, 264 U.S. 219, 238 (1924) (Brandeis, J., dissenting). Like any sensible and productive writer, Brandeis borrowed freely from his own prior work.

[33] 285 U.S. at 406. Brandeis lifted the phrase "more important that a rule of law be settled, than that it be settled right" from a dissent he wrote 5 years earlier in *DiSanto v. Pennsylvania*, 273 U.S. 34, 42 (1927) (Brandeis, J., dissenting).

[34] 285 U.S. at 406–08.

seize the reader's attention. Brandeis drops three footnotes in the short paragraph just quoted—and those notes occupy two full pages of the *United States Reports*. The first footnote follows the sentence suggesting that stare decisis is especially wise policy when Court "error[s]" can be corrected by legislation. Dryly observing that the Court has "occasionally overruled its earlier decisions although correction might have been secured by legislation," this footnote catalogs over a dozen non-Constitutional precedents and the subsequent cases that overruled them.[35] The second footnote lists nearly 30 overruled or abrogated Constitutional precedents as well as the cases that effected the change.[36] The third footnote features quotes from Chief Justice Taney as well as Justices Miller and Field, all approving the revisiting of precedent in light of better reasoning or the test of experience.[37]

Cumulatively, these footnotes demonstrate to an empirical certainty that the Court had historically treated stare decisis as a discretionary principle. Brandeis cites authority *en masse* to prove that overruling was a realistic option and one frequently taken by the Court. Having established these general premises, Brandeis then brings home his specific argument for overruling *Gillespie*. Adherence to stare decisis is not advisable, he argues, when the challenged precedent is based on factual determinations "influenced by prevailing views as to economic or social policy which have since been abandoned."[38] *Gillespie* suffered from this flaw since it rested on an essentially factual judgment that taxing a private company's lease profits would "interfere substantially with the functions of state government."[39] Given that better reasoning suggested that *Gillespie* was wrong about this, Brandeis concludes the case should be overruled.

History shows that Brandeis's argument succeeded brilliantly, if not quite immediately. On the federal income tax question, the Court did indeed frankly overrule *Gillespie* six short years after the *Coronado Oil* majority declined to do so.[40] More than this, Brandeis's influence on the Court's subsequent stare decisis jurisprudence was profound. In three separate opinions written between 1936 and 1944, Justice (and then Chief Justice) Stone specifically cited Brandeis's *Coronado Oil* dissent and its extraordinary footnotes to support propositions about the Court's ability to overrule its constitutional precedents.[41] By 1949, Justice Wiley Rutledge had similarly referred to "the trenchant discussion by Mr. Justice Brandeis of the lesser impact of stare decisis in the realm of constitutional construction" and had noted that the "[i]nstances in which this court has overruled

---

[35] *Id.* at 406 n.1.

[36] *Id.* at 407 n.2.

[37] *Id.* at 408 n.3.

[38] *Id.* at 410, 412.

[39] *Id.* at 412.

[40] See Helvering v. Mountain Producers Corp., 303 U.S. 376, 387 (1938) (overruling *Gillespie*).

[41] See St. Joseph Stock Yards Co. v. United States, 298 U.S. 38, 93 (1936) (Stone, J., concurring); Connecticut General Life Ins. Co. v. Johnson, 303 U.S. 77, 85 & n. 10 (1938); United States v. South-Eastern Underwriters Ass'n, 322 U.S. 533, 579 (1944) (Stone, C.J., dissenting).

prior constitutional determinations are catalogued in" *Coronado Oil*.[42] Brandeis's dissent thus quickly assumed canonical authority.

Brandeis dramatically impacted both the substance and the form of the Court's stare decisis jurisprudence. Substantively, Brandeis's analysis about the proper conditions for adhering to precedent still resonates. Justices to this day quote or paraphrase his most famous aphorisms, including "stare decisis is not an inexorable command" or "it is more important that the law be settled than that it be settled right." Formally, Brandeis made it *de rigueur* for Justices to cite Court authority when discussing stare decisis. After *Coronado Oil*, no Court opinion has ever again described stare decisis as merely a maxim. Abstract debates about overruling precedent instead proceed by reference to the Court's own prior pronouncements on the topic. In short, Brandeis transformed stare decisis from common-law maxim to Supreme Court doctrine.

2.3 Mapping the Dialectic of Stare Decisis Doctrine

Contemporary stare decisis doctrine may owe its existence to Brandeis, but it also exhibits a dialectical form. As demonstrated by the debate in *Citizens United*, the discourse now features two distinct general views regarding when the Court can rightly overrule its own precedents. The first view advocates what I call a "weak" conception of stare decisis that sanctions overruling if a challenged precedent suffers from "bad reasoning." The second view promotes what I call a "strong" version of stare decisis—one that requires a "special justification" for overruling beyond mere belief that the challenged precedent was "wrongly decided." Given the existence of two competing approaches to stare decisis, it seems unlikely that *Coronado Oil* alone—a single source—gave rise to contemporary doctrine.

So how did these weak and strong conceptions of stare decisis emerge in modern discourse? This section answers this question by tracing back to their doctrinal roots the competing stare decisis approaches advocated by Justices Kennedy and Stevens in *Citizens United*. This process of doctrinal tracing is visually represented through a series of "opinion maps" that illustrate the relationships among the competing opinions in the weak and strong stare decisis traditions. The opinion maps initially confirm that both traditions share common ancestry in Brandeis's *Coronado Oil* dissent. However, analysis of the doctrinal history also reveals that the stare decisis debate in *Citizens United* effectively carries on an argument first engaged between Chief Justice William Rehnquist and Justice Thurgood Marshall in 1991's *Payne v. Tennessee*. It is the debate in *Payne* that provides the real blueprint for the Court's contemporary dialectic of stare decisis doctrine.

---

[42] See National Mut. Ins. Co. of District of Columbia v. Tidewater Transfer Co., 337 U.S. 582, 618 n. 11 (1949) (Rutledge, J., concurring).

As of this writing, *Citizens United* stands as the latest major installment in the Court's ongoing argument over stare decisis. The stare decisis debate in the case stemmed from the majority's controversial decision to expand the First Amendment rights of corporations. To reach this result, the majority had to overrule a 1990 precedent called *Austin v. Michigan Chamber of Commerce*.[43] Writing for the majority, Justice Kennedy applied a weak stare decisis approach to conclude that overruling *Austin* was justified. In dissent, Justice John Paul Stevens relied upon a strong conception of stare decisis when he protested that the Court's doctrine actually required adherence to *Austin*. Since Kennedy and Stevens invoked competing opinions to establish their competing approaches, it makes sense to look back at those opinions, as well as the opinions they in turn relied on, to uncover the roots of the dialectic between the strong and weak schools.

Before applying this citation-tracing method to the stare decisis approaches advocated by Kennedy and Stevens in *Citizens United*, I should emphasize that neither jurist used the adjectives "weak" or "strong" to describe their competing conceptions. Rather, I have introduced these terms to distinguish between conflicting doctrinal formulations of the proper inquiry the Court should use when deciding whether to overrule one of its precedents. The weak approach is so called because it effectively grants stare decisis less constraining power to prevent overruling than the strong approach. Once again, I want to be clear that the actual doctrinal formulations do not use phrases like "constraining power." Instead, as shown below, the linguistic difference turns on the role of "reasoning" or "justification."

2.3.1 The Weak and Strong Traditions

Consider first the origins of the weak stare decisis approach. Directly quoting 2009's *Montejo v. Louisiana*, Kennedy posited in his *Citizens United* majority opinion that the "relevant factors in deciding whether to adhere to the principle of *stare decisis* include the antiquity of the precedent, the reliance interests at stake, and of course *whether the decision was well reasoned*."[44] (The emphasis on the soundness of the precedent case's reasoning signals that Kennedy is adopting the weak approach.) As it happens, Justice Scalia wrote the majority opinion in *Montejo*—and he, in turn, relied on at least two earlier opinions to authorize this formulation of the appropriate stare decisis approach. Those earlier opinions again invoked prior cases, and so on. This chain of opinions that effectively constitute the weak tradition is represented in Fig. 2.1 below.

---

[43] See *Citizens United*, 130 S. Ct. at 913 (overruling Austin v. Michigan Chamber of Commerce, 494 U.S. 652 (1990)). The Court notably also overruled another, more-recent precedent, *McConnell v. Federal Election Commission*, 540 U.S. 93 (2003).

[44] *Citizens United*, 130 S. Ct. at 912 (quoting Montejo v. Louisiana, 129 S. Ct. 2079, 2088–89 (2009)) (latter emphasis added).

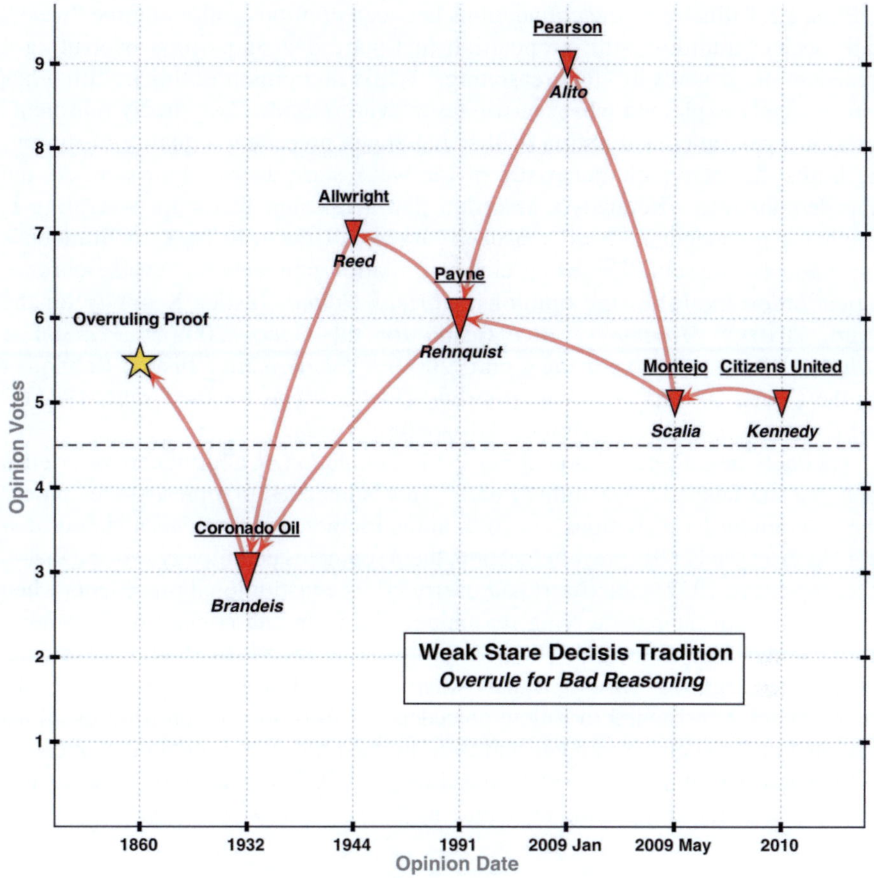

Fig. 2.1 Weak stare decisis tradition: Overrule for bad reasoning

Since this is the first opinion map presented, a brief introduction to the schema is in order.[45] Each triangle on the map represents a Court opinion; the case name appears above the opinion and its author's name appears below. The X-axis indicates the year the opinion case was decided. The Y-axis shows the number of votes the opinion received on the Court—how many of the Court's nine Justices joined in the opinion. Under this schema, all points above the dashed line are thus majority opinions. Solid arrows connecting opinions indicate that the latter opinion directly cited the earlier one. The resulting picture is of continuous lines of authority that stand for a particular proposition in Court discourse.

---

[45] For a thorough discussion of the theory animating this doctrinal mapping schema, see "Exile on Main Street: Competing Traditions and Due Process Dissent" (Starger 2012a) and "Expanding Stare Decisis: The Role of Precedent in the Unfolding Dialectic of *Brady v. Maryland*" (Starger 2012b).

Figure 2.1 illustrates the connections between opinions endorsing the "weak" stare decisis tradition—the proposition that stare decisis permits overruling a precedent on grounds of "bad reasoning." While no opinion in this tradition has ever precisely explained what constitutes a "well reasoned" or "badly reasoned" decision, specific consideration of the challenged precedent's quality of reasoning is the distinctive characteristic of the weak stare decisis approach. As the map demonstrates, Kennedy's assertion that a relevant factor in overruling is whether a precedent is "well reasoned" traces all the way back to Brandeis's *Coronado Oil* dissent. The exact chain of citation connects, in reverse-chronological order, the following opinions: *Citizens United* (Justice Kennedy for the Court, 2010);[46] *Montejo* (Justice Scalia for the Court, 2009);[47] *Pearson v. Callahan* (Justice Alito for the Court, 2009);[48] *Payne* (Chief Justice Rehnquist for the Court, 1991);[49] *Smith v. Allwright* (Justice Reed for the Court, 1944);[50] and *Coronado Oil* (Justice Brandeis dissenting, 1932).[51]

Although the earliest opinion in Fig. 2.1 is *Coronado Oil*, a further arrow extends back to a star labeled "Overruling Proof." This is intended to represent the "proof" (the voluminous case citations) set forth in the footnotes of Brandeis's famous dissent. As discussed in the previous section, these footnotes definitively showed that—at least prior to 1932—the Court had overruled its constitutional precedents when dissatisfied with their underlying reasoning. The form and content of Brandeis's proof exerted great influence over the subsequent discourse. In 1944, for example, Justice Reed argued in *Allwright* that "when convinced of former error, this Court has never felt constrained to follow precedent."[52] To prove this proposition, Reed first cited to Brandeis's footnotes and then dropped his own footnote documenting a dozen new overrulings that had occurred since 1932.[53] Then in 1991, Chief Justice Rehnquist employed the same technique in *Payne* when he carefully cataloged 33

[46] 130 S. Ct. 876 (2010). *Citizens United* was a five-to-four decision. Justice Kennedy wrote the majority opinion. Chief Justice Roberts wrote a separate concurrence, which was joined by Justice Alito. Justice Stevens's dissent received four votes.

[47] 556 U.S. 778 (2009). *Montejo* was a five-to-four decision. Justice Scalia wrote the majority opinion. Justice Alito wrote a separate concurrence. Justice Stevens's dissent received four votes.

[48] 555 U.S. 223 (2009). *Pearson* was a nine-to-zero decision. Justice Alito wrote the majority opinion.

[49] 501 U.S. 808 (1991). *Payne* was a six-to-three decision. Chief Justice Rehnquist wrote the majority opinion. Justice Scalia wrote a separate concurrence that received three votes. Justice Marshall's dissent received three votes.

[50] 321 U.S. 649 (1944). *Allwright* was an eight-to-one decision. Justice Reed wrote the majority opinion which received seven votes. Justice Frankfurter concurred in result only. Justice Owen Roberts wrote a solo dissent.

[51] 285 U.S. 393 (Brandeis, J., dissenting). *Coronado Oil* was a five-to-four decision. Justice McReynolds wrote the majority opinion. Justice Stone's dissent received four votes. Justice Brandeis's dissent received three votes.

[52] *Allwright*, 321 U.S. at 665.

[53] *Id.* at 665 n.10.

constitutional decisions that had been overruled in the prior 20 years.[54] The empirical reality of the Court's overruling practice thus stands as the ultimate backing for the weak stare decisis tradition.

What about the competing strong tradition? To uncover the doctrinal origins of the strong stare decisis tradition, it makes sense to once again start with *Citizens United* and work backward. In his *Citizens United* dissent, Stevens argued that stare decisis demands "significant justification, beyond the preferences of five Justices, for overturning settled doctrine."[55] Directly quoting 1992's *Planned Parenthood of Southeastern Pennsylvania v. Casey*, Stevens elaborated, "[a] decision to overrule should rest on some special reason over and above the belief that a prior case was wrongly decided."[56] *Casey*, of course, rejected a constitutional challenge to the right to an abortion and adhered to *Roe v. Wade* primarily on stare decisis grounds. To support its view that in the absence of "special justification" stare decisis requires adherence to precedent, the joint opinion in *Casey* inevitably cited earlier decisions.

Figure 2.2 represents the connections among opinions endorsing the strong stare decisis proposition that overruling Court precedent is prohibited absent "special justification." At the outset, it is apparent that this map is more complicated than that presented in Fig. 2.1. This reflects the rather complex origins of the "special justification" formulation of the stare decisis test. To understand the map's depiction of this origin story, further explanation is required. Note how the map uses both blue and red triangles to depict opinions. The blue triangles point upward to indicate that they are opinions that affirmed a challenged precedent case (or, if written in dissent, advocated affirming the precedent). By contrast, the red triangles point downward to indicate that they are opinions that overruled a challenged precedent (or advocated overruling).[57] Thus, although the chain of citation extends from Stevens's dissent in *Citizens United* back to Brandeis's dissent in *Coronado Oil*, the map shows that Justice O'Connor's 1984 opinion in *Rumsey v. Arizona*[58] is actually the earliest opinion in the strong stare decisis tradition that adhered to a challenged precedent.

This reveals a key difference between the strong and weak traditions. While all the opinions in the weak stare decisis line ultimately advocate overruling a challenged precedent, the opinions in the strong stare decisis line are not similarly uniform in advocating adherence to a challenged precedent. Before I explore this apparent contradiction, a formal listing of the opinions in Fig. 2.2 will be useful. In reverse chronological order, they are: *Citizens United* (Justice Stevens dissenting,

---

[54] See *Payne*, 501 U.S. at 828 n.1.

[55] *Citizens United*, 130 S. Ct. at 938 (Stevens, J., dissenting).

[56] *Id.* at 938 (quoting *Planned Parenthood of Southeastern Pa.* v. *Casey*, 505 U.S. 833, 864 (1992)).

[57] This second map also introduces dotted arrows to connect opinions despite the lack of a formal citation relationship. I use dotted arrows to assert that the opinions are nonetheless connected and form part of the same tradition. Specific justifications for these dotted arrows are provided below in discussions of the particular opinions.

[58] 467 U.S. 203 (1984).

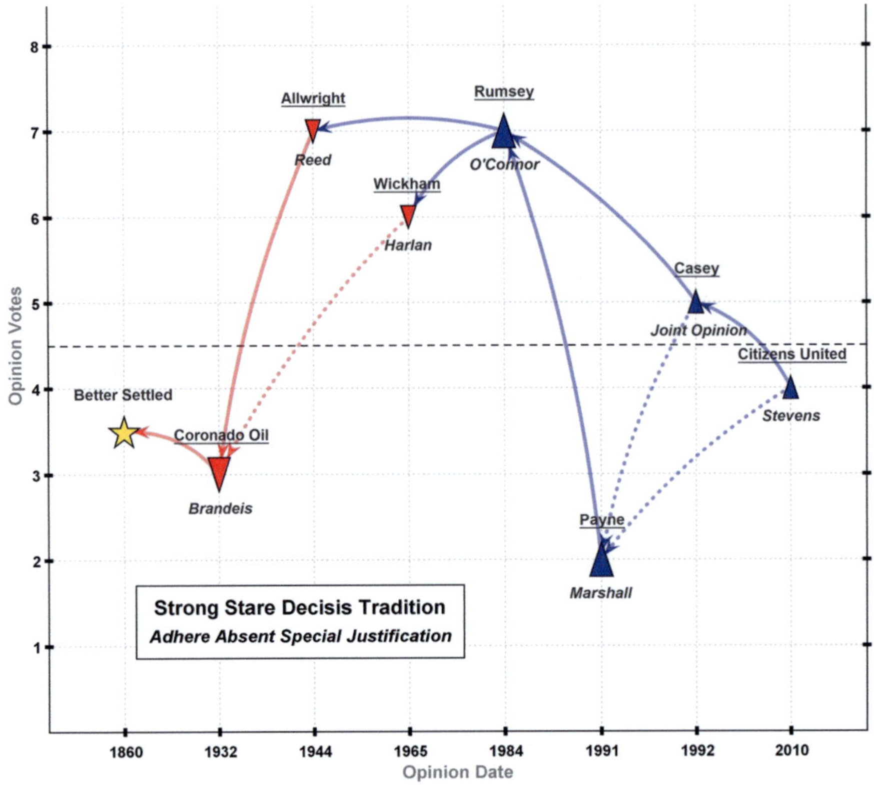

Fig. 2.2 Strong stare decisis tradition: Adhere absent special justification

2010);[59] *Casey* (joint plurality opinion by O'Connor, Kennedy, and Souter, 1992);[60] *Payne* (Justice Marshall dissenting, 1991);[61] *Rumsey v. Arizona* (Justice O'Connor for the Court, 1984);[62] *Swift & Co. v. Wickham* (Justice Harlan for the Court, 1965);[63] *Allwright* (Justice Reed for the Court, 1944);[64] and *Coronado Oil* (Justice Brandeis dissenting, 1932).[65]

[59] See note 46 above.

[60] 505 U.S. 833 (1992). *Casey* was a five-to-four decision. No single opinion commanded a majority. Justices O'Connor, Kennedy, and Souter authored a joint plurality opinion. Justices Stevens and Blackmun wrote separate solo opinions concurring in part. Chief Justice Rehnquist and Justice Scalia both wrote dissents that each received four votes.

[61] See note 49 above.

[62] 467 U.S. 203 (1984). *Rumsey* was a seven-to-two decision. Justice O'Connor wrote the majority opinion. Chief Justice Rehnquist wrote a dissent that received two votes.

[63] 382 U.S. 111 (1965). *Wickham* was a six-to-three decision. Justice Harlan wrote the majority opinion. Justice Douglas dissented and his opinion received three votes.

[64] See note 50 above.

[65] See note 51 above.

As noted, the apparent contradiction presented by Fig. 2.2 is that the strong stare decisis tradition traces its origins to three opinions that did not advocate adhering to precedent: *Wickham*, *Allwright*, and *Coronado Oil*. This contradiction is not altogether surprising given the tensions in Brandeis's foundational *Coronado Oil* dissent. Though the dissent clearly bowed to the force of better reasoning in constitutional decisionmaking, Brandeis also famously described stare decisis as the wise default policy because "in most matters, it is more important that the applicable law be settled than that it be settled right." On its own, this aphorism is consistent with the strong stare decisis notion that a decision to overrule should rest on more than "the belief that a prior case was wrongly decided." Figure 2.2 represents the connection between this aspect of *Coronado Oil* and the strong stare decisis tradition by extending an arrow back from the dissent to a star labeled "Better Settled."

Clearly, Brandeis's polite nod to the wisdom of stare decisis does not adequately explain the origins of the strong tradition embraced by Stevens in *Citizens United*. A more complete explanation requires a closer analysis of the doctrine. The focus should be etymological. This is because one hallmark phrase—"special justification"—is repeated enough in the doctrine that it fairly stands as shorthand for the entire strong stare decisis tradition. In the roots of this phrase lie the origins of the strong tradition's most consistent theme.

2.3.2 *Special Justification*

The basic etymological inquiry is simple enough. As scholars have previously acknowledged, Justice O'Connor introduced the phrase "special justification" into Court discourse in 1984's *Rumsey*.[66] O'Connor's opinion for the majority had granted relief to a criminal defendant via a relatively straightforward application of a 1981 double-jeopardy precedent. Seeking to avoid this result, the State of Arizona had in its briefing urged the Court to overrule the precedent. In response, O'Connor wrote: "We decline the invitation. Although adherence to precedent is not rigidly required in constitutional cases, any departure from the doctrine of stare decisis demands special justification."[67]

This simple sentence is the sole source of the Court's current "special justification" language, but it provoked no stare decisis debate at the time. Indeed, the phrase did not assume any real significance in the discourse until the doctrine-defining clash between Chief Justice Rehnquist and Justice Marshall 8 years later in *Payne*. It really was Marshall's dissent in *Payne* that provided the first unambiguous articulation of the strong stare decisis test. A review of O'Connor's

---

[66] See Emery G. Lee III's (2002) "Overruling Rhetoric: The Court's New Approach to Stare Decisis in Constitutional Cases," tracing the origin of "special justification" to *Rumsey*.

[67] *Rumsey*, 467 U.S. at 212.

citations in *Rumsey* confirms that the earlier doctrine essentially adopted a weak stare decisis perspective.

For her "special justification" proposition, O'Connor directly cited two cases: *Wickham* and *Allwright*. As noted, both of those cases overruled rather than affirmed precedent. Yet O'Connor apparently relied on language in, rather than the results of, these decisions to support the "special justification" proposition. In *Wickham*, the Court overruled a 3-year-old precedent penned by Justice Frankfurter. Only tacitly admitting the stare decisis implications of this move, Justice Harlan wrote in his majority opinion: "The overruling of a six-to-two decision of such recent vintage, which was concurred in by two members of the majority in the present case, and the opinion in support of which was written by an acknowledged expert in the field of federal jurisdiction, demands full explication of our reasons."[68] Harlan then explicated his reasons: Since it had been decided, the challenged precedent had sown confusion in the lower courts and proved unworkable. Though the unworkability of a precedent certainly counts as a special justification for overruling under current doctrine, it bears emphasis that Harlan did not frame his *Wickham* discussion as a general reflection on stare decisis. Instead, his insistence on a "full explication of [the Court's] reasons" was inextricably linked to the enormity of overruling a 3-year-old Frankfurter opinion.

O'Connor's "special justification" formulation is even more tenuously supported by her citation to *Allwright*. Decided in 1944, *Allwright* held that the Fifteenth Amendment prohibited racial discrimination in primary elections run by political parties, thereby overruling a unanimous 1935 precedent that had permitted such discrimination. The only language in Justice Reed's majority opinion that even arguably promoted stare decisis was this: "In reaching this [overruling] conclusion we are not unmindful of the desirability of continuity of decision in constitutional questions."[69] However, Reed then strenuously insisted on the propriety of overruling precedent when convinced of former error. This discussion more squarely locates *Allwright* in the weak stare decisis tradition—an orientation confirmed by *Allwright*'s depiction in Fig. 2.1 above. Given this, O'Connor's citation to *Allwright* is indeed puzzling. Perhaps she regarded the correction of a rank racial injustice as exemplifying a "special justification."

In any event, it is clear that neither *Wickham* nor *Allwright* supports a strong view of stare decisis. This mattered little at the time because *Rumsey* did not provoke a stare decisis debate: O'Connor's general argument for adhering to precedent was not challenged on its merits. The reality is that in *Rumsey*, O'Connor did not use the phrase "special justification" in a rhetorically or doctrinally significant sense. The phrase only assumed such significance in *Payne*. Because of its centrality to the modern dialectic, *Payne* deserves a more detailed analysis.

---

[68] *Wickham*, 382 U.S. at 116 (overruling Kesler v. Dep't of Public Safety, 369 U.S. 153 (1962)) (internal footnotes and citations omitted).

[69] *Allwright*, 321 U.S. at 665 (overruling Grovey v. Townsend, 295 U.S. 45 (1935)).

2.3.3 *Payne v. Tennessee*

The specific legal controversy in *Payne* turned on whether the Eighth Amendment permits jury consideration of victim-impact evidence. Previous majorities had prohibited victim-impact evidence in cases called *Booth* and *Gathers*.[70] Writing for a six-Justice majority, Chief Justice Rehnquist overruled these cases. In so doing, the Chief Justice advanced two central propositions about stare decisis doctrine. First, he argued that "[c]onsiderations in favor of *stare decisis* are at their acme in cases involving property and contract rights, where reliance interests are involved," while "the opposite is true in cases such as the present one involving procedural and evidentiary rules."[71] Second, Rehnquist suggested that *Booth* and *Gathers* were ripe for overruling because they had been "decided by the narrowest of margins, over spirited dissents challenging the basic underpinnings of those decisions."[72]

In dissent, Justice Marshall loudly objected to Rehnquist's articulation of the stare decisis inquiry. Marshall accused Rehnquist of creating a "radical new exception to the doctrine of *stare decisis*" by suggesting that the Court could freely "discard any principle of constitutional liberty which was recognized or reaffirmed over the dissenting votes of four Justices and with which five or more Justices *now* disagree."[73] Rejecting Rehnquist's weak test, Marshall posited that "[t]he overruling of one of this Court's precedents ought to be a matter of great moment and consequence.... Consequently, this Court has never departed from precedent without 'special justification.'"[74] For this last proposition, Marshall naturally quoted Justice O'Connor's opinion in *Rumsey*.

Marshall then elaborated on what he believed constituted "special justification." In the main, legitimate justifications were major factual or legal developments that undermined a challenged precedent's essential rationale. Turning to the precedents at hand, Marshall argued that no legal or factual developments justified overruling *Booth* and *Gathers*. He boldly suggested that the only notable change since those cases had been handed down was in the Court's own personnel. Rather than provide the special justification required by stare decisis, this new majority had simply—and illegitimately—elevated the dissents from *Booth* and *Gathers* into the law of the land.

The razor-sharp vehemence of Marshall's dissent attracted the attention of the other Justices. In his separate concurrence, Justice Scalia suggested that Marshall acted hypocritically by "demand[ing] of us some 'special justification.'"[75] Justice Souter, who also concurred, took a less personal tack and argued that the Court did

---

[70] See Booth v. Maryland, 482 U.S. 496 (1987); South Carolina v. Gathers, 490 U.S. 805 (1989).

[71] *Payne*, 501 U.S. at 828 (emphasis in original).

[72] *Id.* at 829.

[73] *Id.* at 845 (Marshall, J., dissenting) (emphasis in original).

[74] *Id.* at 848–49 (Marshall, J., dissenting) (quoting *Rumsey*).

[75] *Id.* at 834 (Scalia, J., concurring).

indeed possess "special justification" for overruling *Booth* and *Gathers*.[76] The substantive merits of these competing claims are not relevant for this inquiry. What is relevant is that the language of "special justification" suddenly took center stage. Although the phrase had only been politely echoed in two cases since *Rumsey*, it now became the linguistic axis around which the stare decisis debate turned.[77] And it has played a lead role in the discourse ever since.

While this etymological account helps explain the original split between the strong and weak stare decisis traditions, the doctrinal history is not yet complete. Grasping the full rhetorical context requires one final look at Marshall's *Payne* dissent. Confronting Rehnquist's proposition that stare decisis has greater force in "cases involving property and contract rights," Marshall warned that the majority was "send[ing] a clear signal that essentially *all* decisions implementing the personal liberties protected by the Bill of Rights and the Fourteenth Amendment are open to reexamination."[78] Furthermore, he argued,

> [t]aking into account the majority's additional criterion for overruling—that a case was decided or reaffirmed by a 5–4 margin "over spirited dissen[t]"—the continued vitality of literally scores of decisions must be understood to depend on nothing more than the proclivities of the individuals who *now* comprise a majority of this Court.[79]

To dramatize this charge, Marshall proposed a specific list of "endangered precedents" that he suggested might soon be overruled. The endangered precedents identified by Marshall were all liberal constitutional decisions potentially threatened by the new conservative majority. Marshall presciently included on his list three cases that the Rehnquist Court did in fact overrule within the decade after *Payne*.[80] And while the most prominent decision on his list—*Roe v. Wade*—has so far survived all overruling challenges, Marshall's concern for *Roe* under a weak stare decisis framework was well warranted at the time. After all, Marshall retired from the Court months after *Payne* and a Republican President (George Bush) appointed a conservative successor (Clarence Thomas). And in the Term immediately following *Payne*, the Court in fact entertained a very serious challenge to *Roe*. As it happens, the debate in *Payne* effectively anticipated—perhaps even consciously—the epic stare decisis confrontation in that case, 1992's *Planned Parenthood v. Casey*.

---

[76] *Id.* at 842 (Souter, J., concurring).

[77] For the only other invocations of *Rumsey*, see Patterson v. McLean Credit Union, 491 U.S. 164, 172 (1989), and Garcia v. San Antonio Metropolitan Transit Authority, 469 U.S. 528, 557 (1985) (Powell, J., dissenting).

[78] 501 U.S. at 851 (Marshall, J., dissenting) (emphasis in original).

[79] *Id.* (emphasis in original).

[80] See Agostini v. Felton, 521 U.S. 203 (1997) (overruling Aguilar v. Felton, 473 U.S. 402 (1985)); Adarand Constructors v. Pena, 515 U.S. 200 (1995) (overruling Metro Broadcasting v. F.C.C., 497 U.S. 547 (1990)); United States v. Dixon, 509 U.S. 688 (1993) (overruling Grady v. Corbin, 495 U.S. 508 (1990)).

2.3.4 *Planned Parenthood v. Casey* and Stare Decisis Doctrine After *Payne*

In *Casey*, the Court reviewed the constitutionality of Pennsylvania laws restricting abortions. Although the Court was explicitly invited to overrule *Roe v. Wade*, a majority of the Court declined to do so. The majority opinion in *Casey* probably represents the zenith of the strong stare decisis tradition. This is because the opinion's joint authors (O'Connor, Kennedy, and Souter) explicitly argued that "the force of *stare decisis*" compelled them to accept *Roe* despite "the weight of the arguments" for its overruling and even their own "reservations" in reaffirming its central holding.[81] In other words, the majority hinted that *Roe* might be "wrong" but argued that stare decisis compelled them to affirm it anyway. Given that *Roe* is also the Court's most persistently controversial constitutional precedent, the significance of the majority's strong stare decisis stance cannot be overstated.

At the same time, significance should not be confused with originality. The majority in *Casey* essentially advocated the same strong view of stare decisis that Marshall had championed in *Payne*. *Casey*'s now-famous analysis looked to "a series of prudential and pragmatic considerations" to decide whether overruling a precedent was appropriate, including the precedent's workability, reliance interests, related doctrinal development, and changed factual circumstances.[82] This approach built upon Marshall's stare decisis considerations and relied on much of the same "precedent about precedent"—including *Rumsey*—that Marshall had invoked. And yet, the *Casey* joint authors noticeably failed to cite Marshall's dissent in their opinion. (To reflect this absence of a formal citation relationship, the arrow pointing from *Casey* to *Payne* in Fig. 2.2 is dotted rather than solid).

This failure-to-cite on the part of the *Casey* majority should not obscure the fact that Marshall's dissent in *Payne* effectively ushered in a doctrinally distinct strong stare decisis approach. Building on *Rumsey*, Marshall's *Payne* dissent had dubbed certain considerations as properly part of an overruling inquiry. The *Casey* majority further developed these same considerations. And like Marshall, the *Casey* majority did not include the "bad reasoning" of a precedent case as a relevant stare decisis consideration. Given that Marshall's *Payne* dissent also loudly signaled stare decisis as an important means of protecting liberal precedents targeted for overruling—*Roe* chief among them—it seems evident that the *Casey* majority picked up where Marshall left off.

On the flip side of the dialectic, the *Casey* dissenters clearly followed the example set by the *Payne* majority. In his dissent in the case, Chief Justice Rehnquist proclaimed that "authentic principles of *stare decisis*" require the Court "to bo[w] to the lessons of experience and the force of better reasoning."[83] Although he did not repeat his claim from *Payne* that constitutional precedents have less stare decisis

---

[81] See *Casey*, 505 U.S. at 853 (emphasis in original).

[82] *Id.* at 844–45.

[83] See *Casey*, 505 U.S. at 955 (Rehnquist, C.J., dissenting) (emphasis in original).

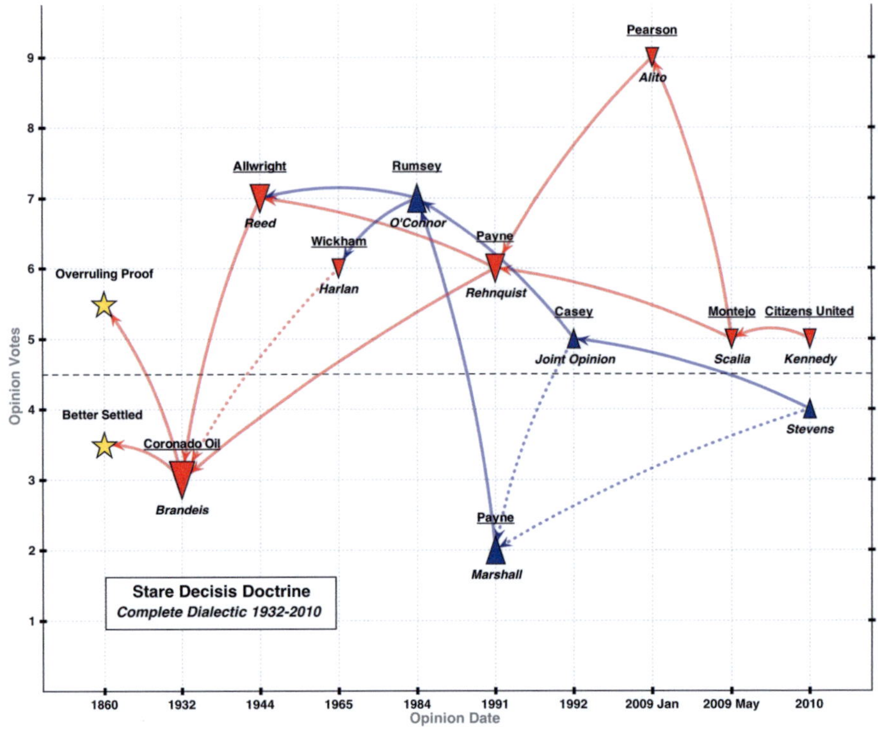

Fig. 2.3 Stare decisis doctrine: Complete dialectic 1932–2010

value when reached over "spirited dissents," Rehnquist's own spirited dissent in *Casey* quite obviously embraced the proposition. Meanwhile, Justice Scalia's separate *Casey* dissent echoed similar core themes. After noting that the joint opinion failed to "squarely contend" that *Roe* was a correct application of "reasoned judgment," Scalia suggested that a legitimate stare decisis inquiry would ask, "how wrong was the [original] decision on its face?"[84]

After *Payne* then, the blueprint for the modern stare decisis dialectic was in place. Strong and weak schools split over whether "authentic principles" of stare decisis properly looked to the "correctness" of a precedent's reasoning in overruling determinations. Put another way, the split concerned whether the strength of a prior dissent properly factored into decisions to adhere to a challenged precedent. This split emerged in *Payne* and has continued to play out in Court discourse from *Casey* to *Citizens United.*

Figure 2.3 combines Figs. 2.1 and 2.2 to provide a visual summary of the analysis in this section. It bears emphasis, however, that Fig. 2.3 does not purport to

[84] *Id.* at 982–83 (Scalia, J., dissenting).

represent every opinion in the dialectic of stare decisis doctrine. The map is not the territory. Complete accounts of both the weak and strong stare decisis traditions would undoubtedly include other opinions.[85] But the point of the map is not exhaustive detail. Rather, the idea is to represent the most influential and important opinions in the ancestry of the stare decisis debate in *Citizens United*. To deploy an analogy, Fig. 2.3 is like a constellation map. From a sparkling universe of opinions, it draws lines between the brightest stars in the dialectic. As has been shown, the brightest stars in stare decisis doctrine are Justice Brandeis's *Coronado Oil* dissent and the competing majority and dissenting opinions in *Payne*.

2.4 The Precedential Value of Stare Decisis Doctrine

With the origins of the strong and weak stare decisis traditions now mapped, this section critically examines the competing claims in the contemporary stare decisis dialectic. Specifically, this section confronts the question: Is either side "right" about what the doctrine of stare decisis really requires?

Given that the Court itself ultimately defines the requirements of stare decisis doctrine, the most literal answer to this question is "no." As shown in the previous section, the Court does not speak with one voice about stare decisis. Debate rages on and outcomes are mixed. Since *Payne* initiated the modern dialectic, both traditions have won victories and suffered losses. Some controversial precedents have been affirmed (like *Roe* in *Casey*) while others have been overruled (like *Austin* in *Citizens United*). In this sense, stare decisis is like due process, equal protection, or any other endlessly contested Court doctrine—inherently subjective and utterly immune to "right" interpretation.

However accurate this answer may be as a descriptive matter, it fails to satisfy any normative yearnings. To scratch the normative itch, some judgment—even an imperfect one—is required. Here, judgment is called for on the central question that apparently divides the weak from strong approaches: the degree to which the soundness of a challenged precedent's reasoning is properly part of the stare decisis calculus. Of course, pinning down the precise disagreement between the competing traditions on this question is tricky since neither side speaks in absolutes. Both traditions pay lip service to adhering to precedent when necessary *and* to

---

[85] Figure 2.3 does not include all opinions from the weak stare decisis tradition. See, for example, *Casey*, 505 U.S. at 955 (Rehnquist, C.J., dissenting), and Vasquez v. Hillery, 474 U.S. 254, 269 (1986) (Powell, J., dissenting). For other affirmations of the strong stare decisis perspective, see Dickerson v. United States, 530 U.S. 428 (2000) (affirming Miranda v. Arizona, 384 U.S. 436 (1966)); Patterson v. McLean Credit Union, 491 U.S. 164 (1989) (affirming Runyon v. McCrary, 427 U.S. 1960 (1976)); Garcia v. San Antonio Metropolitan Transit Authority, 469 U.S. 528, 557 (1985) (Powell, J., dissenting). *Dickerson* was interesting at the time because Chief Justice Rehnquist—a proponent of the weak stare decisis school in *Payne* and *Casey*—wrote the majority opinion. However, its enduring appeal seems limited, as no Justice cited it in *Citizens United*.

overruling precedent when justified. There is ambiguity in how the dueling stare decisis traditions understand "justification" and its relationship to the "reasoning" of precedent decisions.

Given this ambiguity, it makes sense to reframe the inquiry. A useful alternate framework for judgment concerns the competing attitudes toward the reasoning in dissents. After all, the weak stare decisis tradition generally has had no compunction about citing the dissents associated with challenged precedents and frankly adopting the dissent's view of the argument when overruling. On the other hand, opinions in the strong stare decisis line have loudly decried the invocation of prior dissents as an illegitimate move incompatible with the rule of law. The competing sides thus seem to have staked out clear and conflicting positions on whether the force of a dissent's reasoning should be given real weight when faced with an overruling decision. The question thus remains: Who has the better argument?

At the outset, the weak tradition's approach of admitting the force of prior dissents' reasoning into the stare decisis calculus seems the presumptive victor. This is because Justice Brandeis clearly embraced this position in *Coronado Oil*. Since Brandeis effectively transformed stare decisis from a common-law maxim into Court doctrine, his word on the doctrine's content demands special deference. Of course, Brandeis did acknowledge, as all inheritors of the weak stare decisis tradition do, that sometimes the law is better settled than settled right. Yet Brandeis notably did not object to a subsequent overruling of a precedent based on the analysis in a prior dissent. After all, Brandeis was a famously successful dissenter himself, and the force of reasoning in his dissents—*Coronado Oil* not the least among them—helped change many areas of Court doctrine for the better.

In order to overcome Brandeis's presumptive authority, then, a pointed response to his dissent-embracing analysis is needed. Perhaps the best response here appeals to consistency as a means to preserve Court legitimacy. Though still invoked by the strong tradition, this argument has noble roots that pre-date Brandeis. Consider *Smith v. Turner*, a case decided in 1849. In the reported argument, counsel for one side asserted that his opponent could win only if the Court overruled an 1832 precedent called *Miln*. In the course of his argument for stare decisis, he observed:

> This court remains, but its members change. Three of the five members who decided in favor of State rights in the case of *Miln* are gone. Where is Thompson? Where is Baldwin? Where is Barbour, who gave the opinion of the court in that case? Had these judges remained in the seats which they once adorned, this suit would never have been brought. Is it wise thus to invite speculation upon the sad changes which the inevitable doom that awaits us all must produce in this tribunal? If temporary majorities are to give the law of this court, its decisions, which should be as permanent as the republic, will become as fluctuating and mortal as its members.[86]

The idea that Court precedent should not change with every new majority has intuitive appeal. Constitutional law should have more consistency than politics. As

[86] Smith v. Turner, 48 U.S. 283, 364 (1849) (argument of counsel).

Justice Brewer succinctly put it in 1893, "[a] change in the personnel of a court should not mean a shift in the law."[87]

Though advocates for the weak stare decisis tradition would likely agree with Brewer, his observation nonetheless presents a real challenge to Chief Justice Rehnquist's *Payne* argument, which assigned less stare decisis value to precedents obtained by "the narrowest of margins, over spirited dissents." By definition, five-to-four decisions are most vulnerable to changes in Court personnel. And new lineups can all too easily look to prior dissents to find "better reasoning" to rationalize a change in law actually motivated by ideology.

Major opinions in the weak stare decisis tradition can be plausibly interpreted as ideological overrulings made possible by change in the composition of the Court. In *Citizens United*, for example, Justice Stevens persuasively argued that the majority overruled *Austin* simply because it did not "like" *Austin* and characterized Justice Kennedy's majority opinion as "essentially an amalgamation of resuscitated dissents."[88] In fact, Justice Kennedy in *Citizens United* did favorably cite his very own dissent from *Austin* and did adopt its reasoning while making his case for overruling.[89] Similarly, Justice Scalia's majority opinion in *Montejo* overruled *Michigan v. Jackson* while citing to Chief Justice Rehnquist's prior *Jackson* dissent.[90] Finally, Rehnquist in *Payne* justified overruling *Booth* by directly invoking Justice White's *Booth* dissent.[91] In all of these cases, a new Court lineup looked to prior dissents to rationalize overruling liberal precedents.

Despite this, it would be a mistake to regard the weak stare decisis tradition as a ruse perpetrated by a conservative Court majority. While the post-*Payne* dialectic has frequently seen the members of the Court's liberal wing appeal to stare decisis to defend older liberal precedents, the pattern is not monolithic. Over time, liberal Justices also have frequently advocated overruling based on prior dissents. Indeed, there is a flip side to the empirical reality of overruling first demonstrated by Brandeis: Changes in the composition of the Court demonstrably have facilitated overruling, and Justices of all political stripes have taken advantage of this reality.

More than this, individual Justices often have taken inconsistent positions on stare decisis doctrine. In *Payne*, for example, Justice Scalia observed that the "response to Justice Marshall's strenuous defense of the virtues of stare decisis can

---

[87] Cadawalader v. Wannamaker, 149 U.S. 541, 547 (1893) (Brewer, J., dissenting). The *Casey* plurality made an essentially similar point almost a century after Brewer's pronouncement when they controversially argued that the Court's legitimacy required it to follow precedent in the face of political pressure. See *Casey*, 505 U.S. at 865–66 ("The Court must take care to speak and act in ways that allow people to accept its decisions on the terms the Court claims for them, as grounded truly in principle, not as compromises with social and political pressures having, as such, no bearing on the principled choices that the Court is obliged to make.").

[88] *Citizens United*, 130 S. Ct. at 941–2 (Stevens, J. dissenting).

[89] *Id.* at 903 (citing *Austin*, 494 U.S. at 695 (Kennedy, J., dissenting)).

[90] See *Montejo*, 129 S. Ct. at 2091 (overruling *Michigan v. Jackson*, 475 U.S. 625 (1986)). See also *id.* at 2087 (citing *Jackson*, 475 U.S. at 1404 (Rehnquist, CJ., dissenting)).

[91] See *Payne*, 501 U.S. at 830, 825 (citing *Booth*, 482 U.S. at 517 (White, J., dissenting)).

be found in the writings of Justice Marshall himself."[92] Scalia quoted Marshall's prior observation that stare decisis "is not an imprisonment of reason" and concluded that Marshall really agreed with the proposition that precedents "with plainly inadequate rational support" should be overruled.[93] In essence, Scalia charged Marshall with adopting the weak approach when he disapproved of the precedent in question and the strong approach when he approved. Meanwhile, though Chief Justice Rehnquist articulated a weak test in *Payne*, he later took a surprisingly strong stance toward stare decisis in *Dickerson v. United States*—a case that affirmed the notably liberal precedent *Miranda v. Arizona*.[94] When Justice Scalia dissented from this stare decisis analysis in *Dickerson*, Rehnquist subtly pointed to Scalia's own inconsistency by quoting Scalia's observation that a ruling's "wide acceptance in the legal culture … is adequate reason not to overrule it."[95]

Such examples of inconsistency could be multiplied. However, the basic point is brought home by the fact that Justice Kennedy both wrote the *Citizens United* majority opinion *and* was one of the joint opinion authors in *Casey*. He has thus advocated for and against including an analysis of a challenged precedent's reasoning in the stare decisis calculus. In other words, the Court's most prominent swing vote has swung wildly on the question of what authentic principles of stare decisis really require.

The widespread inconsistency of Justices towards the proper stare decisis test suggests that the Court's "precedent about precedent" itself has little precedential value. From one case to the next, a single Justice may analyze overruling questions using different stare decisis tests. Whether the test advocated is weak or strong depends almost entirely on the result being justified. Strong stare decisis tests—disavowing inquiry into the reasoning of a challenged precedent—appear almost exclusively in opinions urging adherence.[96] On the flip side, weak tests that emphasize the force of reasoning in prior dissents only show up in opinions pushing for overruling.

Choosing sides in the debate over stare decisis doctrine is thus ill-advised. Consistency about stare decisis doctrine may sound like a good rule-of-law idea, but its theoretical value is challenged by the practical bottom line of strong versus weak views of stare decisis. When all is said and done, a weak view of stare decisis authorizes change in doctrine through overruling precedent while a strong view promotes stability by affirming precedent. It seems unfair (if not absurd) to expect any jurist to universally commit ahead of time to always supporting doctrinal change or

---

[92] *Payne*, 501 U.S. at 833 (Scalia, J., concurring).

[93] *Id.* (quoting Guardians Ass'n. v. Civil Service Comm'n of New York City, 463 U.S. 582, 618 (1983) (Marshall, J., dissenting)) (internal citation omitted).

[94] See Dickerson v. United States, 530 U.S. 428, 443 (2000) ("Whether or not we would agree with *Miranda*'s reasoning … in the first instance, the principles of *stare decisis* weigh heavily against overruling it now.")

[95] *Id.* (quoting Mitchell v. United States, 526 U.S. 314, 331 (1999) (Scalia, J., dissenting)).

[96] Some exceptions are depicted in Fig. 2.1 (Sect. 2.3.1 above) and discussed in the accompanying text.

always supporting doctrinal stability. Sometimes change is good. Sometimes stability is. Context matters immensely.

In the final analysis, stare decisis doctrine is all about context. It is a way of arguing about context—a rhetorical mode for debating first-order Court doctrine.[97] The competing opinions in the stare decisis dialectic effectively provide a list of ready-made arguments for and against overruling any given precedent. Justices frame their own particular cases for overruling or adhering to precedent by citing to earlier stare decisis discussions. These earlier discussions themselves cite back to even earlier opinions, and so on, in a chain, all the way back to Brandeis's dissent in *Coronado Oil*. Yet no opinion in the chain can ever stand completely apart from the particular overruling debate that precipitated it.

References

Aristotle (2007) On rhetoric: a theory of civic discourse, 2nd edn (trans: Kennedy GA). Oxford University Press, New York

Lee EG III (2002) Overruling rhetoric: the court's new approach to stare decisis in constitutional cases. Univ Toledo Law Rev 33(3):581–619

Starger C (2012a) Exile on main street: competing traditions and due process dissent. Marquette Law Rev 95(4):1253–1328

Starger C (2012b) Expanding stare decisis: the role of precedent in the unfolding dialectic of *Brady v. Maryland*. Loyola Los Angeles Law Rev 46(1):77–161

[97] Aristotle's term for this kind of rhetorical mode was *topoi*—topics of invention (2007).

Chapter 3
Did *Casey* Strike Out? Following and Overruling Constitutional Precedents in the Supreme Court

Larry Alexander

Abstract This chapter challenges the supposed normative justifications of constitutional stare decisis in the Supreme Court. The author contends that a Justice who believes the Constitution must be obeyed even when it would produce what she believes to be unjust results should, for the same reasons, presumptively reject a supposed obligation to follow incorrect constitutional precedents. The author acknowledges that this presumption might in theory be overcome, if the consequences of overruling a precedent would be calamitous. But he suggests that this will rarely be the case, as the Court could delay implementation of an overruling in order to mitigate its effects or to allow the enactment of a corrective constitutional amendment. The author then specifically addresses the arguments for stare decisis advanced by the well-known plurality opinion in *Planned Parenthood v. Casey*, finding them poorly reasoned and unpersuasive.

3.1 Precedent and Legal Transitions

The topic of legal transitions is one of the most difficult to theorize. Just as we need determinate legal rules to avoid the costs of uncertainty, unpredictability, and lack of coordination, so too we also need those legal rules to be relatively stable over time. Legal rules that are changing from moment to moment fail to provide the benefits and avert the costs that are their *raison d'être*. On the other hand, legal rules can be infelicitous in many ways. They may have been defective from the outset. Or they have become anachronistic due to various changes in the circumstances to which they are applicable. And when legal rules are or have become infelicitous, we need to be able to change them.

L. Alexander (✉)
School of Law, University of San Diego, 5598 Alcala Park,
San Diego, CA 92110, USA
e-mail: larrya@sandiego.edu

C.J. Peters (ed.), *Precedent in the United States Supreme Court*, Ius Gentium: Comparative Perspectives on Law and Justice 33, DOI 10.1007/978-94-007-7951-8_3,

So we want our legal rules to be impermanent but not ephemeral. But how to determine where that sweet spot is between those undesirable poles is a theoretical puzzle. It overhangs the law of takings, the law of impairment of contracts, the doctrine of vested rights, and the problem of whether various legislative changes (in, for example, the tax code) should avoid retroactivity and to what extent (Alexander 2003). (Even laws that are prospective in form can upset expectations formed prior to their enactment. So, for example, a law to eliminate the home mortgage tax deduction allowed by current U.S. tax law—even if it is not to go into effect for 30 years—can negatively affect current property values.)

The problem of when to overrule precedent is another problem of legal transitions, and it is no easier to theorize than the others (Alexander and Sherwin 2001, 136–56; Alexander and Sherwin 2008, 58–63). Precedents, like other legal rules, can be or become infelicitous. And when they are infelicitous, there is obviously a reason—their infelicitousness—to overturn them. On the other hand, if precedents could be overruled merely because the courts believed them to be infelicitous, there would be no doctrine of stare decisis, and the benefits it provides would be lost. (Stare decisis has its force only in those cases in which the court believes that the result demanded by the precedent is worse than the opposite result; or, put differently, if precedents are followed only when the court agrees with the results they reached, stare decisis is doing no work.)

My topic here will be that of precedents in constitutional law. Moreover, I will be concerned only with constitutional law precedents established by the U.S. Supreme Court. And the issue I will explore is under what conditions should the Supreme Court overrule its constitutional precedents.

3.2 Infelicitous Precedents

The Supreme Court should overrule its constitutional precedents only if they are infelicitous in some way. That much is obvious. But constitutional precedents can be infelicitous in three basic ways.

First, they may be infelicitous because, although they faithfully implement the Constitution, the Constitution itself is infelicitous in the sense that it dictates bad policy or even injustice. The Supreme Court would in such a case be faced with the dilemma that besets all law, namely, whether to follow its legal obligations or whether to disobey them for the sake of good policy or justice. I have written extensively about this dilemma (Alexander and Sherwin 2001, 53–95), but here I shall put it aside. I shall assume in what follows that the Court will follow any precedent that it believes correctly interprets and implements the Constitution, even if it believes the provision of the Constitution at issue is itself bad policy or unjust.

The second way a constitutional precedent may be infelicitous occurs when the constitutional provision at issue is correctly interpreted by the Court to be a vague standard, and the precedent case created a more determinate rule to implement that standard, a rule about which the Court now has second thoughts. The Court may believe that, say, equal protection is such a standard, and that its doctrines regarding levels of scrutiny are judicially crafted rules for implementing that standard, rules that it now believes should be rethought.[1] Overturning precedents of this type raises pretty much the same issues as are raised by overturning common-law precedents, which can themselves be conceptualized as rules for implementing standards of wise and just policy. Put differently, standards invite the decisionmaker to employ first-order practical reasoning and "do the right thing" within the rule-bounded domain governed by the standard. In the course of implementing standards, however, the courts might attempt to convert them into sets of rules, rules that later courts might deem infelicitous.

The third kind of constitutional infelicity occurs when the Court's precedent assumes that the constitutional provision in question (1) is a standard when the Court now believes it to be a rule; (2) is a standard of broad scope when the Court now believes it to be a standard of much narrower scope; (3) is a standard that refers to value A when the Court now believes it refers to value B; or (4) is a rule with meaning A when the Court now believes it to be a standard or a rule with meaning B. In all of these examples, the Court now believes its precedent rests on a misinterpretation of the Constitution rather than on a misimplementation of it. Precedents that (the Court believes) misinterpret the Constitution in these ways will be my focus in this chapter.

So I am interested here in Supreme Court errors of misinterpretation (of the Constitution) rather than errors in implementing correct interpretations. "We said in our precedent case that this constitutional provision means A, and now we believe it means B." When the Court is in that position, under what conditions should it overrule the erroneous precedent, and under what conditions should it follow that precedent?

3.3 Precedents that Misinterpret the Constitution

One necessary condition for overruling an erroneous interpretive precedent is that the interpretation of the Constitution that the precedent declares is now believed to be erroneous. That much is obvious once one accepts that one's belief in the infelicity of the Constitution, correctly interpreted, is itself not a sufficient condition for departing from it. But is the necessary condition of interpretive error also a sufficient condition for overruling a constitutional precedent?

Some, whom I shall call constitutional purists, might say that it is (Lawson 2007; Paulsen 2005). But what if overturning an incorrect constitutional interpretation

[1] In U.S. equal-protection jurisprudence—judicial decisionmaking under the Equal Protection Clause of the Constitution's Fourteenth Amendment—the courts scrutinize some laws more closely than others. The laws they more closely scrutinize are laws that employ racial, alienage, or gender classifications or that infringe so-called "fundamental rights."

would wreak economic and social havoc? Consider the *Legal Tender Cases*,[2] an 1871 decision in which the Supreme Court upheld the constitutionality of paper money. The Court's constitutional interpretation on this matter was, and is, controversial. It is quite possible that the Court erred.

So suppose that the Court in the *Legal Tender Cases* did err, and paper money's constitutionality as legal tender is again challenged. Should the present Supreme Court, convinced that interpretive error was committed in the *Legal Tender Cases*, repudiate that earlier holding and declare paper money to be unconstitutional?

On first impression, this seems like a rhetorical question. Of course the Court should stick with the precedent even if the precedent Court misinterpreted the Constitution. Getting rid of paper money would be economically and socially disastrous. The Court or the Constitution, perhaps both, would likely cease to be regarded as authoritative, in which case a (bloodless) revolution of sorts would have occurred.

But the purist would say, "Not so fast. The Court can delay implementing the new (really the old) regime for a time period sufficient for adopting a constitutional amendment affirming the *Legal Tender Cases* and the validity of paper money. So the sky needn't fall if the Court repudiates erroneous constitutional precedents."

"Moreover," the purist might continue, "you have just said that the Court should not deviate from the Constitution just because in its eyes some constitutional provisions are infelicitous. Were infelicity (in the Court's eyes) a sufficient ground for departing from the Constitution, correctly interpreted, we would have substituted the Court's views of justice and wise policy for the Constitution as the 'supreme law of the land.' But what is the difference between adhering to the Constitution despite belief in its infelicity and overturning precedents that are inconsistent with the Constitution even if overturning them would in some way be infelicitous?"

I used to believe there was an answer to the purist's points. To see how that answer went, one must put oneself in the position of the Court in the *Legal Tender Cases*. Suppose the Court believes that using paper money as legal tender is good policy but that the Constitution does not allow that. If there is a point to having a constitution, the Court must declare the attempt to make paper money legal tender to be invalid. That is the point I made earlier.

On the other hand, once the Court upholds the use of paper money as legal tender, and institutions and practices grow up premised on the assumption that paper money is legal tender, the constitutional question arguably looks different. Now, overturning the *Legal Tender Cases* would not merely be infelicitous. It would be calamitous.

However, the purist would respond that the difference between "calamitous" and "infelicitous" is one of degree, not kind. It is surely not a sufficiently bright-line distinction to be judicially administrable. Rather, the Court will be tempted, consciously or not, to find "calamity" lurking behind overturning any precedent it likes on policy grounds. The vagueness of the infelicitous/calamitous distinction will make the overturning of erroneous precedents into a one-way ratchet. Precedents

---

[2] 79 U.S. 457 (1871).

will be overturned only if the Court thinks them infelicitous and never if the Court thinks them felicitous.

The purist will also point out that the response does not take into account the possibility of delaying the overturning of precedents for a period sufficient for amending the Constitution.[3] After all, if overturning a precedent will really be calamitous, will not there be the requisite supermajority to amend the Constitution ready to act to preserve the status quo? Conversely, if there is not such a supermajority in favor of departing from the Constitution as now properly interpreted, will not that rebut the claim that overturning the erroneous precedent would be catastrophic?

One reply to the purist would be to argue that a decision prospectively overruling a constitutional precedent in order to allow time for a constitutional amendment would violate the "case or controversy" requirement of Article III.[4] It would be equivalent to an advisory opinion in that it would not resolve the particular case brought by the challenger of paper money.

There are cases, however, where the Court has not granted immediate relief but has instead ordered compliance with the new constitutional order to take place "with all deliberate speed."[5] That would imply that the Court accepts that a judgment declaring that paper money as legal tender is unconstitutional, and then ordering the dismantling of institutions built on paper money "with all deliberate speed," complies with the case or controversy requirement. And "all deliberate speed" could be gauged to allow time for a constitutional amendment, or so the purist might argue.

Here's another possible reply to the purist. Some erroneous constitutional precedents are so popular that they have been accepted as the supreme law of the land and have in effect become nonorganic constitutional amendments. By nonorganic, I mean that they have not become amendments to the Constitution in the manner prescribed by Article V.[6] Rather, they have become amendments merely through their popular acceptance, just as the Constitution itself is only supreme law because it is accepted as such. (Just because it was ratified in the manner prescribed by its Article VII and declares itself to be "the supreme law of the land" in Article VI does not make it the supreme law of the land. If I write down a bunch of norms and declare them to be the supreme law of the land upon my raising my right hand and singing "God Bless America," my raising my right hand and so singing will not

[3] Prospective and delayed-implementation overrulings are not unknown (Maltz 1987–1988, 368–69; Keeton 1969, 25–53). On delayed-implementation overrulings, see the discussion of *Brown v. Board of Education* in the text accompanying note 5 below. Of course, even prospective changes can cause present uncertainty (Alicea 2012, 811). Yet, if the changes are delayed sufficiently, that uncertainty can be significantly reduced.

[4] U.S. Const. art. III, § 2. The Supreme Court has held that the Constitution's extending federal judicial power only to cases or controversies precludes federal courts from issuing merely advisory opinions.

[5] Brown v. Board of Education, 349 U.S. 249, 301 (1955).

[6] U.S. Const., art. V sets forth the formal requirements for amending the Constitution.

make my norms supreme law—unless, that is, they are accepted as such by most of the population. The Constitution is no different.)

The purist will reply that the assertion that some erroneous precedents have been accepted as nonorganic constitutional amendments is a theoretical possibility.[7] But in order to tell if that is the case with any particular erroneous precedent, one must distinguish precedents that are revered despite the knowledge that they are misinterpretations of the Constitution from those that are revered because it is believed, erroneously, that they are faithful interpretations. In the absence of that distinction, one cannot say of the polity's "acceptance" of an erroneous constitutional precedent that it is not conditional on a belief in its correctness, a belief that by hypothesis is mistaken. And perhaps the only way to make that distinction, other than by highly sophisticated polling, is to have the Court overrule the precedent but stay the effect of the overruling to allow time for an organic constitutional amendment.

There is another possible arrow in the anti-purist's quiver: the value of settlement. Just as the Constitution settles disagreements about what shall be the supreme law of the United States, so, too, Supreme Court decisions settle what the Constitution itself means. Or, those decisions interpreting the Constitution settle the matters in dispute so long as they themselves are accepted as supreme law, on par with the Constitution itself. If settlement is a good thing in the case of the Constitution, is it not an equally good thing in the case of Supreme Court interpretations of the Constitution?

Supreme Court settlement of the meaning of the Constitution *is* a good thing. Fred Schauer and I have strongly, though controversially, endorsed *Cooper v. Aaron*'s[8] holding to that effect (Alexander and Schauer 1997). However, *Cooper* does not answer the question before us. *Cooper* held that officials must act as though the Court's interpretations of the Constitution are correct. It rejected strong departmentalism, which would allow officials outside the judiciary to act contrary to the Court's commands if they disagree with the Court's constitutional decisions. *Cooper* did not hold that the Court itself was so bound, and nothing in the logic of the judicial supremacy asserted in *Cooper* demands that later Supreme Courts be bound by erroneous (in their eyes) decisions of earlier Supreme Courts.

Of course, if the Court routinely overturned its earlier decisions, the benefits of settlement would be diminished, particularly in domains in which long-term predictability of constitutional requirements is important. Even so, the benefits of diachronic settlement pale in comparison to those of synchronic settlement. For if each branch and level of government—federal, state, and local—insisted on following its own interpretation of the Constitution, such interpretive anarchy would prove intolerable. By contrast, the Supreme Court's overturning its own precedents will likely happen infrequently, especially with recent precedents,

---

[7] See, for example, Frederick Schauer's "Amending the Presuppositions of a Constitution" (1995, 145).

[8] Cooper v. Aaron, 358 U.S. 1 (1958). The Supreme Court in *Cooper* held that its constitutional interpretations must be treated by other governmental actors as tantamount to the Constitution itself and not restricted to controlling only the cases in which they were announced.

and the accompanying reliance setbacks can be cushioned by making the overruling decisions prospective in effect.

Another tack for defending adherence to erroneous constitutional precedents would be to argue that even staying an overruling for a period sufficient to get a constitutional amendment would not avert the deleterious effects of unsettling a precedent upon which so much has been staked. After all, even with a sufficient period of time, and even with the threat of cataclysmic costs if the amendment is not ratified, it is still possible that the amendment will fail to get through the many "veto gates" in the path of constitutional amendments. And uncertainty that it will do so will produce its own costs.[9]

I have tentatively come to believe that if the case-or-controversy argument fails, then this last argument is the best argument available for following precedents that misinterpret the Constitution. It is not a knockdown argument by any means, and I'm not sure it is persuasive. The purist's case against following precedents that misinterpret the Constitution is a strong one, at least when buttressed by the possibility of staying the overruling for a period of time.[10]

3.4 The Supreme Court and Constitutional Misinterpretations

At this point I shall put aside the theoretical question regarding the precedential force of constitutional misinterpretations and turn to what the Court itself thinks about the issue. The most recent and extensive Supreme Court discourse on the matter occurs in *Planned Parenthood of Southeastern Pennsylvania v. Casey*.[11] In that case, the Court's then three swing Justices—Kennedy, O'Connor, and Souter—issued

[9] A "veto gate" here refers to the various institutions that must approve a proposed constitutional amendment for it to become part of the Constitution. Article V of the Constitution typically requires approval of the amendment by two-thirds of each house of Congress and by three-fourths of the states. Put negatively, that means that one-third of either house or 12 states can veto a proposed amendment. (I call this set of requirements "typical" because the alternative method for amending the Constitution, through state conventions, has never been employed; and in any event, the convention method will likely be just as difficult an obstacle course for getting an amendment approved as is the typical method.)

[10] I should say a word about my colleague Mike Rappaport's and his co-author John McGinnis's (2009) recent argument in favor of following erroneous constitutional precedents. They believe that either when, because of reliance, overruling an erroneous constitutional precedent would impose enormous social costs, or when a precedent has become "entrenched" (widely accepted as equivalent to the Constitution in terms of authority), the Court should follow the precedent. With respect to reliance costs, they do not consider the possibility of a stayed overruling. They also realize that it is difficult to discern when a precedent has been accepted in the manner required for entrenchment rather than on the assumption that the Court has correctly interpreted the Constitution. And although they cite evidence that the "judicial power" granted the Court by the Constitution includes the power to establish binding precedents, there are many domains in which that power could be asserted other than the domain of constitutional interpretation.

[11] 505 U.S. 833 (1992).

an opinion in which they hinted that they believed *Roe v. Wade,*[12] the 1973 case recognizing a constitutional right to an abortion, had been wrongly decided. They went on, however, to argue that even if that were true, they would not overrule it but would adhere to its basic holding.

The basic holding of *Roe* to which these three Justices pledged fealty was its deeming as a violation of the Fourteenth Amendment's Due Process Clause any state effort to ban early-term abortions. Other aspects of the *Roe* decision—most notably, its specific rules for each trimester of pregnancy—these Justices were willing to abandon, and they did so in *Casey*. But they refused to abandon the basic holding even if it was an erroneous one. That holding was a precedent to which they believed they should adhere.

The three Justices not only did not come out and say explicitly that *Roe*'s basic holding was erroneous; they also declined to elaborate on exactly why it might be erroneous. So perhaps it is worthwhile to review *Roe*'s basic holding and see what aspect of it the *Casey* plurality might have found questionable.

One aspect of the holding in *Roe* was its deeming a woman's control over her reproduction a fundamental liberty.[13] This aspect, however, which follows naturally enough from *Eisenstadt*'s[14] gloss on *Griswold,*[15] was almost assuredly not what the *Casey* plurality had in mind. Nor is it by itself what is so controversial about *Roe*.

The real weak link in *Roe*'s basic holding was not its giving great weight to women's control over reproduction but rather its rejection of the state's assertion of a compelling interest in protecting the life of the fetus. If such a compelling interest had been recognized, it would have vindicated the state's ban on early abortions notwithstanding the woman's opposed fundamental interest.

One line of argument in *Roe*, given short shrift in the majority opinion by Justice Blackmun, was that fetuses were "persons" within the meaning of the Due Process Clause and therefore protected against deprivations of life without due process of law.[16] The upshot of finding fetuses to be persons under the Due Process Clause would perhaps be an affirmative obligation on the state to protect their lives by banning the intentional killing of them. *A fortiori*, if the state has a constitutional *duty* to protect the lives of fetuses, it is *permitted* to do so.

In any event, Justice Blackmun rejected that interpretation of the "persons" to whom the Due Process Clause refers. That rejection may or may not have been correct, but I do not read the *Casey* plurality as regarding that aspect of *Roe* as its weak link.

Of course, even if fetuses are not persons within the meaning of the Due Process Clause, that does not settle the question of whether the state has a compelling

---

[12] 410 U.S. 113 (1973).

[13] 410 U.S. at 169–70.

[14] Eisenstadt v. Baird, 405 U.S. 438 (1972), held that unmarried persons have a right to obtain contraceptives.

[15] Griswold v. Connecticut, 381 U.S. 479 (1965), held that married couples have a right to obtain contraceptives.

[16] 410 U.S. at 157–58.

interest in protecting their lives. E.T., Steven Spielberg's cute extraterrestrial, is surely not a person in the Due Process Clause sense. Nor is Koko, the gorilla who communicates using sign language and at one time had a pet kitten. But that they are not persons in the constitutional sense surely does not mean their lives are not worth protecting, and protecting at the expense of serious human interests.

The question of whether the state has a compelling interest in protecting the life of the early fetus was misleadingly characterized by Justice Blackmun as the question of when human life begins, a question that, according to Blackmun, divides the medical profession and scientists.[17] But there is no such question and no such division. No one denies that fetuses are alive. If they were not alive, then abortions could not kill them. Abortions *do* kill them, however, so they *are* alive. Nor is there any question about fetuses' humanity. They are, after all, *human* fetuses.

The real question is whether early fetuses are morally protectable beings who are no different in that respect from human adults, and that is a philosophical question, not a medical or scientific one.[18] And, of course, that question is hotly debated among philosophers. Some believe that early fetuses *are* morally protectable, and aborting them is a serious wrong, on par with killing post-natal humans.[19] Others believe that fetuses are not morally protectable for reasons that entail that very young children are also not morally protectable.[20] Presumably, these philosophers would deny that the state has any compelling interest in banning infanticide, at least in circumstances where the infant can only be cared for by its mother using her body. (Think of a young mother shipwrecked with an infant, who cannot be rescued for 9 months, and who can only keep the infant alive by nursing it.) And there are many philosophical positions regarding the moral protectability of fetuses that lie in between these polar camps. Finally, there are some philosophers who argue that even if fetuses are fully morally protectable, women do not have affirmative duties to use their bodies to keep fetuses alive.[21] (Because the Court has accepted the constitutional legitimacy of compelling bodily labor,[22] this libertarian philosophical position, however persuasive philosophically, has no constitutional traction and therefore cannot support *Roe*.)

The most charitable reading of Justice Blackmun's opinion in *Roe* is that when you have a woman's fundamental interest on one side of the balance, and you have a philosophically controversial position on the state's side, the woman wins. In other words, a philosophically controversial state interest, even if it would be a compelling interest were one side of the philosophical controversy correct, cannot count as a sufficiently compelling interest to override an opposed fundamental interest. But even that charitable reading leaves Blackmun's opinion quite vulnerable. For one thing, as I have just shown—recall my shipwrecked nursing mother

---

[17] *Id.* at 160–61.

[18] See, for example, George Parkin Grant's *English-Speaking Justice* (1985, 71–73).

[19] See, for example, Don Marquis's "Why Abortion is Immoral" (1989).

[20] Including Michael Tooley (1973, 51), Mary Anne Warren (1979, 35), and Jeff McMahan (2002, 254).

[21] One such philosopher is Judith Jarvis Thomson (1971).

[22] See Selective Draft Law Cases, 245 U.S. 366 (1918).

example—the ban on infanticide can conceivably intrude on women's liberty interests, including their control over their bodies. But some quite respectable philosophers believe infants are no more morally protectable against painless killing than are fetuses. Would Blackmun conclude that therefore bans on infanticide are unconstitutional?

The more general worry about this reading of Blackmun's opinion is this: Even if the state's side of the balance is a controversial proposition, one might still conclude that its side of the balance should prevail against the woman's side of the balance. For if it is possible that the controversy should be resolved in favor of the fetus's protectability, then a ruling in favor of a woman's right to abort will result in the death of a morally protectable being. A ruling in favor of protecting the fetus, however, if it has resolved the controversy incorrectly, will result in forced pregnancy and childbirth—a huge unjustifiable cost, but not nearly as huge a cost as an unjustifiable death.

3.5 Reliance?

I shall assume that this last, most charitable reading of Justice Blackmun's opinion in *Roe* is what the *Casey* trio had second thoughts about. Yet, they declined to overrule *Roe* on this point. Why did they decline?

With respect to when the Court should overrule its constitutional precedents, the trio admitted that, quoting Justice Brandeis dissenting in *Burnet v. Coronado Oil & Gas Co.*, "*stare decisis* is not an 'inexorable command,' and certainly it is not such in every constitutional case."[23] They continued:

> Rather, when this Court reexamines a prior holding, its judgment is customarily informed by a series of prudential and pragmatic considerations designed to test the consistency of overruling a prior decision with the ideal of the rule of law, and to gauge the respective costs of reaffirming and overruling a prior case. Thus, for example, we may ask whether the rule has proven to be intolerable simply in defying practical workability …; whether the rule is subject to a kind of reliance that would lend a special hardship to the consequences of overruling and add inequity to the cost of repudiation …; whether related principles of law have so far developed as to have left the old rule no more than a remnant of abandoned doctrine …; or whether facts have so changed, or come to be seen so differently, as to have robbed the old rule of significant application or justification ….
>
> So in this case we may enquire whether *Roe*'s central rule has been found unworkable; whether the rule's limitation on state power could be removed without serious inequity to those who have relied upon it or significant damage to the stability of the society governed by it; whether the law's growth in the intervening years has left *Roe*'s central rule a doctrinal anachronism discounted by society; and whether *Roe*'s premises of fact have so far changed in the ensuing two decades as to render its central holding somehow irrelevant or unjustifiable in dealing with the issue it addressed.[24]

---

[23] Planned Parenthood of Se. Pa. v. Casey, 505 U.S. 833, 854 (1992) (emphasis in original).

[24] 505 U.S. at 854–55.

What is striking about the trio's list of considerations is that nowhere do they refer to whether the precedent misinterpreted the Constitution. Perhaps they are assuming that the precedent is a misinterpretation but implying that these additional conditions are necessary before overruling is proper. Thus, if a precedent is both a misinterpretation and, in addition, unworkable in practice, it should go without saying that it should be overruled. On the other hand, if there are serious reliance interests that would be in jeopardy were the misinterpreting precedent overruled, that would be a reason for not overruling. (Recall the example of the *Legal Tender Cases.*) I shall return to the reliance point in a moment.

The third and fourth conditions—whether the law or the facts have developed in a direction that leaves the precedent an isolated, narrow, doctrinal remnant—seem more applicable to rules developed by the Court to implement constitutional interpretations than to constitutional interpretations and misinterpretations themselves.[25] After all, if there will be no reliance harms in overruling a misinterpretation of the Constitution, why should we care whether that misinterpretation has also been left orphaned by doctrinal and factual changes?

One possibility is that "orphaning" of a precedent might make it less likely that people have reasonably relied on it. For that reason, the fact that *Roe* had not been orphaned made the inference of detrimental reliance on it at least less implausible than had *Roe* been orphaned. Orphaning would just be an evidentiary consideration; reliance would be the material one.

Another possibility is that orphaning is evidence for the decision's being a misinterpretation of the Constitution. Thus, *Roe*'s not having been orphaned strengthens the case that it was a correct interpretation.

The trio, of course, was writing its opinion based on the contrary hypothesis, namely, that *Roe* was incorrectly decided. Perhaps, however, its doubts about the truth of that hypothesis weighed heavily on them and affected what they wrote. I am assessing their opinion on the assumption that they believed *Roe* was incorrectly decided and thus that unencumbered by that precedent, they would have decided *Casey* and the abortion issue generally differently. Of course, constitutional interpretation is a difficult matter, and due consideration should be given to the opinions of one's predecessor interpreters. Nonetheless, the ultimate question is what one should do when, having considered the contrary evidence, including the opinions of the precedent courts, one concludes that the precedent courts erred in their constitutional interpretations.

Having listed the conditions for overruling constitutional precedents, the trio then turns to assessing whether overruling *Roe* satisfies those conditions and concludes that it does not. The basic holding of *Roe* has not proved "unworkable." Nor has it by any means become a doctrinal orphan. And, of course, neither the facts about unwanted pregnancies nor those regarding the nature of fetuses have changed since *Roe*.

---

[25] See Mitchell N. Berman's "Constitutional Decision Rules" (2004), distinguishing interpretations, which set forth the *meanings* of the provisions at issue, from decision rules, which are judicially crafted doctrines for implementing those meanings.

The trio was correct about all of this, but, as I said, I fail to see the relevance of these points if *Roe* is a misinterpretation of the Constitution. I have discussed orphaning. "Workability" seems to bear on whether the Constitution is good policy, something that I said courts should treat as immaterial. Reliance on *Roe*, on the other hand, *is* relevant, or so I have indicated, at least if one rejects the purist's position. But the trio's discussion of the reliance condition for overruling is nothing short of risible.

The trio begins its discussion of reliance sensibly enough by downplaying as *de minimis* any reliance on *Roe* by individuals engaged in sexual activity that might result in an unwanted pregnancy. As the Justices recognize, "reproductive planning could take virtually immediate account of any sudden restoration of state authority to ban abortions."[26]

That point, however, does not dispose of the reliance interest in the eyes of the trio. For they go on to say the following:

> To eliminate the issue of reliance that easily, however, one would need to limit cognizable reliance to specific instances of sexual activity. But to do this would be simply to refuse to face the fact that for two decades of economic and social developments, people have organized intimate relationships and made choices that define their views of themselves and their places in society, in reliance on the availability of abortion in the event that contraception should fail. The ability of women to participate equally in the economic and social life of the Nation has been facilitated by their ability to control their reproductive lives. ... The Constitution serves human values, and while the effect of reliance on *Roe* cannot be exactly measured, neither can the certain cost of overruling *Roe* for people who have ordered their thinking and living around that case be dismissed.[27]

That is all the trio says about what, in my opinion, has to be the pivotal consideration in the decision whether to overrule a misinterpretation of the Constitution. "[P]eople have organized intimate relationships" around *Roe*? "[P]eople have ... made choices that define their views of themselves and their places in society" in reliance on *Roe*? It is hard for me to take these statements seriously, especially the latter one. Indeed, reliance on an erroneous interpretation of the Constitution to form one's view of oneself and one's place in society is arguably not the kind of reliance interest that should be protected by constitutional stare decisis. Many white Southerners no doubt formed their view of themselves and their place in society around the constitutional legitimacy of Jim Crow laws. That such a reliance interest should have blocked overruling *Plessy v. Ferguson*[28] would not pass the straight-face test. Why is the unconstitutionality of bans on abortion, if an error, any different from *Plessy* in this respect? Where constitutional issues of great moment are at stake, it seems inappropriate to consider whether people have relied for their self-conception on existing incorrect interpretations.

And is the unconstitutionality of bans on abortion really necessary for "[t]he ability of women to participate equally in the economic and social life of the

---

[26] 505 U.S. at 856.

[27] *Id.*

[28] 163 U.S. 537 (1896). *Plessy* upheld the constitutionality of *de jure* racial segregation.

nation"? Overturning *Roe* does not by itself make abortion illegal; that requires the states to act to ban it. But even if all 50 states do so—a quite unlikely scenario—it is hard to believe that in this era of "the pill" and other quite effective forms of birth control, the availability of abortion is necessary for women to achieve economic and social equality. It is almost insulting for the trio to imply otherwise. At the very least, the Court should not have rested its reliance case on unsupported empirical assumptions.

Finally, the trio's implication that many people "have ordered their thinking and living around [*Roe*]" is, quite frankly, ludicrous. The "cost" to such people, if any exists, is surely not one that should be countenanced. There probably actually were people who "ordered their thinking and living" around Jim Crow. Should that have given the Court pause before acknowledging the constitutional error of *Plessy*?

3.6 Consistency?

Having attempted to justify not overruling *Roe* on the implausible ground of reliance, the plurality next attempts to distinguish its invocation of stare decisis to uphold *Roe* from its willingness to overrule the precedents of *Plessy v. Ferguson* and *Lochner v. New York*[29] and their progeny.[30] Assuming *Plessy* and *Lochner* were erroneous constitutional interpretations, I have no quarrel with the plurality's case for their overruling. However, the plurality's attempt to rest the distinction between *Plessy* and *Lochner* on the one hand, and *Roe* on the other, on the basis of changes in circumstances or the understanding of those circumstances is simply a dodge. The basic question in all these cases is whether they rest on correct interpretations of the Constitution. And the reason *Plessy* and *Lochner* were overruled was not because of changed factual circumstances or changed views of the original factual circumstances. They were overruled because they were deemed to have interpreted the Constitution incorrectly. The fact that there have been no changes in our understanding of the nature of fetuses since the *Roe* decision does not suggest that the decision was correct.

3.7 Legitimacy?

The plurality's final argument for not overruling *Roe* is perhaps its most controversial one. In essence, the plurality argued that given the controversy surrounding the *Roe* decision, overruling it would make the Court appear susceptible to popular pressure and unprincipled, with the result that its legitimacy as the authoritative interpreter of

[29] 198 U.S. 45 (1905). *Lochner* struck down as an unconstitutional deprivation of liberty a state law setting maximum hours for bakers.

[30] 505 U.S. at 861–64.

the Constitution would be undermined.[31] The plurality described the role of the Court as that of an arbiter of major political controversies, whose authority so to act would be undermined were it to reverse course after having announced its resolutions. In essence, the plurality was saying, better to stick to our guns rather than to admit error, even if we believe we did err.

But consider the implications of the plurality's stance. Even if *Roe* misinterpreted the Constitution, and even if, as a consequence, millions of lives of possibly morally protectable human beings hang in the balance, the Court must not admit error for fear that doing so will diminish its authority.[32] No wonder that Michael Paulsen (2003, 1032) regards the plurality's refusal to overrule *Roe* on that basis as an "atrocity" and indicts *Casey* as "[t]he worst constitutional decision of all time."

Paulsen (1035) is scathing in his criticisms of *Casey*: "As a practical matter, *Casey* may have made, and certainly appears to have been intended to make, the constitutional right to abortion *irreversible* by our legal system—even though a majority of the Court apparently believed that *Roe* was wrongly decided." Paulsen goes on to point out that the doctrine of stare decisis set forth by the plurality not only did not compel affirming *Roe* but was indefensible on its own terms—manipulable and inconsistent with its announced *desiderata* of workability, reliance, stability, consistency, and the appearance of judicial integrity (1035). I concur.[33]

3.8 Conclusion

The practice of following precedent sits uneasily in a system governed by a Constitution that is the supreme law of the land. If the Constitution, properly interpreted, blocks the achievement of justice and good government, we can blame that on the Constitution and seek to change it. If, as is much more likely, the Constitution merely permits but does not compel unjust and imprudent policies, we can blame our elected representatives. If judicially overturning an

[31] *Id.* at 864–69.

[32] The policy stakes in a constitutional interpretation should not bear on it, or so I have argued. If *Roe* were a correct interpretation of the Constitution, the moral status of fetuses and aborting them would be immaterial to the Court's job. If, however, *Roe* was wrongly decided, the policy stakes in refusing to overrule it surely compound the Court's error.

[33] It is also very difficult to square the plurality's position for not overruling *Roe* with its willingness to overrule *Bowers v. Hardwick*, 478 U.S. 186 (1986) (which upheld anti-sodomy laws), in *Lawrence v. Texas*, 539 U.S. 558 (2003) (which held anti-sodomy laws unconstitutional). The *Casey* plurality all supported the decision in *Lawrence*, although the case for overruling *Bowers* surely was not easily distinguishable from the case for overruling *Roe* according to the criteria to which the plurality claimed adherence in *Casey*, a point hammered home by Justice Scalia in his *Lawrence* dissent. 539 U.S. 558, 586–92 (Scalia, J., dissenting). There was an ongoing controversy over *Bowers* just as there was over *Roe*. And *Bowers* was surely not undermined by other decisions or factual changes. Justice Kennedy, in his opinion for the Court in *Lawrence*, claimed there had been no reliance on *Bowers*. But the reliance argument in *Casey* was, as I argued above, a ludicrous one.

erroneous interpretation of the Constitution would upset reasonable reliance on that erroneous interpretation, there are, as my imaginary purist suggested, possible ways to mitigate the harms of that reversal.

Judicial supremacy in constitutional interpretation may be desirable as compared with departmentalism or other more "protestant" regimes. But the supremacy of an earlier Supreme Court interpretation of the Constitution over what a later Supreme Court now believes is the correct interpretation, while it partakes of the value of settlement, partakes too much of its disvalue. *Casey*'s version of stare decisis untethers constitutional law in the Supreme Court from the Constitution itself without acknowledging that it is doing so, much less justifying it.

References

Alexander L (2003) Introduction to the conference on legal transitions. J Contemp Legal Issues 13(1):1–4

Alexander L, Schauer F (1997) On extrajudicial constitutional interpretation. Harv Law Rev 110(7):1359–1387

Alexander L, Sherwin E (2001) The rule of rules: morality, rules, and the dilemmas of law. Duke University Press, Durham

Alexander L, Sherwin E (2008) Demystifying legal reasoning. Cambridge University Press, Cambridge

Alicea J (2012) Stare decisis in an originalist Congress. Harv J Law Publ Policy 35(2):797–819

Berman M (2004) Constitutional decision rules. Vaa Law Rev 90(1):1–168

Grant GP (1985) English-speaking justice. University of Notre Dame Press, Notre Dame

Keeton RE (1969) Venturing to do justice: reforming private law. Harvard University Press, Cambridge

Lawson G (2007) Mostly unconstitutional: the case against precedent revisited. Ave Maria Law Rev 5(1):1–22

Maltz E (1987–1988) The nature of precedent. N C Law Rev 66(2):367–93

Marquis D (1989) Why abortion is immoral. J Philos 86(4):183–202

McGinnis J, Rappaport M (2009) Reconciling originalism and precedent. Northwest Univ Law Rev 103(2):803–856

McMahan J (2002) The ethics of killing: problems at the margins of life. Oxford University Press, New York

Paulsen MS (2002–2003) The worst constitutional decision of all time. Notre Dame Law Rev 78(4):995–1044

Paulsen MS (2005) The intrinsically corrupting influence of precedent. Const Comment 22(2):289–298

Schauer F (1995) Amending the presuppositions of a constitution. In: Levinson S (ed) Responding to imperfection: the theory and practice of constitutional amendment. Princeton University Press, Princeton, pp 145–161

Thomson JJ (1971) A defense of abortion. Philos Publ Aff 1(1):47–66

Tooley M (1973) A defense of abortion and infanticide. In: Feinberg J (ed) The problem of abortion. Wadsworth Publishing Co., Belmont, pp 51–91

Warren MA (1979) On the moral and legal status of abortion. In: Wasserstrom RA (ed) Today's moral problems, 2nd edn. MacMillan Publishing Co., New York, pp 35–51

Chapter 4
An Epistemic Defense of Precedent

Deborah Hellman

Abstract This chapter presents a normative justification of stare decisis, that is, of a court's presumptive deference to its own prior decisions. Critics often contend that valid epistemic reasons to follow precedent—reasons based on the notion that following precedent will lead to better decisions—do not exist. The author argues, however, that a judge may have both "procedural" and "substantive" epistemic reasons to follow precedents with which she disagrees. Procedurally, a presumptive obligation to follow precedent can force a judge to confront opposing arguments and articulate strong reasons for disagreeing with them, thus improving her own decisionmaking. Substantively, the case-by-case process of generating precedent, involving the input of many judges over time, may generally be superior to ad hoc decisionmaking by a single judge or court. As a conceptual matter, the author argues, these epistemic reasons truly are reasons to follow precedent, because they might apply even when a judge believes a given precedent was decided incorrectly.

4.1 Introduction

To most people who write about precedent, the claim that judges should follow precedent for epistemic reasons is a non-starter. It is derided on the grounds that epistemic reasons for deference to precedent don't really constitute deference to precedent *as precedent*. Alternatively, following precedent for epistemic reasons is mocked and treated as patently unjustified. It smacks of the worst form of blind adherence to tradition. Instead, the judicial practice of according some weight to precedent is usually defended on other grounds, including its value in protecting

D. Hellman (✉)
School of Law, University of Virginia, 580 Massie Road,
Charlottesville, VA 22903, USA
e-mail: dh9ev@virginia.edu

C.J. Peters (ed.), *Precedent in the United States Supreme Court*, Ius Gentium: Comparative Perspectives on Law and Justice 33, DOI 10.1007/978-94-007-7951-8_4,

liberty, equality, stability,[1] predictability,[2] and legitimacy.[3] In this essay, I argue that epistemic reasons for deference to precedent are reasons for according some weight to precedent because it is precedent, and thus constitute a genuine defense of the practice of precedent. In addition, I argue that the practice of deferring to precedent is justified, at least in part for reasons that are epistemic in nature.

A system of decisionmaking that incorporates precedent is one that requires a judge to accord some weight to precedent. For example, if there is a precedent case C1 that is relevantly similar to the case currently before the court, C2, then the judge deciding C2 must count the fact that a prior court decided C1 a particular way as a reason to decide C2 the same way. Whether deference to precedent must take the form of a rule,[4] or instead can take the form of a reason that counts in favor of deciding C2 as C1 was decided,[5] is a further issue that is itself the subject of controversy but which will not be my focus here.

It is important to distinguish genuinely precedential reasoning from reasoning that uses precedents in other ways. For example, a judge deciding C2 may think that C1 was rightly decided, that the reasons affecting the decision in C1 were properly weighed, etc. and thus that the relevantly similar case C2 should be decided in the same manner. Such a decision is not an instance of following precedent, however. The judge decides C2 in the same manner as C1 but not *because* that is how C1 was decided. Rather, she decides this way because she believes it is the correct resolution of the case. Thus Gerald Postema (1991, 1160) asserts that genuinely precedential reasoning must satisfy what he calls the "independence thesis." In order to count as an instance of precedential reasoning, the fact that C1 was decided in a particular way must count in favor of deciding C2 the same way "*independent* of the merits of the decision" in C1 (1160).

The question posed by precedential reasoning then is this: Why should the fact that a prior case was decided a particular way count as a reason, on its own, for deciding a relevantly similar case the same way? The question is most pressing in

---

[1] Frederick Schauer (1987, 601) thinks that the arguments in favor of deference to precedent that work (reliance, predictability, and conservation of judicial resources) all relate to stability. For that reason, Schauer (602) thinks that a system of precedent involves trade-offs: "Stability may be unimpeachable in the abstract, but in reality stability comes only by giving up some of our flexibility to explore fully the deepest corners of the events now before us."

[2] Anthony Kronman (1990) is an outlier to this trend as he defends precedent on the grounds that following tradition ties us to the past and is thus valuable in itself. But Kronman defends traditionalism not for its usefulness (in leading to truth or anything else of value) and thus also rejects an epistemic defense.

[3] In "Stare Decisis and Constitutional Adjudication," Henry Paul Monaghan (1988, 752) describes the function of stare decisis as demonstrating "at lease to elites—the continuing legitimacy of judicial review."

[4] Schauer (1987, 594) argues that "the set of cases in which a precedent is applicable but overridden appears to be an empty one" because we distinguish a case rather than override its precedential force.

[5] For example, Gerald Postema (1991, 1158) describes his project as explaining "in moral terms why we believe that the fact that a decision of a certain sort was taken in the past provides a sound reason for reaching a similar decision in the situation currently facing us."

cases where the judge faced with deciding C2 believes that C1 was wrongly decided. In such cases, why should the fact that C1 was decided this way count even as a reason, let alone a decisive reason, to decide C2 the same way?

It is often thought that epistemic reasons are conceptually unable to provide a justification for following precedent. If there are good reasons to believe that precedent is epistemically valuable, then the judge who follows the precedent case for these reasons is not doing so because of a rule or practice that requires that he defer to precedent. Rather, he follows the precedent because there are good epistemic reasons to decide the latter case the same way as the precedent case. As Schauer explains, a judge who thinks "If Cardozo decided this way, who am I to argue?" has a reason to believe that C2 should be decided as Cardozo decided C1. When the current judge credits Cardozo's judgment, expertise, or experience in this way, and thus counts the fact that Cardozo decided C1 in a particular way as a reason to decide C2 similarly, this isn't an instance of precedential reasoning. Rather, the judge in C2 reaches the result he thinks is best, all things considered, in C2. It is just that the fact that C1 was decided a particular way causes him to change his mind about how C2 ought to come out.

In Sect. 4.2, I argue that this rejection of the possibility of an epistemic defense of genuinely precedential reasoning is flawed. This account fails to consider an important distinction between reasons to believe and reasons to act, and attending to this distinction shows that epistemic reasons can provide a justification for precedential reasoning that satisfies Postema's independence thesis.

While an epistemic defense of precedential reasoning is possible, is it justified? Are there good reasons to believe that a legal system which includes the requirement that judges accord some weight to precedent will reach better decisions than a system without it? Section 4.3 takes up this question. I argue that precedent does have epistemic value for reasons that are similar to those one might have for thinking, as Lord Mansfield did, that the common law "works itself pure."[6] I also argue, however, that *even if* precedent cases are no more likely to be right than are the decisions of individual judges today, still the process of requiring judges to defer to precedent yields better decisionmaking than would a system without it. In other words, there are substantive reasons to think that precedent is epistemically valuable and procedural reasons to think that a legal system with a practice of following precedent will make better decisions than one without it.

4.2 A Genuinely Epistemic Defense of Precedent

Epistemic reasons to follow precedent are often rejected on the grounds that they cannot provide a justification for precedential reasoning at all. The argument goes as follows. An epistemic justification for precedent rests on the claim that there are good reasons to believe precedent has epistemic value. If this is right, then there are

[6] Omychund v. Barker, (1744) 26 Eng. Rep. 15 (Ch.) 23; 1 Atk. 21, 33.

good reasons to believe that the precedent case C1 is rightly decided notwithstanding the fact that the current decisionmaker tasked with deciding C2 thinks that C1 was wrongly decided. But if this is the case, these reasons should affect what the judge in C2 *thinks* is the right resolution of C2. If so, then he follows the precedent not because it is precedent, but instead because the fact that C1 was decided in the way it was gives him reason to believe that this resolution is correct (because precedents have epistemic value) and thus that C2 ought to be decided the same way. But, as Frederick Schauer (1987, 576) argues, stressing the same independence thesis as Postema: "A naked argument from precedent … urges that a decisionmaker give weight to a particular result regardless of whether that decisionmaker believes it to be correct and regardless of whether that decisionmaker believes it valuable in any way to rely on that previous result."

Epistemic reasons for precedential reasoning typically are rejected precisely because they are epistemic in nature. Because they are reasons to *believe* that the precedent case is correct, and thus that the current case should be decided in the same manner, they obviate the need to defer to or rely on precedent *as precedent*, or so the argument goes. What we are looking for in a justification for precedential reasoning is a reason *to act* a particular way rather than a reason *to believe* that a particular result is correct. For precedent to function as precedent, it must provide a reason for a judge to decide C2 as C1 was decided regardless of what he believes. (This is Postema's independence thesis.) By this logic, epistemic reasons are thought to be ill-suited to the task.

What this dismissal of epistemic grounds for precedential reasoning misses, however, is the fact that while the practice of precedent must instantiate an action-guiding principle, the reasons to adopt such a principle could themselves be epistemic in nature. For example, one could adopt either the rule of deferring to precedent or the practice of according some weight to precedent because one believes that, in general, adoption of this rule or practice will produce better decisions than not doing so. If precedent is more likely to be correct than is the judgment of contemporary judicial decisionmakers, then one has good epistemic reasons to either defer to or accord some weight to precedent. The epistemic reasons provide a justification for the rule or practice. However, having adopted the rule "follow precedent" or the principle "accord some weight to precedent," this rule or principle directs the current decisionmaker to do certain things, rather than influencing her to believe certain things. As a result, the justification for genuinely precedential reasoning can be epistemic in nature.

One might wonder, however, why the fact that precedent is epistemically justified, if it were true, wouldn't provide a reason for the judge also to believe that C2 should be decided in the same way as was C1. If so, the judge in C2 would be deciding as she thinks best, all things considered, and precedential reasoning wouldn't be doing the work. It is possible, of course, that the epistemic justification for the practice of precedent would induce any particular judge to change her mind about the how the case before her ought to come out, and in such instances the judge would be deciding as she thinks best and thus not deferring to precedent after all. While this may happen in some instances, surely not in all. A judge who accepts the epistemic justification for the practice of precedent believes that following precedent over the run of cases is more likely to yield correct results than deciding as she thinks best in each case. However, accepting this fact need not provide sufficient reason for the judge to believe that her judgment in the particular case before her is mistaken. This is especially so when we consider that an epistemic defense of precedential reasoning could justify the practice of according some weight to precedent only weakly. It might be the case, for example, that following precedent yields correct answers only slightly more often than if each current judge makes an independent decision about what result she thinks is correct.

Moreover, an individual judge might accept that there are epistemic reasons for a rule or practice of precedent-following on the grounds that judges, as a whole, tend to overestimate their confidence in their own reasoning ability and be insufficiently attentive to the reasons that count against it. Yet, this same judge might believe—perhaps erroneously—that she doesn't suffer from these human frailties. In other words, the judge may accept the need for a rule or practice of following precedent, and may think that as a judge, she too is obliged to follow the rule or practice (just as she believes other judges are), but nonetheless *believe* that she would reach better results by not following it. Therefore, the epistemic defense of stare decisis provides a reason for each individual judge to actually follow precedent even though the individual judge continues to believe she will decide more cases in error by doing so. This is because there are epistemic reasons that justify the rule or practice of precedent-following that don't directly translate into reasons for any individual judge to believe that doing so will yield the right outcome in the particular case.

The above argument simply demonstrates that a judge might have an epistemically grounded reason to defer to the practice of precedent-following while at the same time believing that her own decisions would be better, in the aggregate, by sticking with her own judgment. The judge might think that precedent-following is justified because judges (other judges, especially) are benefitted by a rule that requires following precedent, while simultaneously believing that she herself would do better deciding each case as she thinks best. This sort of defense is possible because the fact that the practice of precedent is epistemically justified in general provides her with an epistemic reason to support and maintain that practice. She does so by herself deferring to precedent.

A less arrogant judge could also think stare decisis is justified for epistemic reasons (i.e., she might think, "I'll reach the correct answer in more cases by according some weight to precedent than simply deciding how I think best each time"), but also believe that following this rule or practice *in a particular case* before her will yield the wrong answer. The rule or practice of according some weight to precedent in all cases, even when one believes the precedent case was wrongly decided, would then be a form of self-paternalism. The judge ties herself to the mast of stare decisis precisely because in an individual case she will be tempted to simply decide how she thinks best (ignoring precedent because she believes it unhelpful *in this case*). To constrain and manage my own hubris, I could well commit myself, or believe the legal system justified in committing itself, to a practice of precedent-following in order to bind both my future self and other judges who would otherwise be tempted to ignore precedents they believe to be incorrect, and thereby to reach more wrong results in the aggregate than they would reach if they accorded some weight to precedent.

If epistemic reasons can in fact provide reasons to adopt a rule or policy of according weight to precedent, why has this justification been so roundly rejected? In part, others have failed to recognize that there can be epistemic reasons that justify a rule or practice that itself then operates independently as a reason to act in a particular way, as discussed above. In other words, once the practice of precedent is epistemically justified, this practice can work as a reason to act a particular way, no matter what one believes.

In addition, the way the issue of precedent often is posed may be a culprit. A justification for deference to precedent must explain why a judge should decide C2 as C1 was decided even though she believes that C1 is incorrect. This characterization of the issue stresses the perspective of the judge and thus makes the practice of precedent appear to involve some cost. The judge, after all, is deciding the case in what seems to her to be a suboptimal way. What this perspective leaves out (or at least does not emphasize) is the fact that the judge who is faced with deciding C2, and who believes that C1 was incorrectly decided, may well be mistaken. From the perspective of the individual decisionmaker in C2, it looks like precedent-following involves some cost or loss. The practice of following precedent exerts pressure on the judge to decide in a way that she believes is erroneous. But from the systemic perspective, it is not at all clear that the practice of precedent involves a cost in terms of *actually* erroneous decisionmaking. At least at this point in our inquiry, we have no reason to believe that the decisions of individual judges today are more likely to be correct than the decisions of prior judges that constitute the relevant precedents. If precedent in fact has epistemic value, then there is no loss when a judge defers to precedent rather than deciding the case as she thinks best. But of course, that remains to be seen. The point to stress now is that when we emphasize that we don't know whether the C2 judge's view that C1 is erroneous is itself correct, the problem of justifying precedent begins to take on a different cast.

The focus on the individual decisionmaker may itself be misguided. When we ask whether the fact that a prior court has decided a particular way provides an individual judge with good reason to decide a current case in a way that she believes is incorrect, we don't really ask whether the rule or practice of following precedent is justified. The individual judge has good reason to accord weight to (or follow) precedent if that is what the norms of judicial decisionmaking dictate within our system, whether or not deference to precedent is justified for epistemic reasons or any other reasons. In other words, the question of what the judge should do in this situation is, at least in part, a question of professional ethics rather than a question about whether the practice of following precedent is normatively justified.

In order to focus on whether the practice of precedent is normatively justified, we should look at the question from a systemic perspective and ask the following question: Are there good reasons to adopt a rule or practice requiring judges to accord some weight to precedent? Such a rule or practice would give judges a reason to decide a current case as a prior case was decided, even when the judge believes the prior case is a mistake. This formulation allows us to see more clearly that the current judge's belief that the prior decision is in error is simply that—her belief, which may be correct or incorrect.

In this section, I have argued for the possibility of a genuinely epistemic justification for the practice of following precedent. An epistemic justification of precedent is possible and is truly a defense of precedent. It is at least plausible to suppose that by adopting a rule of according some weight to precedent, decisionmakers will reach better decisions than without that rule. If so, the legal system has epistemic reasons for adopting this rule. These epistemic reasons do not, at least necessarily, seep into the individual cases. A judge may believe that the rule of precedent-following is epistemically justified and still believe that by following precedent in the case before her she will reach the wrong result. This is because the epistemic reasons for following precedent are reasons that support the rule. The rule, once adopted, provides each judge with an action-guiding reason to follow the rule, whether or not she believes doing so will improve decisionmaking in the individual case.

The epistemic justification for the practice of according weight to precedent thus provides an individual decisionmaker with a reason to act (to decide a case in line with precedent) rather than a reason to believe that deciding that way is correct. But, as a justification for the doctrine of stare decisis, it is only as good as the strength of the epistemic reasons themselves. In the next section, I consider whether there are good epistemic reasons for the rule or practice of following precedent.

4.3 Are There Epistemic Reasons for Deference to Precedent?

The natural way of thinking about the question whether our legal system ought to include a practice of according some weight to precedent would be to ask whether the decisions of past judges have epistemic value. One might think that in order for deference to precedent to be epistemically justified, precedent cases must be more likely to be right than are decisions of present-day decisionmakers. This view is often ridiculed. For example, Oliver Wendell Holmes, Jr. (1897, 469) complained that it was "revolting to have no better reason for a rule of law than that so it was laid down in the time of Henry IV." Why, critics ask, would we suppose that precedent is a repository of wisdom? Rather, there are good reasons to suspect that past decisionmakers made decisions that were morally compromised by prejudices that were common in the past but which we have now recognized as faulty. For example, judges of prior eras may well have imbibed the racism and sexism of their time and brought those flawed moral views to bear on their decisions. If we think that society makes some progress in moral insight, a view I share, then there are good reasons to think that present-day decisionmakers will make better decisions than past decisionmakers. As a result, one might conclude that precedent is not epistemically valuable.

So there are good reasons to suppose that the decisions of individual judges today are likely to be better than the decisions of individual decisionmakers of the past. But, whether present-day judges make better decisions than prior judges isn't the question we should be considering. Rather, in exploring whether deference to precedent can be justified on epistemic grounds, we need to ask a slightly different question: Will the decisions of present-day judges be improved or worsened by a judicial practice of according some weight to precedent? Nevertheless, as to this question too there is cause for concern. If the decisions of past decisionmakers are likely to be worse, in the aggregate, than the decisions of present-day decisionmakers, then one might worry that the practice of following precedent will make it more difficult to correct mistakes in our law than it would be if our legal culture did not accord any weight to precedent. Past mistakes are likely to become entrenched, as the doctrine of stare decisis means that later decisionmakers must have especially strong reasons to depart from prior, mistaken, case law. If so, it looks as if there is an epistemic cost to the practice of precedent, albeit a cost that may be outweighed by benefits of a different kind—the traditional values of stability, predictability, and equality that are commonly used to defend the doctrine of stare decisis—but a cost nonetheless.

If this argument is correct, the case for an epistemic justification for the doctrine of stare decisis looks weak. In what follows, I suggest two reasons—one procedural and one substantive—to think that it is not.

4.3.1 A Procedural Argument for the Value of Precedent

In this section, I offer an argument for the value of the practice of according some weight to precedent that does not depend on a claim that precedent itself has epistemic value. How could this be? If the *process* of requiring judges to accord some weight to precedent produces better decisions than if judges simply decide as they individually think best in each case, then stare decisis has epistemic value.

The practice of according some weight to precedent requires current decisionmakers to do two things. First, it requires them to take seriously the opinion and reasoning of prior courts. Second, it forces them, in cases in which their own view of the legally best outcome departs from precedent, to have an especially good reason before they can depart from the precedent case. These two effects on today's judges may improve their decisionmaking because a judge deciding a case today, like anyone at any time, is likely to be overconfident in his own decisionmaking ability and to bring to the question at hand a partial and limited perspective. The practice of according weight to precedent checks judicial overconfidence by requiring that the judge have an especially good reason before departing from precedent, and it expands the partial perspective by forcing the judge not only to listen to but also really to hear the perspective of a person who has a different view.

Frederick Schauer presents horizontal precedential reasoning—the situation in which the judge in the latter case defers to a decision of a prior judge at the same level in the judicial hierarchy—as an oddity. When the Supreme Court follows the reasoning of its earlier opinion, despite the fact that it thinks that reasoning erroneous, this is the working of horizontal precedential reasoning. Schauer (2009, 42) notes that "[s]cientists, for example, are not expected to reach the same conclusions as their predecessors just because their predecessors have reached them" and that "[i]t would be surprising if Congress were to make the same decisions as previous Congresses only because previous Congresses had made them." Schauer uses these examples to illustrate the strangeness of reasoning from precedent and in particular to show that it needs special justification because it flies in the face of good epistemic practice. However, this comparison to the practices of scientific inquiry and the procedures of politics provides a clue to why the practice of precedent is justified on epistemic grounds.

Both science and politics employ methods that help insure the truth or wisdom of the conclusions or decisions reached, methods that are, for the most part, lacking in judicial practice. The culture of scientific inquiry is organized in such a way that the conclusions of individual scientists are reviewed, challenged, critiqued, and discussed. Articles announcing scientific results are published in journals only after extensive peer review. Even before they reach that stage, scientists present their work at academic conferences at which their conclusions and reasoning are examined and vetted by their peers. Both within individual institutions and more broadly within the profession, individual scientists present their work to others in formats designed to encourage critical review. This process both sharpens the arguments and refines the conclusions of published work and thus helps to insure that this work is free of error. Of course, even with this process in place mistakes are made, but there is good reason to think that this gauntlet of criticism makes it more likely that published work is true than it would be without it.

Politics also has similar checks that help to insure the wisdom of its decisions. It is certainly true that the current Congress does not defer to the decisions of past Congresses. If the current Congress believes a law should be changed, it simply does so. However, the structure of Congressional decisionmaking works to insure that the decisions of the current Congress are vetted and critiqued. Any new law will be the subject of debate and discussion. Given our two-party system, we can be assured that the view of the majority who support a particular law will be vigorously challenged by the minority who oppose it.

The judiciary, by contrast, makes decisions that are not subject to formal checks or critique. While of course the opinions of lower-court judges are reviewed by appellate and supreme-court judges, the opinions of the highest court, and of lower courts when they are not reviewed, are the product only of one judge or one group of judges. But if critique, discussion, and multiple perspectives help to insure accuracy and sound judgment, then it would be a welcome development if judicial practice included a structural mechanism to provide something analogous.

But is such a mechanism needed? There are, of course, familiar ways in which judicial decisionmaking is checked. First, judges are to decide according to law, rather than simply as they would like. But in cases in which a precedent case says that the law requires X and the judge in the relevantly similar case at issue thinks the law requires Y, it is, by definition, unclear what the law requires. So while the law provides some check on judicial decisionmaking, the very problem we are considering presupposes that the law is uncertain enough that it will be an insufficient check in difficult cases.

Second, judicial judgment is checked by its lack of power. Having neither sword nor purse (Hamilton 1826, 433), the judiciary cannot make its decisions stick without the cooperation of the other branches of government. Nonetheless, the judiciary has a fair amount of power. When we recognize that what the law requires is often uncertain (how much so may depend on one's view of the nature of law), then the ability to render judgment in such cases means judges wield significant power. Moreover, in a country such as ours in which so-called "rule of law values" are deeply entrenched, the check envisioned by the Founders (i.e., the fact that the judiciary has "no direction either of the strength or of the wealth of the society; and can take no active resolution whatever" (Hamilton 1826, 433)) may be less than one would have thought. It is hard to imagine a judicial decision being ignored. At the same time, perhaps the entrenchment of the rule of law is itself in part the result of relatively good judicial decisionmaking. If so, we have a virtuous cycle in which strong emphasis on the rule of law means that it is especially important that judges make good decisions and good judicial decisions strengthen the rule of law.

Judicial decisionmaking also is checked by the fact that it is not always exercised by solo judges. Appellate courts routinely use groups to reach decisions—the nine members of the Supreme Court, for example. The fact that a group of judges rather than a single judge decides is important. There are (at least) two familiar reasons why this might be the case. First, as Condorcet's jury theorem demonstrates, if each person voting on the decision has a probability of reaching a correct decision that exceeds 50 %, then increasing the number of people "voting" on the decision will improve the likelihood of a correct decision.[7] The theory presupposes that the decisionmakers are independent, however, which may limit the usefulness of this account. Appellate judges are not independent in that they discuss a case together. However, both juries and democracy, for which Condorcet's theory is thought to provide support, include decisionmakers who are not independent. Whether groups improve decisionmaking for the reasons Condorcet thought when decisionmakers are not independent is a controversy I will not wade into here. I suspect that the group may well make a better decision than the individual judge. Nevertheless, we may get better decisionmaking still if we augment the ways in which judges' decisions are subject to critique.

The decisions of individual judges or groups of judges suffer from two related problems. First, each judge brings a partial perspective to bear on the issue. While judges may endeavor to view the cases before them objectively, taking the "view from nowhere" as Thomas Nagel (1986) calls it, this is difficult to do. A wise judge, or decisionmaker of any sort, may tell herself to try to see things from the perspective of others, and especially from the perspective of someone who

[7] For a good explanation of Condorcet's theorem, see Paul H. Edelman's "On Legal Interpretations of the Condorcet Jury Theorem" (2002, 328).

disagrees fundamentally with her conclusions, in order both to test her reasoning and to challenge her intuitions. Someone who is wiser still will recognize that this is a difficult process to engage in alone and that creating a structure to force one to engage in this process will likely improve one's decisions. Examples of endeavors of this kind are legion. You ask your friend to "play devil's advocate," forcefully taking a view that contrasts with your own when you have an important decision to make. The structure of legal decisionmaking builds on this insight. In a trial, each litigant presents the events from her own perspective and argues for the legal outcome she thinks is correct. The "case or controversy" requirement limiting the jurisdiction of federal courts to live cases in which two sides of an issue will be vigorously presented can also be defended on epistemic grounds along these same lines. The decisionmaking of the judge is enhanced, one might think, by hearing both sides of the issue presented fully and vigorously. The practice of stare decisis can also be defended along similar lines. We add yet another layer of debate, criticism, and forced engagement with another's perspective and reasoning when we require judges today to take seriously the decisions of prior judges on relevantly similar questions.

The doctrine of stare decisis provides a built-in structure requiring today's judges to seriously consider alternative viewpoints—at least in those cases in which their view about the correct resolution of a case differs from the view of past judges. It creates an artificial conversation across time and space in which the judge in the precedent case gets to "play devil's advocate," challenging the judgment and intuitions of the judge in the case under consideration. Just as the adversarial system and the case-or-controversy requirement are, in part, justified by the view that presentation of opposing viewpoints and testing of ideas through articulation of contrary views helps to produce better outcomes, so too, one can defend the doctrine of stare decisis for these same reasons. Deference to precedent requires today's decisionmakers to broaden their partial perspectives to include the viewpoints of others that they may not disregard.

The key point here is that stare decisis *requires* the judge to engage in this process. The doctrine provides a structure that forces consideration of the opposing view. If the judge in the case under decision believes the case ought to come out differently than the precedent case would indicate, then this doctrine requires real and serious engagement with that view. While the current judge would do well to consider the prior cases even without such a doctrine, a realistic appraisal of human behavior tells us that we tend to be overly confident in our own views and to dismiss too easily the conclusions of those with whom we disagree. If this is right, then from a systemic perspective, we would do well to force decisionmakers to take opposing views seriously. One way to do that—not the only way to be sure but *a* way nevertheless—is to require a judge to follow precedent except if she has special or especially strong reasons for rejecting the precedent. Because judges are not required to follow horizontal precedent, the doctrine functions as a thumb on the scale in favor of the result of the precedent case. If human nature will automatically put a thumb on the scale in favor of the judge's own reasoning, this doctrine may be a much-needed antidote to judicial hubris that improves judicial decisionmaking.

But, one might wonder: Aren't past judges as likely to be overly confident in the correctness of their own reasoning and judgment as are present-day decisionmakers, such that there is no reason to suppose the past judges are correct more often than current judges? At this point, I am not resting the argument on any claim to the contrary. I am not defending deference to precedent on the grounds that past decisions are better decisions. Rather, I am defending a system that requires that current judges defer to precedent on the grounds that by so doing, these current judges will make better decisions than if they were unconstrained by precedent. This is because a system that forces decisionmakers to engage with a contrary point of view and take that view seriously improves decisions. In addition, the natural human tendency to think we are right needs a counterweight. The doctrine of stare decisis provides that counterweight.

4.3.2 A Substantive Argument for the Value of Precedent

In the prior section I argued that the practice of according some weight to precedent may be justified even if there is no reason to suppose that the decisions of prior judges are more likely to be correct than the decisions of current judges. But perhaps that isn't the case. Perhaps precedent cases *are* a repository of wisdom. The reason that precedent itself (as contrasted with the practice of deference to precedent) may be epistemically valuable is that precedent is often not simply the static decision of one prior judge or court. Rather, precedent cases evolve from prior cases via the common-law tradition in which the rule of the case is refined and critiqued, extended or distinguished. As no latter case is exactly the same as the precedent case, the application of a precedent to latter cases in fact refines the precedent. The process of arguing that a precedent doesn't cover Y because Y is relevantly different but does cover Z because Z is relevantly similar is the development of the principle that the precedent stands for, so that the precedent is an accumulation of the work of several decisionmakers and the testing of principles by seeing how they apply to diverse particulars on the ground. This was certainly Lord Mansfield's view (though that doesn't insure that it is correct): "[A] statute very seldom can take in all cases, therefore the common law, *that works itself pure* by rules drawn from the fountain of justice, is for this reason superior to an act of parliament."[8]

This confidence in the epistemic value of the common law at first seems based on a skepticism about rule-based decisionmaking—in that the product of the legislature will necessarily be defective. But this isn't quite right, as the judge in the case under decision will articulate a new rule, informed by the particulars of the case before him. Rather, Lord Mansfield's confidence in the wisdom of the common law *over time* seems to be based on two observations. First, that the view from any particular time and place is necessarily limited. Second, that the view of any individual or group (the legislature) is also limited. As a result, the accretion of insight provided

[8] Omychund v. Barker, (1744) 26 Eng. Rep. 15 (Ch.) 23; 1 Atk. 21, 33 (emphasis added).

by the common-law process of refinement and critique by multiple minds over time will yield superior judgment than would the decision of any particular person or group today. If so, then precedent itself, and not simply the process of deferring to precedent, may have epistemic value.

4.4 Conclusion

In this chapter, I have argued for the possibility of a genuinely epistemic defense of deference to precedent. The doctrine of stare decisis can be justified on epistemic grounds if there are epistemic reasons for a judicial system to include such a doctrine. Once such a doctrine becomes part of the legal doctrine of a jurisdiction, then it provides a reason for judges to accord some weight to precedent even when they believe the precedent case is wrongly decided.

In the second section of the chapter, I provided some reasons to think that a legal system will reach better decisions if judges must accord some weight to precedent than if they are not required to do so. In particular, there are good reasons to be worried about the beliefs of individual judges that a particular case should be decided a particular way. They may well believe it and be unpersuaded by the fact that others see it differently or disagree, but their confidence should not necessarily inspire our confidence. The question I focus on is this: How can we design a system to maximize, within the limits of human frailties, the likelihood that judicial decisionmakers will make legally correct and morally justified decisions? In Sect. 4.2, I argued that the procedure of according weight to precedent forces the kind of engagement with opposing views that improves decisions. In Sect. 4.3, I suggested that there may be substantive reasons to think that precedents have epistemic value, especially those precedent cases that have been refined and critiqued over time.

This last substantive claim about the epistemic value of precedent is the one I offer most tentatively. Even if it turns out to be false, the procedure of according weight to precedent may be a needed counterweight to the natural human tendency to believe one is right. If so, we can add epistemic reasons to the array of reasons that count in favor of according at least some weight to precedent.

References

Edelman PH (2002) On legal interpretations of the Condorcet jury theorem. J Legal Stud 31(2):327–349

Hamilton A (1826) Federalist no.78. In: Federalist, on the new constitution. Glazier & Company, Hallowell, pp 432–39

Holmes OW (1897) The path of the law. Harv Law Rev 10(8):457–478

Kronman AT (1990) Precedent and tradition. Yale Law J 99(5):1029–1068

Monaghan HP (1988) Stare decisis and constitutional adjudication. Columbia Law Rev 88(4): 723–773

Nagel T (1986) The view from nowhere. Oxford University Press, New York
Postema G (1991) On the moral presence of our past. McGill Law J 36(4):1153–1180
Schauer F (1987) Precedent. Stanford Law Rev 39(3):571–605
Schauer F (2009) Thinking like a lawyer: a new introduction to legal reasoning. Harvard University Press, Cambridge, MA

Chapter 5
Private-Rights Litigation and the Normative Foundations of Durable Constitutional Precedent

Maxwell L. Stearns

Abstract This chapter contends that there is both a causal correlation and a normative relationship between the relative ease of obtaining a Supreme Court precedent and the relative durability of that precedent. Public-law scholars often argue that justiciability barriers should be lowered to allow the Court to rule on important constitutional issues. The author contends, however, that lowering justiciability barriers has the unintended consequence of making Court decisions more vulnerable to overruling in subsequent cases, after an intervening change in the Court's composition. In contrast, preserving the justiciability requirements associated with traditional private-rights adjudication makes rulings more costly to obtain but also more resistant to subsequent overruling. The author draws a contrast with the Court's *Chevron* doctrine of deference to federal agency decisions, which decreases both the cost of obtaining favorable policies and the durability of those policies. And he suggests that precedents that are difficult to obtain for justiciability reasons therefore should, as a normative matter, be treated with greater deference by subsequent Courts.

The author would like to thank participants at the University of Baltimore School of Law Precedent on the U.S. Supreme Court Symposium and at the George Mason School of Law Austrian Economics Research Roundtable for helpful comments. David McAloon provided excellent research assistance.

M.L. Stearns (✉)
Francis King Carey School of Law, University of Maryland,
W. Baltimore St., Baltimore, MD 21201, USA
e-mail: mstearns@law.umaryland.edu

C.J. Peters (ed.), *Precedent in the United States Supreme Court*, Ius Gentium: Comparative Perspectives on Law and Justice 33, DOI 10.1007/978-94-007-7951-8_5,

5.1 Introduction

This chapter advances a simple thesis, albeit one that runs against the grain of much American public-law scholarship: Holding all else constant, the more difficult (or costly) a constitutional ruling is to obtain, the more valuable the resulting precedent; and conversely, the easier (or less costly) a constitutional ruling is to obtain, the less valuable the resulting precedent.

Most public-law scholarship implicitly rests on the opposite premise that the relative ease or difficulty of obtaining a constitutional ruling should correlate positively, rather than negatively, with the relative importance or unimportance of the claimed constitutional right. In the conventional public-law analysis, important constitutional precedents—the sort that should be afforded durable status—justify relaxing barriers to their procurement, and thus should be less costly to obtain. Conversely, within a private-rights adjudicatory model, judicial rulings, however important, are legitimated by the need to resolve actual cases or controversies that presumptively arise from circumstances beyond the claimant's control.

This chapter will argue that the public-rights adjudicatory model, while motivated by the admirable desire to generate valued constitutional precedent, produces an important unintended consequence. To the extent that the timing of constitutional litigation is driven by the happenstance of ideological sympathies of deciding jurists, the normative justification for affording durable status to the resulting precedent is compromised once those conditions change in a manner that favors the other side. By contrast, the private-rights model makes constitutional precedent more costly to obtain on all sides, thereby enhancing the normative foundation for affording durable status to precedent.

One reason why public-law scholars tend not to focus on this unintended consequence is that they typically view the underlying problem—the relationship between the importance of claimed rights and rules governing the creation of precedent—from the perspective of the precedent-setting case, while ignoring the perspective of subsequent opportunities to overrule that case. Public-rights scholars typically frame the inquiry as follows: The more important the constitutional ruling being sought, the fewer the impediments that should stand in the way of obtaining it.[1] In this analysis, when doctrinal stakes are high, traditional limitations on the ability to obtain precedent—ripeness, mootness, and standing principally among them—should be treated, at best, as avoidable nuisances that obstruct the litigation of pressing constitutional claims. What this perspective overlooks, however, are the systemic consequences of relaxing the barriers to constitutional rulings. While lowering these barriers makes it easier to procure a ruling in the first instance, it also makes it easier to undermine or reverse that ruling in subsequent cases, thus reducing the value of the ruling.

---

[1] See, for example, Siegel (2007), which critiques the application of various timing-based justiciability doctrines to delay the resolution of several high-profile constitutional issues, and Winter (1988, 1510), which assails the use of standing doctrine in *City of Los Angeles v. Lyons* to dismiss a challenge to a police chokehold policy that subsequently resulted in several deaths.

Before proceeding, it is important that I clarify the concept of *cost* as I will use it in this chapter. In this analysis, cost refers to the burdens of complying with formal, and often technical, doctrines that are preconditions to litigating a case in federal court in the United States. The specific set of relevant doctrines arises under the broad heading of justiciability, and within that category includes those doctrines that inform the timing of federal litigation.[2] Among justiciability doctrines—ripeness, mootness, and standing—standing has proved the most important. Justiciability doctrines require that those seeking to litigate in federal court show a presently live claim, meaning one that is ripe and not moot,[3] and that the claimant demonstrate an injury in fact, causation, and redressability.[4] In addition, the claim must be specific and personal, meaning that it should not belong to a third party or be legally diffuse.[5] While these elements may appear abstract and malleable,[6] compliance costs are nonetheless quite real. Satisfying the combined justiciability requirements can delay, and in some cases prevent, litigation that otherwise would lead to a desired constitutional precedent.[7]

Lowering the cost of obtaining precedent thus means relaxing the demands of these individual or combined requirements of justiciability as a means of litigating a case. The motivation for seeking to lower these costs is generally associated with the seemingly attractive composition of the relevant appellate court, or of the Supreme Court, which will ultimately resolve the case and, in so doing, potentially create the desired precedent. Conversely, these justiciability doctrines raise the cost of precedent procurement by presumptively divorcing the triggers to federal court litigation from such factors as beneficial appellate-court composition.

Assuming that the justiciability criteria combine to demand something like fortuity as the dominant driver in timing federal-court litigation, and given the pendulum-like changes in judicial composition over time through the appointments and confirmation processes, adhering to the various justiciability criteria makes it harder, and thus more costly, to optimally time cases for maximum doctrinal effect. Conversely, relaxing such criteria when cases present compelling claims lowers the cost of obtaining desired precedent by allowing litigants to better match desirable claims with a sympathetic appellate court.

Most public-law scholars implicitly assume that lowering the costs of obtaining desired constitutional rulings will not adversely affect the value of the precedent obtained. This chapter instead argues that the legal system is faced with an

---

[2] This chapter does not discuss the political question doctrine, which, although falling under the broad umbrella of justiciability, is not connected to the timing of constitutional litigation.

[3] This briefly captures the requirements of ripeness and mootness. For a general discussion of these doctrines, see notes 12–13 below and the citations therein.

[4] These are the constitutional prerequisites to standing. See, for example, Lujan v. Defenders of Wildlife, 504 U.S. 555, 560–62 (1992), and Allen v. Wright, 468 U.S. 737, 751–52 (1984).

[5] These are the prudential barriers to standing. See *Allen*, 468 U.S. at 750–51.

[6] In a series of works, I have demonstrated that these arguments are often, although not invariably, overstated (Stearns 1995a, b, 2002).

[7] For some specific case illustrations, see Sect. 5.2.1 below.

inevitable choice between a regime of low-cost/low-value or high-cost/high-value precedent. Although I personally conclude that the high-cost/high-value precedent regime is preferable on the grounds that it generally improves stability of law, sharpens legal claims, and renders the overall process of both legislative and adjudicatory decisionmaking more fair, that claim is the subject of a separate body of work (Stearns 1995a, b, 2002). The central goal of this chapter is to demonstrate the inevitability of this choice.

The analysis that follows holds important implications for the history of litigation leading to *Brown v. Board of Education*[8]; for the framing of the stare decisis inquiry in the jointly authored plurality opinion in the 1992 decision *Planned Parenthood v. Casey*[9]; and for the Supreme Court's agency-deference rules.

5.2 Public-Rights Versus Private-Rights Adjudicatory Models

Several notable scholars, including Winter (1988), Siegel (2007), and Elliott (2008),[10] embrace what I will refer to throughout this chapter as the "public-rights model" of constitutional adjudication. Based on that model, these and other scholars have argued for relaxing barriers to justiciability, with a specific focus on standing. Their goal is to broaden access to the federal courts among claimants with pressing constitutional claims in the hope of establishing desired constitutional precedent. Within the framework of the public-rights model,[11] standing presents a set of unnecessary impediments to the formation of public law, and most notably to the development of constitutional doctrine.

The combined justiciability doctrines—ripeness, mootness, and standing—often stand in the way of desired constitutional precedent. These Supreme Court doctrines require claimants who otherwise meet the jurisdictional criteria for litigating in federal court to further establish that their suit is ripe, meaning not premature[12]; that it

[8] 437 U.S. 483 (1954).

[9] 505 U.S. 833, 854–61 (1992).

[10] Heather Elliott suggests that the use of standing in cases like *Allen v. Wright* undermines democratic values by preventing the litigation of pressing claims affecting the interests of particular minority groups (2008, 487–88).

[11] To be clear, these thoughtful scholars each have independent analyses worthy of individual consideration. In this discussion, I am focusing on a foundational assumption undergirding the public-rights adjudicatory model that each of their respective approaches shares in common. For a more focused response to Elliott's and Siegel's critiques of my standing analysis, see Stearns (2013).

[12] To establish that a claim is ripe, it is necessary to show that the claim is premised on a legal violation, most likely a constitutional one, that arises from the actual, rather than potential, application of a law. See Thomas v. Union Carbide Agric. Prod. Co., 473 U.S. 568, 580–81 (1985) (discussing ripeness requirements). With some exceptions, the mere fact that a law has the potential to be

is not moot, meaning that it remains live[13]; and that it satisfies the constitutional and prudential standing requirements. Although ripeness and mootness sometimes present their own complex analyses, in general, standing has emerged as the most stringent justiciability barrier.

Standing has been described as governing the "who" and the "when" of constitutional litigation (Monaghan 1973). Perhaps a more apt description is that standing identifies the necessary attributes for raising a presently live claim. In other words, once we ensure that the claim is ripe and not moot, standing focuses on the circumstances under which the federal judiciary is or is not permitted to adjudicate those claims that remain.

The historical origins of the doctrine have been amply surveyed elsewhere (Winter 1988, 1417–58; Sunstein 1998, 1434–51; Sunstein 1992), and the specific contours of the doctrine have changed several times since its inception. Legal scholars generally trace the origins of standing to judicial efforts to stave off novel constitutional challenges targeting new forms of regulation in the Progressive Era (Winter 1988, 1457–58; Sunstein 1992, 179).[14] Although the earliest incarnation of the doctrine in the New Deal was presumptive,[15] thus allowing Congress to broaden or narrow standing by statute, beginning in the late Warren Court period and most notably in the Burger and Rehnquist Courts,[16] the standing requirements came to be embedded in constitutional doctrine.[17] By the early 1990s, the Court had extended the standing limits that govern claims arising under the Constitution itself to also cover federal statutory claims.[18] These specific rulings remain in flux, as does standing more generally. Despite this, there are some relatively fixed parameters or guidelines, and it is these guidelines that often provide the fodder for the doctrine's detractors.

---

applied in an unconstitutional manner is generally insufficient to justify a constitutional challenge to that law.

[13] Mootness doctrine requires that the claimant show that the relief will remedy an ongoing harm, unless the claim is subject to one of two exceptions: first, that the defendant has voluntarily suspended activity that, upon dismissal of the suit, she is apt to resume; or second, that the claim itself is capable of repetition yet evading review. See, for example, Roe v. Wade, 410 U.S. 113, 125 (1973), which illustrates the "capable of repetition yet evading review" exception, and Northeastern Fla. Chapter of Associated Gen. Contractors v. City of Jacksonville, 508 U.S. 656, 662 (1993), which illustrates the "voluntary cessation" exception.

[14] Winter (1988, 1457–58) traces formalization of standing doctrine to the New Deal period.

[15] Specifically, the Court presumed in favor of standing in cases presenting claims analogous to those arising in the common-law contexts of tort, contract, or property, and presumed against standing more generally (Fletcher 1988, 226–27). In this regime, Congress generally had broad discretion to flip these presumptions by statute, thus conferring standing more broadly or more narrowly, as it saw fit.

[16] For a more detailed discussion of the timing of the development of standing doctrine, see Stearns (2008), which traces to several cases in the early 1970s the attribution of constitutional status to elements of standing doctrine.

[17] Winter (1988, 1451) claims that "[i]t was not until *Doremus v. Board of Education* [1952] that a full Court dealt with standing in exclusively constitutional terms, and not until *Baker v. Carr* [1962] and *Flast v. Cohen* [1968] that the Court fully discussed the new doctrine."

[18] See Lujan v. Defenders of Wildlife, 504 U.S. 555, 578 (1992).

The Supreme Court has identified as constitutional standing elements the requirements of injury in fact, causation, and redressability, and as prudential standing barriers the presumptions against raising the claims of others, raising diffuse claims, and raising claims challenging laws that distort particular markets in a manner that is alleged to injure the claimant.[19] Critics argue that these combined constitutional and prudential standing barriers are, at worst, serious impediments to the development of desired constitutional doctrine, and at best troublesome nuisances that merely cause unnecessary delays in developing doctrine.[20] Either way, these scholars contend, the doctrines should be relaxed or abandoned, especially when doctrinal stakes are high. Although these two positions—standing as a serious impediment and standing as a petty annoyance to developing doctrine—are arguably in tension, that is not my immediate or primary concern. Instead, I will focus on the first and more troublesome objection, which presents standing and other timing-based justiciability barriers as significant obstructions en route to developing constitutional precedent.

5.2.1 A Tale of Two Cases[21]

Two historical case sequences nicely illustrate the preceding point. First, consider the case trajectory reflecting the NAACP's strategy to bring an end to state-mandated segregation of public schools,[22] a regime long sanctioned under the *Plessy v. Ferguson* separate-but-equal doctrine.[23] This trajectory ultimately culminated in *Brown v. Board of Education*,[24] which ended race-based segregation in the South, at least as a matter of formal law. The NAACP strategists initially rejected a plan to present frontal attacks on one racially segregated primary school in each southern state on the ground that, under *Plessy*, each separate suit was destined to fail. Instead, they devised the ingenious plan to attack the most egregious denial of race-based equal protection by targeting graduate programs for which there was simply no counterpart for blacks, and then to work down toward the most pressing cases of segregation at the high-school, middle-school, and elementary-school levels. Not only did this plan present the most obvious denials of state largesse as vehicles for

[19] See, for example, Allen v. Wright, 468 U.S. 737, 750–51 (1984) (setting out constitutional and prudential standing barriers).

[20] Siegel (2007, 75) belongs in the latter camp, positing that the standing rules "throw a few grains of sand into the workings of the judicial branch but do not prevent it from grinding out a judgment."

[21] Portions of this discussion are adapted from Stearns (2013).

[22] For a classic treatment of this historical period, see Kluger (1977).

[23] 163 U.S. 537 (1896). To be clear, nothing in *Plessy* itself mandated the "but equal" part of this formulation; instead, the statute mandating segregated railway cars, which the Court sustained, nominally required separate but equal. Nonetheless, *Plessy* has long been associated with this doctrinal formulation.

[24] 347 U.S. 483 (1954).

distinguishing *Plessy*, but also it presented early challenges in contexts in which parental sensitivities over school choice were less pronounced, given that the early challenges involved institutions educating adults rather than school-aged children.

This strategy ultimately proved successful, so much so that others mimicked it in other contexts (Stearns 2002, 189–90). Despite this, the history of the litigation highlights the considerable costs that traditional justiciability criteria, of the sort we now associate with standing doctrine, ultimately imposed. One of the most significant cases in the trajectory was *Missouri ex rel. Gaines v. Canada.*[25] In that case, Lloyd Gaines successfully challenged the regime for state-funded legal education in the State of Missouri. Missouri had offered its flagship state law school to qualified white law students, but had no counterpart law school for qualified black students. This case was particularly attractive as part of the litigation sequence because rather than focusing on the substantive differences between programs, here the claim was direct and to the point: Whites had a program; blacks did not. Instead, Missouri provided a tuition voucher and transportation costs for attendance at an out-of-state law school. Gaines's lawsuit made its way to the Supreme Court, and the result was to strike down the Missouri program.

That ruling, however, ultimately left the state with a choice. Missouri could elect to admit black students into its flagship school, or instead, it could create a separate in-state law school for blacks. Missouri chose the latter course. After Missouri created an obviously inferior blacks-only law school, the NAACP lawyers were most anxious to challenge it in a follow-up equal protection suit. Alas, Lloyd Gaines had disappeared (Bluford 1959). What happened to Lloyd Gaines has ever since been a mystery; what happened to the NAACP strategy, however, is well known.

The loss of Gaines as the named litigant suspended the careful case sequencing that would have allowed the challenge to progress from a complete denial of programming based on race to the denial of comparable-quality programming based on race. Instead, the NAACP had to await another litigant, and another case. It took a full 10 years until the Supreme Court revisited the issue that began with the *Gaines* litigation in Missouri. In *Sipuel v. Board of Regents of the University of Oklahoma*,[26] a black woman who had been denied admission to the flagship Oklahoma state law school because of her race succeeded before the Supreme Court. Like Missouri a decade earlier, Oklahoma had the choice to admit black students or to create an alternative black law school. It chose the latter. That same year, in *Fisher v. Hurst*,[27] the Supreme Court rejected the challenge that Oklahoma's new law school for blacks was unequal to the flagship state law school for whites.

Although of course there is no way to know for sure whether the result would have differed had Gaines been available as a litigant in the earlier case, it very well might have. In both cases, the states, Missouri and Oklahoma, behaved similarly in response to the Supreme Court's decision demanding either that a qualified black student be admitted to the existing state law school or that the state create

[25] 305 U.S. 337 (1937).

[26] 332 U.S. 631, 632 (1948).

[27] 333 U.S. 147, 148–49 (1948).

a black law school. In the intervening decade, the Supreme Court had undergone major compositional changes. These involved appointments by Democratic Presidents, Franklin Delano Roosevelt and Harry Truman. Although it is tempting to assume that desegregation cases are a liberal project, that greatly oversimplifies the matter. Progressive liberalism, which dominated much of that era, often equated to judicial restraint as a means of affording legislative choice over policy. The shift in the Court's membership between *Gaines* and *Fisher*, then, might well have determined the outcome.

Ultimately, even the loss of Lloyd Gaines proved only a temporary setback as far as the case-law trajectory is concerned. Eight years following *Fisher*—with a series of cases in between, including most notably *Sweatt v. Painter*[28]—the Supreme Court ultimately announced an end to race-based segregation in public schools in the landmark decision *Brown v. Board of Education*.[29] Of course that case, and perhaps especially the egregious inadequacy of the "with all deliberate speed" formulation that followed reargument over the remedy in *Brown II*,[30] generated another case trajectory designed to effectuate the *Brown* mandate.[31] The larger point for our purposes is that the conventional understanding of standing, requiring a specific litigant with an actual injury caused by the government that is redressable by the courts, is indeed burdensome for those seeking to bring a constitutional challenge.

The second illustration involves the later case-law trajectory that resulted in locating a right of privacy within the Fourteenth Amendment's Due Process Clause, and ultimately established the rights of married couples to use contraceptives and of women to terminate unwanted pregnancies prior to viability. Unlike the sequence of cases leading to *Brown*, these right-of-privacy cases did not arise as part of a coordinated litigation campaign. Despite this, the individual cases built upon each other in a similar fashion, with the right to marital privacy creating a foundation for an expansion outside the marital context, and for a reconceptualization to include the controversial right to abort an unwanted pregnancy.

In *Poe v. Ullman*,[32] the Court rejected an early challenge to the same Connecticut contraception-ban statute that the Supreme Court eventually struck down, concluding that the challenge was not ripe. The result was a 4-year delay in addressing that challenge even though the later case, *Griswold v. Connecticut*,[33] was presented

[28] 339 U.S. 629 (1950) (holding that Texas's start-up blacks-only law school was not substantially equal to the whites-only University of Texas Law School, in part because of intangible factors such as faculty reputation and alumni influence).

[29] 347 U.S. 483, 493–95 (1954).

[30] Brown v. Board of Education of Topeka, 349 U.S. 294 (1955).

[31] See, for example, Swann v. Charlotte-Mecklenburg Board of Educ., 402 U.S. 1, 15 (1971) (providing broad equitable powers for purposes of enforcing southern school desegregation decrees), and Keyes v. School Dist. No. 1, 413 U.S. 189, 209–10 (1972) (determining who bears the burden to prove that state policies did or did not produce predominantly one-race schools in districts that had not mandated segregation).

[32] 367 U.S. 497 (1961).

[33] 381 U.S. 479, 485–86 (1965).

under circumstances that appear contrived, involving a claim by the prescribing physician who contended that the couple using contraceptives would be unwilling to press such a claim on their own behalf.[34] In this instance, the intervening judicial appointments were far less dramatic than those that followed *Gaines* and might even have been beneficial from the perspective of those bringing the constitutional challenge. Notably, President Kennedy had replaced Felix Frankfurter with Arthur Goldberg and Charles Whitaker with Byron White. Although both Goldberg and White filed separate concurrences, they did join the seven-to-two majority opinion striking down the Connecticut statute in *Griswold*.

Even if one takes the view that *Poe* and *Griswold* are primarily, or exclusively, symbolic—despite Justice Douglas's alluring prose, there does not appear to be any contemporaneous evidence of Connecticut sex police searching the "sacred precincts of marital bedrooms for telltale signs of the use of contraceptives"[35]—that is certainly not true of the far more significant cases that arose later in the privacy case-law trajectory. Of course, this case sequence culminated in *Roe v. Wade*, holding that the right of privacy extends far enough to include a woman's right to terminate an unwanted pregnancy.[36] A different ruling in *Poe v. Ullman* might have changed this eventual case trajectory.

As is always so with counterfactuals, we can only speculate as to how these two well-known case trajectories might have played out absent a set of justiciability barriers. And it is notable that in the Lloyd Gaines litigation, it was not a judicial decision that thwarted standing; rather it was the clear understanding among the lawyers that absent an actual affected litigant the case could not proceed. Although there are other illustrations of this basic insight, these cases amply demonstrate the central contention of public-rights scholars: These and other important constitutional claims are, at best, delayed, as in *Poe*/*Griswold*, when the federal judiciary interposes justiciability barriers between willing litigants and the constitutional claims they seek to advance; and, at worst, denied, as in *Fisher v. Hurst*, if the changed circumstances between the initial presentation and the eventual opportunity—with "i"s dotted and "t"s crossed—result in an adverse ruling as compared with how an earlier case presenting the same substantive issue might have been resolved absent the justiciability barrier.

5.2.2 *The Public-Rights View*

I am classifying the group of scholars advancing this understanding of justiciability as embracing a "public rights" adjudicatory model. The central premise of the public-rights model is that constitutional claimants present these and other important constitutional claims specifically to generate valued constitutional precedent, or, stated differently, to create "public rights." The specific cases, along with any

[34] See *id*. at 480.

[35] *Id*. at 485.

[36] 410 U.S. 113 (1973).

particular interests that litigants hold, whether in the form of expected damages or injunctive relief, are ultimately a byproduct, and in the broader scheme an inconsequential one at that, of the larger adjudicatory mission of establishing desired constitutional precedent. Whatever private benefits inure to the nominal litigants are merely the justificatory vehicle or trigger that creates the opportunity for the sought-after ruling. In this model, allowing technical details about justiciability defects to undermine such litigation misconceives both the means and ends of the process of constitutional adjudication.

Within this public-rights model, the normative justification for resolving a dispute implicating a constitutional right is positively correlated with the normative importance of the claimed constitutional right itself. For pressing claims, therefore, standing should be relaxed so that the federal judiciary can fulfill its core mission of articulating constitutional precedent. And by negative implication, for ordinary litigation, which tends to involve more mundane claims, constitutional or otherwise, it is acceptable to burden litigants with traditional impediments, or such business-as-usual requirements as the strictures of standing, ripeness, and mootness.

5.2.3 The Private-Rights Alternative View

Let us now consider an opposing perspective on the nature of constitutional adjudication, which I will refer to as the "private rights" adjudicatory model. In this camp, I will include Brilmayer (1979), Pushaw (2010), and myself (1995a, b). For those embracing a private-rights model, the fundamental premises about the nature of the adjudicatory process are generally unaffected by the level of importance associated with the underlying substantive claim, constitutional or otherwise. Whether we are discussing ordinary litigation—of the A hits B; B sues A sort—or high-level constitutional adjudication, the adjudicatory process itself remains centered on dispute resolution.

To be clear, this is not to say that those embracing the private-rights model are systematically duller than public-rights scholars (at least I hope not). Scholars in this camp are well aware that those litigating high-profile constitutional claims are doing so to establish high-profile constitutional precedents. Instead, within the private-rights framing, judicial creation of precedent, including constitutional precedent, is, as a formal matter, treated as the byproduct of case resolution, rather than the other way around. Because cases more generally (setting aside the sort of cases I have previously described) are triggered by stochastic events, meaning that they are largely randomly driven responses to circumstances beyond the control of the claimant,[37] in general case law is not "timed." The process of timing is passive,

[37] Of course criminal defendants often "control" the circumstances that give rise to the litigation in which their legal claims, including constitutional defenses, arise. With rare exception, however, they do not engage in criminal activity with the purpose of creating precedent. Quite the contrary,

not active, and the consequence is that precedent is subject to a never-ending set of factors—docket delays; discovery delays; motion delays; changes in judicial appointments; randomly comprised appellate panels; unpredictable grants or denials on relevant discretionary dockets—that individually and collectively are well beyond the control of any litigant.[38] Indeed, many important procedural rulings arise from cases that were themselves centered on altogether unrelated substantive points of law.

In general, we expect regular litigants—those bringing common-law claims, regulatory claims, and statutory claims—to comply with the complex set of rules governing adjudicatory timing. And although constitutional adjudication is undoubtedly motivated by constitutional precedent, within the private-rights model the basic adjudicatory assumptions nonetheless remain. This holds without regard to the importance of the claim that the litigant seeks to advance. Instead, private-rights adjudicatory scholars seek to separate, as much as practicable, the preferred timing of cases from the coincidence of favorable circumstances respecting those who are likely to resolve the dispute.

Even assuming that constitutional precedent is more important than other bodies of precedent,[39] within the private-rights model the relative importance of constitutional claims does not change the essential dynamics required to create precedent. These include a claim that is ripe and not moot, and a litigant suffering a first-person and non-diffuse injury caused by the defendant that is susceptible of meaningful judicial redress. Each of these requirements is subject to considerable criticism among scholars, but the essential insight for our immediate purposes is simply this: Individually and in combination, each captures a characteristic feature of the traditional, non-high-profile lawsuit. When B sues A after having been hit, there is little question of injury, causation, and redressability. There also is no concern about whether B is presenting a claim that is distinctly his. Public-interest litigation certainly complicates these matters, but one way to think about the justiciability requirements is that however imperfect they might be, they are designed to ground litigation in a manner that, as in the ordinary case, seems less likely to be driven by considerations of strategic timing.

those who are guilty of the underlying offenses typically commit them with an eye to evading detection and thus succeeding in their crimes.

[38] For a further exploration of these sorts of adjudicatory delays caused by justiciability, see Stearns (2013), in which I argue that justiciability factors cause impediments to developing doctrine that are potentially more akin to a "butterfly effect" than to the mere tossing of grains of sand into the adjudicatory gears, as Siegel (2007, 75) contends. In chaos theory, the term "butterfly effect" refers to a phenomenon by which a seemingly minor event can, through cumulative, nonlinear means, result in significant consequences, as in the familiar hypothetical example of a hurricane that would not have occurred but for the earlier movement of a butterfly's wings.

[39] This is not an inevitable conclusion. For many, and perhaps most, individuals, non-constitutional rulings and any number of other methods of affecting legal policy might have a greater direct impact on their lives than constitutional decisions. Despite this, for purposes of this analysis, I am assuming there is a special significance to constitutional precedents.

5.2.4 *Form Versus Motive*

The distinction drawn here—between those who embrace a public-rights adjudicatory model and those who espouse a private-rights model—goes to the form of, rather than the motivation behind, the litigation. Otherwise the private-rights model and those who embrace it risk appearing shockingly naïve. There is no doubt, for example, that many cases, including those previously discussed, were motivated more by the desire for precedent than by the desire for specific litigant relief. Those pressing school desegregation or sexual-privacy claims were almost certainly driven by a desire to create public law even if they also hoped that they themselves, or those they cared for, would receive some eventual benefit. Instead, the private-rights model rests on the assumption that the *process* through which all precedent-creating adjudication occurs is improved if the judiciary behaves *as if* the general model of adjudication—grounded in private-rights resolution with precedent as a byproduct—remains intact, without regard to the importance of the sought-after precedent.

We can now revisit this chapter's central thesis: A key premise of the public-rights model—that the relative ease of constitutional lawmaking should be a function of the importance of the claimed constitutional right—creates an unintended and deleterious effect from the perspective of those who care deeply about highly valued constitutional precedent. To the extent that the timing of constitutional litigation is driven by such factors as present political support for developing doctrine or the ideological sympathies of present jurists, the normative justification for respecting the precedential status of a ruling obtained is inevitably relaxed when those conditions change. By contrast, the private-rights model raises the cost of obtaining constitutional precedent and thereby enhances the normative foundation for respecting inevitably hard-fought rulings as precedent, regardless of the fortuity of such changed circumstances, including most notably changes in the ideological composition or predilections of deciding courts.

Precedent that is more costly to obtain should be more durable than precedent that is cheaper to obtain. The analysis thus suggests a normative tradeoff: Those seeking to relax requirements for obtaining constitutional precedent must accept a diminished precedential value, whereas those willing to retain requirements for obtaining constitutional precedent benefit from higher precedential value. The central claim of this chapter is that this tradeoff is an inevitable design feature rather than a bug in the system. It is not possible to benefit from lower-cost constitutional adjudication while also benefiting from durable precedent. And this implies that those who are most eager to employ the federal judiciary to create constitutional precedent might themselves compromise the eventual value of such precedent by successfully claiming that the underlying issues are sufficiently compelling to warrant relaxation of traditional requirements for adjudication.

5.3 Another Look at Justiciability: Linking Standing to the Private-Rights Model

In separate works, I have demonstrated that standing doctrine raises the cost to litigants of manipulating the timing, and thus the substantive development, of constitutional precedent (1995a, b). It does so by making it more difficult to present constitutional cases in a preferred ordering to maximize doctrinal effect. The analysis, which rests largely on social-choice theory, reveals the circumstances under which judicial preferences on an appellate judicial panel are prone to the phenomenon of cycling. Cycling implies that members of a multimember decisionmaking body, including the nine-Justice Supreme Court, will sometimes hold preferences that thwart the general condition of transitivity, or A preferred to B preferred to C implies A preferred to C. When a cycle arises, three persons, each holding internally rational, or transitive, preferences (for example ABC, BCA, CAB), will, when combining their preferences, discover a cycle such that the group as a whole prefers A to B and B to C, but C to A.

In series of individual Supreme Court cases, and in groups of combined cases, the Supreme Court has manifested evidence of underlying cycling preferences (Stearns 2002, 97–156). Within individual cases, the potential for cycling arises when the Justices generally agree to the dispositive issues on which the case turns but disagree as to how those issues should be resolved. The particular—and relatively uncommon—condition that generates the cycle arises when a voting path that follows the separate resolution of each dispositive issue logically compels the dissenting result. This phenomenon arises when those who agree on the actual result, or judgment, nonetheless base their respective judgments on opposite resolutions of both dispositive issues.

Cycling preferences also arise across multiple cases. This phenomenon occurs, most notably, in paired cases in which each has majority support for a seemingly opposite judgment but a crossover majority believes that the two cases cannot be legally distinguished. That crossover majority is inevitably split over how the cases should be resolved, with one subgroup preferring that both challenges be rejected and another preferring that both be sustained, but nonetheless shares in common a rejection of the minority argument that seeks to distinguish the cases.[40]

---

[40] For a pair of case illustrations, see my discussion of *Crawford v. Bd. of Educ.*, 458 U.S. 527 (1982), and *Washington v. Seattle School Dist. No. 1*, 458 U.S. 457 (1982), in Stearns (2002, 170–80). In *Crawford*, a majority rejected a challenge to a California constitutional amendment, enacted through a referendum process, that prevented state courts from ordering busing as a means of integrating public schools unless the court first determined that such a remedy was necessary to avoid violating the Fourteenth Amendment Equal Protection Clause. In *Seattle*, a majority struck down a constitutional amendment enacted as an initiative that prevented local school boards from employing busing as a means of integrating public schools unless doing so was necessary to remedy a violation of either the state or federal equal protection requirements. Although these cases

The phenomenon of cycling across multiple cases is particularly relevant because it helps to explain why ideologically motivated interest groups seek to further their agendas through preferred case orderings. Assume a majority of Justices sincerely believes that two cases that have majority support for opposing rules are nonetheless indistinguishable. Further assume this majority adheres to precedent. If these cases were presented sequentially rather than simultaneously, the case ordering would control the development of doctrine in both cases. Under these conditions, case A followed by case B produces opposite holdings in both cases as compared with case B followed by case A. That is because the crossover majority in the second case (B or A) will vote to resolve that case consistently with the binding precedent established in the first case (A or B). And, most notably, this holds *even assuming* that the cases reach the Supreme Court in rapid succession with no intervening change in membership.

To be sure, pursuing a favorable case trajectory can be a noble endeavor. Perhaps the most notable illustration is the previously discussed series of cases comprising the eventually successful NAACP strategy to rid equal protection of the *Plessy* regime and replace it with *Brown*. The question here, however, is not whether the *Plessy-Brown* trajectory and eventual doctrine were compelling—obviously they were—but rather whether part of what made the doctrine endure, and indeed has made it something of an icon within constitutional law, was the very difficulty of achieving it. The burdens of the traditional private-rights adjudicatory model were not theoretical; they were quite real. That, after all, is the lesson of Lloyd Gaines.

Public-rights scholars maintain that relaxing standing would remove what they regard as the doctrine's pointless constraints, which undermine the judiciary's central lawmaking function. In an important respect, however, this criticism misses both the main insight of the social-choice account of standing and one of the central lessons of the history on which it rests. Although the social-choice model of standing demonstrates the possibility of cycling in a snapshot manner—meaning with no change in Supreme Court membership and no other changes than the order of case decisions—public-rights scholars are sensitive to the more serious problem that losing the opportunity to press a claim today might well result in a far less attractive opportunity (depending on what the Supreme Court looks like) tomorrow. Over a host of substantive constitutional issues, the Roberts Court is less attractive to liberal interests and more attractive to conservative interests than were the Rehnquist Court, the Burger Court, and certainly the Warren Court. As the replacement of

---

were decided on the same day, a crossover majority, comprising four Justices who agreed with the *Crawford* holding and who dissented in *Seattle*, and one Justice who agreed with the *Seattle* holding and dissented in *Crawford*, expressed in separate opinions that the two cases were constitutionally indistinguishable, and thus should have been resolved in the same manner. See *Crawford*, 458 U.S. at 547–48 (Marshall, J., dissenting) (reasoning that there is no distinction between the two cases and disagreeing that California's action could be constitutional while Washington's is not), and *Seattle*, 458 U.S. at 494 n.8 (Powell, J., dissenting) (noting the Court's holding in *Crawford* that "the Equal Protection Clause is not violated by the mere repeal of race-related legislation or policies that were not required by the Federal Constitution" and reasoning that the same logic should apply in *Seattle*) (internal quotations omitted).

Justice O'Connor with Justice Alito amply demonstrates, even a single change in the Court's staffing can potentially alter the conditions for litigating a case.[41]

The implications of the social-choice account therefore should not be misunderstood. Although the model demonstrates conditions under which litigants can benefit from using favorable case orderings to affect precedent even absent any changes in judicial staffing, these incentives are only enhanced by the very real prospect of material changes in Court membership following the imposition of justiciability barriers to a constitutional challenge.[42]

Although standing and other justiciability doctrines raise the cost of procuring precedent, they also enhance the durability of precedent. This is necessarily so for two reasons. First, the cost of procuring a contrary precedent is substantially higher as well in a regime that adheres to requirements of justiciability. Second, normatively burdensome acquisition provides an independent basis for respecting the outcomes of hard-fought battles in the judiciary, as compared with the outcomes of precedents that were merely the product of convenience. The cost of obtaining these precedents thus confers added normative status.

One way to demonstrate this second point is to compare the Supreme Court's alternative approach to rules obtained at the agency level that are procured in response to changing political conditions, rather than to fortuitous circumstances that require a decision to be issued at a given moment in time. We now consider the Supreme Court's approach to rent-seeking legislation and agency-deference rules. We then return for a comparison with the Court's doctrine of stare decisis.

---

[41] It is, of course, impossible to know how any case might have been resolved with different Supreme Court membership. That said, it seems reasonable to suppose that the outcomes in any of the following landmark cases might have differed absent Justice O'Connor's replacement with Justice Alito: *Parents Involved v. Seattle School District No. 1*, 551 U.S. 701, 747–48 (2007) (striking down voluntary race-based affirmative efforts by Louisville, Kentucky and Seattle, Washington to prevent reversion to single-race schools); *District of Columbia v. Heller*, 554 U.S. 570, 592 (2008) (interpreting the Second Amendment to protect an individual right to bear arms as applied against a District of Columbia handgun ordinance, and overturning *United States v. Miller*, 307 U.S. 174 (1939)); *McDonald v. City of Chicago*, 130 S. Ct. 3020, 3050 (2010) (striking down a municipal ordinance restricting access to handguns by, alternatively, incorporating *Heller* or classifying the Second Amendment right as a protected Fourteenth Amendment "privilege[] or immunity[]"); *Citizens United v. Federal Elections Commission*, 558 U.S. 310, 342–43 (2010) (striking down campaign-contribution limits on corporations and holding that corporations are persons for purposes of political spending); *Fisher v. University of Texas*, 133 S. Ct. 2411 (2013) (remanding a decision sustaining the University's partially race-based affirmative-action program and asserting that, although strict scrutiny should not be fatal, nor should it be feeble); *Shelby County v. Holder*, 133 S. Ct. 2612 (2013) (invalidating § 4 of the 1965 Voting Rights Act, which establishes the formula used in § 5 to require federal "preclearance" of voting policies in certain states and municipalities with histories of voting discrimination).

[42] For a more detailed analysis, see Stearns (2013). In that article, I more carefully parse the standing doctrines to respond to claims that they are mere inconveniences, akin to throwing Jonathan Siegel's (2007) "few grains of sand" in the adjudicatory gears. In this chapter, I instead begin with the premise that these rules impose meaningful barriers to the imposition of precedent and ask if they are worth their keep from the perspective of those seeking valued constitutional precedent. Answering this question requires a normative defense—independent of the success of particular standing rules—of the cost-raising function of standing in precedent procurement.

The analysis further supports the intuition that the benefit of a payoff is inversely correlated with the political cost of its procurement.

5.4 From Rent-Seeking to Agency-Deference Rules

As is often the case, it is helpful to look at the question under consideration from another angle. Here we consider the relationship between public- versus private-rights adjudicatory models and the normative foundations for durable precedent by turning to a literature that focuses on judicial payoffs for something far less high-minded, namely special-interest rents procured through the legislative process.

In a landmark paper, Landes and Posner (1975) explored the normative justifications for the independent judiciary. The authors reasoned that an independent judiciary increases the durability of legislation, including, in particular, payoffs to interest groups procured through the congressional lawmaking process or state lawmaking processes, as compared with an alternative dependent judiciary. That is because elected judges are not as meaningfully insulated from political pressures and thus remain answerable to legislatures for renewed appointments and perquisites of office. Landes and Posner reasoned that one benefit of the independent judiciary is extending the durability of legislatively conferred rents. Judicial independence encourages this prolongation of rents by increasing the likelihood that Article III judges will construe ambiguous legislation based on the preferences of the enacting legislature, as compared with an elected judiciary, which is more likely to be solicitous of the concerns of the present legislature. In effect, Landes and Posner claimed that judicial independence increases the durability and thus the value of implicit interest-group bargains.

A number of notable theorists have resisted this account of the independent judiciary on various grounds. Here, I will take up two related arguments. Macey (1986) maintains that federal judges should thwart interest-group payoffs and that doing so is consistent with an overarching theory of constitutional design that makes rent-seeking more difficult or costly to procure. Elhauge (2008, 53, 99) maintains that, contrary to Landes and Posner, federal courts can, and should, construe statutes consistently with the preferences of the present Congress, rather than a Congress long prorogued, as a means of improving overall political satisfaction. According to Elhauge, construing statutes in light of today's congressional preferences rather than those of the enacting legislature enhances present political satisfaction by allowing current members of Congress to influence all presently ambiguous legislation that is interpreted during their term, as opposed to allowing current legislators only to influence the meaning of ambiguous legislation that they themselves have enacted, now and into the indefinite future.[43]

[43] An aside: Each year, I ask my public-choice students which regime they would prefer were they a member of Congress, and the class is generally split. Personally, I'd prefer the contrary regime, meaning having my preferences over bills I passed carry forward rather than having future

One of the most important implications of Elhauge's thesis involves agency-deference rules, and specifically *Chevron* deference.[44] Under *Chevron*, courts defer to agency interpretations of ambiguous statutory provisions within the agency's jurisdictional domain even if the courts would have interpreted those provisions differently. This rule is cabined by *Mead*,[45] which requires as a precondition to *Chevron* deference that the interpretation follow quasi-adjudicatory or quasi-rulemaking procedures, as opposed to a less-formal, and non-vetted, bureaucratic decision. *Brand X* reinforces the *Chevron* rule,[46] holding that even if the agency interpretation comes after a contrary Supreme Court ruling interpreting a federal statute, under *Chevron* the later agency interpretation trumps the prior judicial one.

Although *Chevron* deference appears to be in tension with the famous admonition in *Marbury v. Madison* that "[i]t is emphatically the province and duty of the judicial department to say what the law is,"[47] the propositions are reconcilable. If we accept the *Chevron* premise that agency interpretation trumps judicial interpretation of ambiguous provisions in federal statutes, *Brand X* ensures that the order of decision—court then agency versus agency then court—does not drive the substantive meaning of the statute. Whether the agency interpretation leads or follows, the agency interpretation governs. Conversely the judiciary need only afford lesser deference to agency rulings that are not the product of proper channels, applying *Skidmore v. Swift & Co.*,[48] under which agency constructions are considered for their persuasiveness. Again, this principle holds whether the agency decisions pre- or post-date federal judicial interpretations.

Elhauge's interpretive theory is in tension with the Landes and Posner theory of the independent judiciary. Whereas Landes and Posner contend that the federal judiciary is structured to afford special weight to contemporaneous legislative preferences, thereby prolonging the life of special-interest bargains well past that of the enacting legislature, Elhauge instead maintains that the federal judiciary can, and should, give special weight to "enactable," meaning present-day, congressional preferences.

---

congressional preferences govern the interpretation of those statutes and my preference influence the interpretations of past statutes in cases construing them during my hypothetical congressional term. This choice does not admit of a right or wrong answer, of course, and my preferences might well be idiosyncratic (although my admittedly nonscientific polling seems not to show that). The point is that it is not obvious that members of Congress, as a class, necessarily will hold one preference systematically over the other.

[44] Chevron, U.S.A., Inc. v. Natural Resources Defense Council, 467 U.S. 837 (1984).

[45] United States v. Mead Corp., 533 U.S. 218 (2001).

[46] National Cable & Telecommunications Association v. Brand X Internet Services, 545 U.S. 967 (2005).

[47] 5 U.S. (1 Cranch) 137, 177 (1803).

[48] 323 U.S. 134, 140 (1944) (holding that agency decisions will be weighed by a court depending on "all those factors which give it the power to persuade, if lacking power to control"). Prior to *Chevron*, federal courts applied this considerably more modest *Skidmore* deference to all agency interpretations of statutes.

The debate over the durability of legislative preferences respecting judicial interpretation of ambiguous statutory language bears important parallels to the debate over the durability of judicial precedent. And in the context of agency-deference rules, Elhauge appears to have a trump card: Under *Chevron*, courts do in fact provide special weight to present agency interpretation, and they are expected to do so without regard to their own independent assessment of the preferences of the enacting legislature, at least when the statutory mandate is ambiguous. If, as Elhauge maintains, agency interpretations are a reasonable proxy for enactable congressional preferences, then *Chevron* seems to support the intuition that the goal of judicial decisionmaking is to enhance present political satisfaction. And yet, I will argue, *Chevron* is ultimately reconcilable with the opposite intuition respecting the durability of constitutional precedent.

Notice that *Chevron* deference produces results that are relatively easy to obtain. By easy, I do not mean that less work is involved in generating a quasi-legislative or quasi-adjudicatory agency decision than in obtaining a judicial victory, even in the Supreme Court. The ease or difficulty of obtaining results, as I am using those concepts here, is not a statement about exertion. Rather, it is an assessment of the likelihood of obtaining a preferred outcome as a consequence of changed political conditions, and specifically changed conditions within the relevant institution, court or agency, favoring a desired result, as opposed to awaiting a justificatory trigger to decision that is randomly associated with such favorable conditions. It is certainly easier to have an agency favorably interpret an ambiguous statutory provision than it is to enact clarifying legislation in the event that the agency, or a federal court, gets that interpretation wrong. It also is easier to obtain a favorable agency interpretation than a favorable judicial one. That is because agencies can more freely change policies in response to changed political sensibilities. A newly staffed agency, like a newly staffed Congress, can reverse course consistent with changed ideological predilection. By contrast, courts need a much stronger basis for doing so, and this is especially true when construing a statute,[49] although it is also true when construing constitutional precedent.

Of course there is a flip side to the *Chevron* rule. Although favorable agency interpretations are in this sense more easily obtained, they are also less durable than a judicial interpretation. That is because an earlier judicial interpretation pursuant to a case or controversy can only be reversed by a statute or by judicial overruling, and judicial overruling of statutory interpretation is even more difficult than judicial overruling of constitutional precedent. To change an agency interpretation, simply restaff the agency. Accomplishing that result politically is not easy to do, of course, but the point is that a change in political control is itself generally sufficient for a change in

---

[49] For a general discussion, see Eskridge (1988). Eskridge (1362) observes:

> The Court applies a relaxed, or weaker, form of that presumption [of stare decisis] when it reconsiders its constitutional precedents, because the difficulty of amending the Constitution makes the Court the only effective resort for changing obsolete constitutional doctrine. Statutory precedents, on the other hand, often enjoy a super-strong presumption of correctness.

the direction of regulatory policy. And indeed, I would suggest that this might provide the basis for a more robust account of *Chevron* deference than Elhauge's account of enhanced political satisfaction taking the form of enactable preferences. In this analysis, what *Chevron* accomplishes is raising the stakes of political outcomes. It does so by signaling to interest groups, and ultimately to the electorate, that inasmuch as it affects the direction of regulatory policy, agency construction of myriad federal statutes can be altered when political fortunes, and thus agency staffing, change.

Consider in light of this analysis Stephenson's (2008, 71–75) alternative account of *Chevron* deference. Stephenson maintains that contrary to conventional understanding, tighter presidential control of agency policy through a unitary executive might reduce political satisfaction as compared with a regime of insulated, independent, regulatory agencies. Stephenson measures such satisfaction by the political preferences of the median electoral voter. Stephenson observes that presidential candidates invariably occupy policy space some distance to the right or left of the electoral median voter, and he posits that as a result, the tighter the executive control of agency policy, the more likely such policy is to occupy positions distant from the median voter. By contrast, relatively insulated agencies are more likely, over time, to hold positions that converge on the median voter. This follows from the cumulative effect of Democratic and Republican staffing of agencies that to the extent of independence are afforded some degree of political insulation.

Consider a simple, and stylized, illustration. Imagine a political spectrum evenly spaced at 10 % intervals from liberal to conservative, with elected Democratic Presidents generally occupying positions 40 % from the extreme left end of the spectrum and elected Republican Presidents generally occupying positions 40 % from the extreme right end of the spectrum. Agencies that produce policy as a product of unitary executive influence will, following each election cycle, place policy at or about these positions, 10 % to the left of the median voter for Democratic Presidents and 10 % to the right of the median voter for Republican Presidents. Either way, the result is to thwart the preferences of 60 % of voters. By contrast, a regime of independent agencies would generate policies that tend toward the median voter, and in doing so, this regime would enhance present political satisfaction.

This dynamic is all the more pronounced when we compare the output of agencies, on the one hand, with the output of Article III courts on the other. However insulated independent agencies are, they are certainly less so than life-tenured federal judges. And the cumulative effect of presidential appointments that arise from several consecutive presidential administrations enhances the likelihood that judicial constructions of statutes will more closely track median electoral preferences than agency interpretations, whether executive or independent.

As a result, whereas *Chevron* deference is likely to produce predictable political dissatisfaction, *Skidmore* deference (under which courts defer to agency interpretations only insofar as they are persuasive) is more likely to align with median electoral political satisfaction. Contrary to Elhauge's analysis, this analysis might suggest that *Chevron* is mistaken, but that is by no means a necessary implication. The issue is not whether *Chevron* is right or wrong; rather it is what trade-off the choice between *Chevron* and *Skidmore* reveals.

As stated above, I believe that the critical payoff of *Chevron* is raising the stakes of political outcomes. In a *Chevron* regime, political outcomes matter a lot, as they will result in potentially broad pendulum swings in agency policy that the judiciary is generally required to respect. If, by contrast, judicial interpretation is closer to the median, and if judicial interpretations of statutes were instead durable, then political outcomes matter far less. *Skidmore* placed the burden of interpreting ambiguous federal statutes on the federal judiciary and, along with that, diminished the political stakes of this important interpretive process. *Chevron* placed the burden on relatively more politically sensitive agencies, thereby raising the political stakes of this process. The raised stakes, however, might have been designed not to improve satisfaction by rendering the agency outcomes less relevant, but rather to enhance political *dissatisfaction* by rendering such outcomes—and with them the outcomes of elections—more relevant.[50]

And yet, while *Chevron* invites potentially broader policy swings over the meaning of statutes than *Skidmore*, the resulting cheaper-to-obtain political benefits are also shorter-lived. The judicial construction of statutes yields an even stronger stare decisis norm than the judicial construction of open-ended constitutional provisions. Statutory amending would have a more lasting effect precisely because of the greater difficulty in obtaining it. By contrast, an agency victory is fleeting precisely because it is purchased on the cheap, at least in relative terms.

5.5 *Casey*, the Cost of Precedent, and Stare Decisis Revisited

Let us now return to the question of durability of constitutional precedent. Consider the famous passage from the jointly authored plurality opinion in *Planned Parenthood v. Casey*,[51] which described the attributes of durable constitutional precedent. The plurality stated:

> So in this case we may inquire whether *Roe*'s central rule has been found unworkable; whether the rule's limitation on state power could be removed without serious inequity to those who have relied upon it or significant damage to the stability of the society governed by it; whether the law's growth in the intervening years has left *Roe*'s central rule a doctrinal anachronism discounted by society; and whether *Roe*'s premises of fact have so far changed in the ensuing two decades as to render its central holding somehow irrelevant or unjustifiable in dealing with the issue it addressed.[52]

---

[50] The analysis might also help to explain the resistance of federal judges to the call by various scholars, including Jonathan Macey (1986), to construe statutes in a manner that minimizes interest-group payoffs. Just as there is an inevitable tradeoff between the cost of precedent and its durability, so too there is an inevitable tradeoff between limiting interest-group incentives to participate in legislative procurement, which is often the price of doing business, and the successful procurement of desired public-interest laws. For a related analysis, see Stearns (1992).

[51] 505 U.S. 833 (1992).

[52] *Id.* at 855.

The joint authors thus identified four conditions that must be weighed to ascertain whether a precedent—especially one of the magnitude of *Roe*—warrants overruling: (1) whether the rule proves unworkable; (2) whether overruling would undermine important reliance interests; (3) whether the subsequent history has so eroded the precedent as to render it an anachronism or hollow shell; and (4) whether the factual premises have been reconceived to the point that the solution now appears irrelevant or unjustifiable. For this analysis, the last two conditions prove most important: the effect of subsequent rulings on the status of the precedent and the later understanding of the precedent's factual premises. In fact, the plurality treats these two formulations as part of a common inquiry by comparing the ongoing vitality of *Roe* with the diminished vitality—largely owing, in the plurality analysis, to the problem of faulty premises—of *Plessy* and *Lochner*.[53]

In the *Casey* plurality framing, the stare decisis inquiry is, from the point of view of the precedent in question, forward-looking: It focuses on whether the precedent the Court is called upon to retrench—in that case *Roe*—has been subsequently eroded. In the series of cases from *Plessy* to *Brown* and from *Lochner* to *West Coast Hotel*,[54] the *Casey* plurality reasoned, the Court had eroded the earlier precedent by exposing the flawed factual foundations on which the earlier precedents rested. Later cases continued to cut back on the original precedents in a manner that eventually rendered them hollow shells. The *Casey* plurality went on to compare this trajectory with the post-*Griswold* sequence, which had not only failed to erode the personal right of sexual privacy, but had extended it into other realms, including but not limited to the abortion right declared in *Roe*.

The *Casey* plurality's analysis has come under criticism for, among other reasons, claiming to rely on eroded factual foundations despite historical evidence that the foundations had not changed; rather, the normative premises in viewing them had changed.[55] In addition, as Chief Justice Rehnquist observed in his separate opinion, the *Casey* plurality fumbled over two of its own overrulings, with no real effort to reconcile them with its stare decisis analysis.[56] The point here, however, is not

---

[53] *Lochner* relied upon the Fourteenth Amendment Due Process Clause to strike down a state maximum-hours law for bakers, reasoning that the law interfered with the rights of employers and employees to contract for working conditions on mutually acceptable terms and that bakers were not uniquely in need of state legislative protection. Lochner v. New York, 198 U.S. 45 (1905).

[54] *West Coast Hotel Co. v. Parrish*, 300 U.S. 379 (1937), rejected a Fourteenth Amendment due-process challenge to a minimum-wage law affecting women, thus overturning *Adkins v. Children's Hospital*, 261 U.S. 525 (1923), and signaling an end to the era of substantive economic due process associated with *Lochner*.

[55] Later cases demonstrated the failure of the *Plessy* Court to appreciate that "separate but equal" imposed serious costs, psychological and otherwise, on African Americans. And the *Lochner* regime failed to appreciate that laissez-faire had winners and losers. (As if regulatory regimes have only winners!) And yet, there was clear evidence that these contrary understandings concerning the foundations of *Plessy* and *Lochner* existed at the time of the original decisions. Consider, for example, Justice Harlan's dissent in *Plessy* and Justice Holmes's dissent in *Lochner*, both of which characterized the foundations of these decisions in a manner vindicated in the later Supreme Court overrulings.

[56] See 505 U.S. at 948 (Rehnquist, C.J., dissenting).

to quibble with the application of the *Casey* stare decisis analysis, but rather to challenge the direction of the theory on which it rests. The *Casey* joint authors' justification for affording *Roe* durable precedential status looks forward from *Roe* itself: What happened *after Roe* was announced? Was it eroded or did later cases preserve its integrity? Is it a relic, or is it an ongoing part of a larger body of precedent? The joint authors' perspective on the subsequent history of *Lochner* follows a similar analysis. Certainly there is value in these inquiries. But I would suggest that the private-rights adjudicatory analysis reveals an equal or greater value in a *backward-looking* precedential analysis.

In a backward-looking analysis, the durability of precedent correlates in large measure with the burden of obtaining it. The more costly a precedent is to obtain, holding all else constant, the more entitled that precedent is to respect. In addition to considering why *Plessy* and *Lochner* warranted overruling based on later judicial decisions, we should focus on why *Brown* and *West Coast Hotel* deserve respect based on the heavy burden—a burden driven by the need for actual litigants with actual claims—required to bring those precedents about. In each case, the necessary overrulings to obtain these results, of *Plessy* and *Lochner* respectively, did not come about overnight. A change in Court personnel—one more favorable to the jurisprudence of *Brown* and *West Coast Hotel*—in and of itself was insufficient to force the doctrinal change. Instead, both of these eventual precedents were extremely costly to obtain. They were each the product of a series of cases, separately laying a small piece of the foundation for the eventual result. And even a single disruption in the path, for reasons well beyond the control of the groups motivated to bring about doctrinal change, could produce a substantial delay or even denial of the desired constitutional precedent.

Thus, the painstaking and gradual erosion of the relevant precedents, *Plessy* and *Lochner*, followed from cases with actual litigants presenting claims with stakes framed in traditional terms. Although these cases predated the constitutionalization of standing, they reflect something intuitive about the relationship between the process of judicial decisionmaking and the durability of resulting precedent. Requiring cases to meet traditional adjudicatory criteria, as the Lloyd Gaines story and *Poe v. Ullman* illustrate, unquestionably raises the cost of obtaining sought-after precedent. At the same time, however, it raises the value of the results obtained. This is not to suggest that subsequent erosion is unimportant. Indeed, the gradual erosion in other doctrinal contexts beside *Brown* and *Roe*[57] might someday prove to be the foundation for respecting later-obtained precedents.

The very difficulty of obtaining these precedents, and of the gradual erosion of those that came before, enhances the normative justification for their durability.

[57] One might argue that because *Roe* followed an exception to mootness—"capable of repetition yet evading review"—the precedent was in fact low-cost. Assuming, however, that there is validity to the Court's assumption that the duration of pregnancy—9 months—is too short for ordinary channels of litigation to resolve the constitutional issue presented in *Roe*, then this particular exception appears justified, and the larger analysis, focusing on the line of cases from *Griswold* to *Eisenstadt* to *Roe*, demonstrates that the precedent was obtained at high (or at least relatively high) cost.

More-costly precedent is more durable, and the reverse is also true. Precedent (or rules) purchased on the cheap, like agency construction of ambiguous statutory provisions, is necessarily worth less. The burdens of meeting traditional justiciability criteria—ripeness, mootness, and standing—certainly made the eventual path from *Plessy* to *Brown* and from *Lochner* to *West Coast Hotel* more costly. But they also made the eventual precedents obtained far more worthy of respect.

5.6 Conclusion

Public-rights theorists implicitly assume that lower-cost constitutional rulings will not result in lower-value precedent. This chapter demonstrates why that assumption is mistaken. The issue is not the merit of particular matters of constitutional doctrine. Rather, it is the process through which desired doctrine is obtained.

Those favoring relaxed justiciability to obtain desired public-law precedent should recognize an inevitable tradeoff: They can obtain lower-priced/lower-valued goods or higher-priced/higher-valued goods. What they cannot obtain is lower-priced/higher-valued goods. The reason is simple. If a change in judicial personnel is a sufficient normative justification for revisiting a question of law, that will also be true when those on the other side experience a favorable change benefitting them. Although arising in a regulatory context, this is also a core lesson of *Chevron*.

Constitutional precedent should be more durable than agency interpretations of ambiguous statutes subject to *Chevron* deference. But for that to happen, it should also be more costly to obtain.

References

Bluford LH (1959) The Lloyd Gaines story. J Educ Soc 32(6):242–246

Brilmayer L (1979) The jurisprudence of article III: perspectives on the 'case or controversy' requirement. Harv Law Rev 93(2):297–321

Elhauge E (2008) Statutory default rules: how to interpret unclear legislation. Harvard University Press, Cambridge, MA

Elliott H (2008) The functions of standing. Stanford Law Rev 61(3):459–517

Eskridge WN (1988) Overruling statutory precedents. Georgetown Law J 76(4):1361–1439

Fletcher WA (1988) The structure of standing. Yale Law J 98(2):221–291

Kluger R (1977) Simple justice: the history of *Brown v. Board of Education* and black America's struggle for equality. Vintage Books, New York

Landes WM, Posner RA (1975) The independent judiciary in an interest-group perspective. J Law Econ 18(3):875–901

Macey JR (1986) Promoting public-regarding legislation through statutory interpretation: an interest group model. Columbia Law Rev 86(2):223–268

Monaghan HP (1973) Constitutional adjudication: the who and when. Yale Law J 82(7): 1363–1397

Pushaw RJ Jr (2010) Limiting article III standing to 'accidental' plaintiffs: lessons from environmental and animal law cases. Georgia Law Rev 45(1):1–105

Siegel JR (2007) A theory of justiciability. Texas Law Rev 86(1):73–139
Stearns ML (1992) The public choice case against the item veto. Wash Lee Law Rev 49(2):385–436
Stearns ML (1995a) Standing and social choice: historical evidence. Univ Pa Law Rev 144(2):309–462
Stearns ML (1995b) Standing back from the forest: justiciability and social choice. Calif Law Rev 83(6):1309–1413
Stearns ML (2002) Constitutional process: a social choice analysis of Supreme Court decision making. University of Michigan Press, Ann Arbor
Stearns ML (2008) Standing at the crossroads: the Roberts Court in historical perspective. Notre Dame Law Rev 83(3):875–963
Stearns ML (2013), "'Grains of sand' or 'butterfly effect': standing and the legitimacy of precedent", Alabama Law Rev (forthcoming) 65(2)
Stephenson MC (2008) Optimal political control of the bureaucracy. Mich Law Rev 107(1): 53–110
Sunstein CR (1992) What's standing after Lujan? Of citizen suits, 'injuries', and article III. Mich Law Rev 91(2):163–236
Sunstein CR (1998) Standing and the privatization of public law. Columbia Law Rev 88(7): 1432–1481
Winter SL (1988) The metaphor of standing and the problem of self-governance. Stanford Law Rev 40(6):1371–1516

Chapter 6
Group Formation and Precedent

Neal Devins

Abstract This chapter combines historical evidence and social-psychology insights to contend that "coherent" Supreme Courts—those with five or more Justices who agree on crucial issues—are far more likely to overrule precedents, and to aggressively attempt to create broad precedents, than are "incoherent" Courts. The author explains the social-psychology dynamics that contribute to the formation (or absence) of coherent Court majorities. He then surveys three historical periods to illustrate the divergent behavior of coherent versus incoherent Courts: the post-1936 New Deal Court, which was highly coherent on most issues and thus ambitious in both overturning and establishing precedent; the Warren Court, which was incoherent and cautious before 1962 but became coherent and aggressive thereafter; and the Rehnquist Court, which was incoherent on most issues (dominated by two centrist swing Justices) and thus adopted a minimalist approach toward precedent. The author concludes with a preliminary analysis of the Roberts Court, suggesting that it is generally incoherent and therefore reluctant to formally overrule precedent in most areas.

6.1 Introduction

This chapter advances a common-sense proposition about the U.S. Supreme Court's willingness to either overturn landmark constitutional precedents or to craft rule-like decisions that are intended to bind the Court in subsequent cases. When five or more ideologically like-minded Justices sit on the Court, the Court operates as a

This chapter draws from "Ideological Cohesion and Precedent" (Devins 2008) and "The Supreme Court, Social Psychology, and Group Formation" (Devins and Federspiel 2010). The author thanks C. J. Peters for helping him think through the structure and content of the chapter.

N. Devins (✉)
School of Law, College of William & Mary,
613 S. Henry St., Williamsburg, VA 23185, USA
e-mail: nedevi@wm.edu

C.J. Peters (ed.), *Precedent in the United States Supreme Court*, Ius Gentium: Comparative Perspectives on Law and Justice 33, DOI 10.1007/978-94-007-7951-8_6,

"coherent" Court. A coherent Court is willing to aggressively advance its legal policymaking agenda by overturning precedent and by making doctrinal innovations intended to bind itself and subsequent Courts.

When there is not a coalition of five like-minded Justices committed to some vision of legal policymaking, the Court is "incoherent." Rather than overturn landmark decisions or pursue rule-like doctrinal innovations, an incoherent Court is more likely to issue indeterminate, fact-specific, minimalist opinions or ignore, rather than meet head on, precedents that cut against its reasoning. Correspondingly, an incoherent Court is more likely to distinguish or even misinterpret, rather than overrule, precedent that obstructs its preferred outcomes.

In drawing a distinction between "coherent" and "incoherent" Courts, I do not mean to suggest that a "coherent" Court is in lockstep on every issue and an "incoherent" Court hopelessly divided on every issue. For a coherent Court, there are core issues on which a majority coalition comes together and acts as a unified group. For example, the New Deal Court, while sharply divided on civil rights, was very much coherent on issues involving federal power to regulate the economy. Along the same lines, five or more Justices on an incoherent Court sometimes may come together to undermine or overrule precedent. For example, while there were no core issues around which the Rehnquist Court transformed Supreme Court doctrine, the Court did overturn several precedents.

In this chapter, I will contrast the decisionmaking of coherent and incoherent Courts. I see the Rehnquist Court, the pre-1962 Warren Court, and (albeit to a lesser extent) the Roberts Court as incoherent. I see the post-1962 Warren Court and the New Deal Court as coherent. I will identify some emblematic decisions and patterns of decisionmaking from all these Courts. Before doing so, I will make use of social psychology to highlight some of the barriers to group formation on the Supreme Court—barriers which explain why the Court has generally acted as an incoherent Court through most of the past 60 years.

6.2 The Social-Psychology Model

Before turning to the social-psychology model, I want to highlight the assumptions that underlie the dominant political-science models and call attention to the ways that the social-psychology and political-science models both converge and diverge. To start, political-science models share a basic premise about the Justices' motivations, that is, that Justices care only about the substance of legal policy. Consequently, although there are sharp disagreements among political scientists about whether Justices care about law or policy and the extent to which Justices act strategically to advance their goals, political-science models all agree that Justices devote themselves to the pursuit of their preferred legal-policy goals.[1] Any other goal is of minor importance.

[1] This broad agreement includes the work of Jeffrey Segal and Harold Spaeth (2002), who argue that Justices vote their policy preferences; of Lee Epstein and Jack Knight (1998), who argue that

This premise that Justices seek to advance their legal-policy agendas might be contested by pointing to other goals that the Justices might seek to advance through their choices as decisionmakers. These goals might include power, prestige, reputation, harmonious relations with other Justices, "and the other satisfactions that people seek in a job" (Posner 2008, 36). The social-psychology model emphasizes the motivational basis for the goals that the Justices seek to advance. In particular, the social-psychology model argues that the Justices are not simply interested in pursuing preferred legal-policy outcomes but, instead, are also interested in power and image, especially their reputation in social networks that matter to them.[2]

For reasons I will now detail, social psychology identifies numerous roadblocks that stand in the way of a majority coalition forming on the Supreme Court. The most obvious roadblock (and the one hurdle that political scientists and social psychologists agree on) is ideological diversity among the Justices. An individual will not act in ways that are inconsistent with matters central to her cognitive network. In particular, group membership is a basic part of individual self-conception; it is a key component of how we perceive our place in the world (Forsyth 1999, 66–80). Because of the fundamental importance of group identification in our lives, individuals are only willing to associate themselves meaningfully with groups that are sympathetic to their core beliefs.

A second potential barrier to group formation is tied to an individual Justice's motivations, specifically the need for power. An individual's need to influence others and to control or shape the world around her, the need for power, is a basic psychological need; but it is valued differently by different individuals, and it manifests itself differently in different situations. In some settings, membership in a group may actually provide an outlet for people with strong needs for power because groups present opportunities for leadership (Forsyth 1999, 92). Also, an ideologically like-minded coalition may join together in order to decisively advance the individual preferences of coalition members. However, people with a strong need for power may find it best to refrain from joining a group and instead play the role of power broker, or "decider," between rival factions. And, of course, for some people the need for power is simply not a sufficient enticement to join any group.

Consider, for example, the so-called "swing" Justices who cast the deciding votes in controversial cases. Swing Justices exercise power by writing consequential concurring opinions that limit the reach of the majority's ruling or by insisting that their legal-policy preferences are reflected in the majority opinion. Like any Justice, a swing Justice will not cast votes at odds with core beliefs. But a swing Justice might have comparatively weak legal-policy preferences and a comparatively strong desire to exercise power. In order for a swing Justice to exercise power meaningfully, however, the Court must be ideologically diverse (Epstein and Jacobi 2008).

Justices are policy-seekers who take potential resistance to their decisions into account in order to "move the substantive content of law as close as possible to their preferred policy positions"; and of Howard Gillman (2001), who argues that legal considerations play a significant role alongside policy considerations in Supreme Court decisionmaking.

[2] See Lawrence Baum's *Judges and Their Audiences* for general background (2006).

An ideologically cohesive Court (with a majority coalition of five or more Justices) will not need the swing Justice's vote to advance its legal-policy preferences. In this situation, the swing Justice might seek to exercise power by joining that coalition in the hopes of playing a leadership role in that group (assuming that the coalition is acting in ways consistent with her core beliefs). Alternatively, the swing Justice might not want to join that coalition—even if that will mean fewer opportunities to exercise power. For example, the swing Justice (or, for that matter, any Justice) might place a high value on external variables—most notably, how she is perceived by audiences that she cares about. These audiences might include journalists, law professors, lawyers' groups, other judges and Justices, political parties, interest groups, and even the public (Baum 2006).

In paying attention to "audiences," Justices engage in impression management—that is, the "process of controlling how one is perceived by other people" (Leary 1996, 3). Like group dynamics generally, impression management is a universal phenomenon. Everyone engages in some form of impression management every day. It is an "essential component of social interaction" (ibid.). Like an individual's desire to exercise power, the amount of impression management engaged in by individuals varies significantly with the situation and the individual. For Supreme Court Justices, there are countless opportunities to take into account their sanding with various audiences: oral argument, opinion writing, the giving of speeches and interviews, attending social gatherings, and so on. In other words, judging on the Court is in many ways an exercise in self-presentation, and the behavior of the Justices is shaped in important ways by the opinions of outside groups that the Justices care about. More than that, the very process by which we select Justices tends "to favor those with an especially strong interest in the esteem of other people" (Baum 2006, 32). Accepting a judgeship entails accepting relatively significant constraints on personal activities and behaviors as well as (for most judges) a significant reduction in monetary compensation. The inducement for accepting these losses is an increase in prestige (and an increase in potential power). As a result, the types of people who end up with judicial positions tend to be those who care a great deal about the esteem of others.

Impression management figures prominently in the willingness of a Supreme Court Justice to join forces with others and forge a majority coalition. To start, a Justice will not join a coalition if that will harm her reputation among groups that are important to her. Just as a Justice will not join a group that would require her to vote in ways not consistent with her personal beliefs, a Justice will not hurt her standing with groups she cares about. And while some of these groups may have identifiable ideologies, externally focused Justices are well aware that the norm of judging in the United States is that the judge is a neutral, impartial arbiter of disputes. For some (but not all) Justices, this norm tends to act as a disincentive to be part of a unified, ideologically identifiable subgroup of Justices, because "people try to project images of themselves that are consistent with the norms in a particular social setting and with the roles they occupy" (Leary 1996, 67). In this way, Justices have incentives to act like an independent judge and not a member of an ideologically identifiable group. As such, an externally focused Justice—especially as compared to public officials whose status is tied to political battles that play out in public view—has little reason to curry favor with one or another ideologically identifiable constituency. Justices with strong ideological precommitments, however, will place a higher value on winning the esteem of some ideologically identifiable group. For these Justices, approval by such groups may matter more than engaging in self-presentation that is aimed at reinforcing the norm of neutral, impartial arbiter.

Consider again our so-called swing Justice. If all she cared about was power, she would pay no mind to her reputation. Her decision to join one or another side of a dispute would simply be an exercise in power—her efforts to wield as much influence as possible (either by filing a consequential concurring opinion or by providing an essential vote for the majority). In particular, she would want to maintain her swing-Justice status—so that her vote would be critical to the resolution of any dispute. Along these lines, she would want to locate herself at the Court's median (and, to the extent possible, distance herself from Justices to her immediate right and left) (Epstein and Jacobi 2008, 74–81).

An externally focused swing Justice, instead, would focus on how others perceive her. Perhaps she would cultivate a reputation of neutrality; perhaps she would want to be known as the "critical vote"; perhaps she would want groups with disparate ideologies to view her vote as gettable. Whatever her methodology or motivation, the externally focused swing Justice will place a high value on cultivating a positive image with groups that do not demand ideological conformity.

In contrast, Justices with strong ideological precommitments may be especially likely to join coalitions. Members of ideologically like-minded coalitions will agree with each other on issues of high salience to coalition members; consequently, they will more likely seek to assume power by forcefully advancing a shared agenda. In other words, members of such a group have less interest in exercising individualized power by casting the decisive swing vote; for them, the pursuit of a shared agenda is the most important manifestation of power. Likewise, Justices with strong ideological precommitments may be less interested in fostering the norm of an impartial, independent jurist. Rather, when it comes to impression management, the outside groups they care about are those who share their values and objectives. Compare, for example, Justices Anthony Kennedy and Clarence Thomas. Kennedy—consistent with swing-Justice behavior—places a high value on the opinions of the news media and other elites; Thomas identifies closely with ideologically conservative groups (Baum and Devins 2010, 1543–44, 1534–35).

If there are five or more ideologically like-minded Justices, a majority coalition may form. The key variable, as noted above, is whether these Justices have sufficiently strong ideological precommitments to overcome the basic obstacles to group formation. For example, in determining whether a Justice will join a group, it may require more than the Justice agreeing with other members on the preferred outcome and legal reasoning in any given issue space. A Justice not strongly precommitted to the group's agenda may place a higher value on the exercise of individual power or cultivating a reputation for judicial independence. Perhaps for this reason, Justice Anthony Kennedy broke ranks with the Rehnquist Court's "conservative bloc" by switching his initial conference votes in high-visibility school prayer and abortion cases.[3]

The appointments/confirmation process also stands as a substantial obstacle to the formation of an ideologically like-minded majority coalition, especially with regard to controversial, highly salient issues. Because Justices have life tenure, it is very unlikely that appointments to the Court will be clustered closely together. Such clustering of appointments facilitates group formation (Arrow, McGrath, and Berdahl 2000, 69). In the case of the Court, this is both because people who join an existing organization tend to identify with others who join at the same time and because such clustering means that the same President and Senate will be making the appointments, increasing the likelihood of clustered appointees being relatively closely aligned ideologically. For example, President Roosevelt's clustering of Supreme Court appointments from 1938 to 1943 figured prominently in the New Deal Court's dramatic expansion of government power over the economy. However, this perfect storm of closely clustered appointments and other factors that would help overcome the barriers to group formation rarely occurs.

Given these barriers to group formation, it is little wonder that the Supreme Court has been generally incoherent and dominated by swing Justices for most of the past 60 years. By way of contrast, the New Deal Court's dramatic expansion of government power over the economy was tied to the fact that President Roosevelt was able to nominate eight Justices to the Court between 1938 and 1943. This clustering of appointments made the New Deal Court a coherent Court. For the balance of this chapter, I will draw distinctions between the decisionmaking of coherent and incoherent Courts.

6.3 The New Deal Court

The series of events culminating in the formation of the New Deal Court began with the 1935–1936 power struggle between the "Old Court" and Roosevelt over the fate of the New Deal. "Swept into office with a mandate to repair the ravages of the Depression," Congress and the White House set about to revamp the relationship between the federal government and the American people (Irons 1982). The very name "New Deal" implied, according to Roosevelt (1938), "that the Government itself was going to use affirmative action to bring about its avowed objectives … [and] that a new order of things designed to benefit the great mass … would replace the old order of special privilege." On the Supreme Court, New Deal initiatives were met with skepticism. A cohesive four-Justice bloc of conservatives "despised the New Deal program as anti-American and socialistic and condemned it out of hand as unconstitutional" (Urofsky 2001). One of the Court's two moderates (typically

[3] See Lee v. Weisman, 505 U.S. 577 (1992), and Planned Parenthood of Se. Pa. v. Casey, 505 U.S. 833 (1992). Justice Kennedy's unexpected votes in those cases were discussed in popular media at the time, including Terry Eastland's (1993, 32) article "The Tempting of Justice Kennedy."

Associate Justice Owen Roberts but sometimes Chief Justice Charles Evans Hughes) often joined the conservative bloc to rule against New Deal initiatives.

In 1937–1938, the New Deal Court came of age. By replacing two of the Court's staunchest proponents of laissez-faire (Justices Willis Van Devanter and George Sutherland) with New Dealers Hugo Black and Stanley Reed, Roosevelt guaranteed that the Court would uphold both federal and state efforts to regulate the economy. By 1940, Roosevelt had further solidified his New Deal Court with three more appointments. By 1943, eight of the nine Justices were FDR appointees.

After Roosevelt was able to seize control of the Court in 1937, a coherent Court advanced his New Deal agenda by overturning precedent and pursuing doctrinal innovations that insulated governmental efforts to regulate the economy. From 1937 to 1944, the New Deal Court had created a "new constitutional order," overruling 30 cases—"two thirds as many as had been overruled in the Court's previous history" (Powe 2002, 485–86). Over the course of its 12-year tenure (1937–1949), the Court handed down 42 rulings that overturned at least 59 of its prior decisions. The majority of these overrulings had broad support—with only five of these cases decided by a five-to-four vote (as compared to ten unanimous overruling decisions).

The legacy of the New Deal Court was "free-wheeling adjudication" (Berger 1984, 751). The Court, "[i]n a series of decisive strokes in the late 1930s and early 1940s, … thoroughly repudiated the entire doctrinal system of constitutional limitations on federal power over the national economy" (Ackerman 1999, 47). Rather than reinterpret or work against the backdrop of existing precedent, the Court proclaimed that "the ultimate touchstone of constitutionality is the Constitution itself and not what we have said about it [in past decisions]."[4] Correspondingly, in "swiftly" overruling longstanding precedent, the Court did more than put in place a legal regime backed by the President and Congress. It also overruled important precedents in cases where nobody asked it to do so. *Erie Railroad Co. v. Tompkins*[5] is the most striking example of this practice. In *Erie*, both parties sought to preserve the regime of *Swift v. Tyson*[6]—that is, the federal courts' then-existing practice of applying federal common law in diversity cases. The Court, however, overruled *Swift* without briefing—concluding that the Court itself, and not the parties to a controversy, decides which legal arguments are relevant.

Against this backdrop, it is little wonder that the New Deal Court pursued significant doctrinal innovations—particularly with respect to the power of Congress and the states to regulate economic issues. Consider, for example, the Court's repudiation of *Hammer v. Dagenhart*'s constrained view of federal regulatory power and its embrace of seemingly limitless power in *Wickard v. Filburn*.[7] *Hammer* struck down a federal statute prohibiting the shipping (in interstate commerce) of goods manufactured by children within specified age ranges. Concluding that the production

[4] Graves v. New York *ex rel.* O'Keefe, 306 U.S. 466, 491–92 (1938) (Frankfurter, J., concurring).

[5] Erie R.R. Co. v. Tompkins, 304 U.S. 64 (1938).

[6] Swift v. Tyson, 41 U.S. 1 (1842).

[7] See Hammer v. Dagenhart, 247 U.S. 251 (1918), and Wickard v. Filburn, 317 U.S. 111 (1942).

and manufacture of goods were not part of commerce, the Court boldly claimed that our federalist system would be "destroyed" by such congressional encroachments into the state police power. Nearly 23 years later, the New Deal Court unanimously overruled *Hammer* in *United States v. Darby* and, in so doing, rejected the *Lochner* Court's distinction between intrastate manufacture and interstate shipment.[8]

Even more striking is *Wickard*'s approval in 1942 of efforts by the Secretary of Agriculture to enforce a quota on wheat production against a farmer who grew wheat for home consumption. Not only did the Court in *Wickard* dispense with the requirement that Congress assemble some type of record, it explicitly recognized that Congress may regulate economic conduct "trivial by itself" so long as the aggregation of similar activity by other actors affects interstate commerce. Recognizing (in private correspondence) that the Court had "all but reached an era in the interpretation of the commerce clause of candid recognition that [they had] no legal judgment upon economic effects which [they could] oppose to the policy judgment made by Congress in legislation" (Cushman 2000, 1143), *Wickard*'s author, Associate Justice Robert Jackson, observed: "I really know of no place … where we can bound the doctrine" (ibid., 1145).

Wickard exemplifies what a coherent Court can do. Not needing to engage in horse-trading over votes, a coalition of five or more Justices can advance an expansive view of the law. Furthermore, when precedents are at odds with that view of the law, the Court (as it did in *Darby*) can simply overturn those precedents.

6.4 The Warren Court

There were two Warren Courts. The 1962–1968 Terms featured, as Lucas Powe (2002, 207) put it, "history's Warren Court." That Court was a coherent Court willing both to overturn precedent and to make significant doctrinal advances. The 1953–1961 Terms tell a far different story. During that period, the Court rarely overturned precedents (doing so only 11 times) and was sharply divided. In its 1960 Term, for example, the Court split five to four in 25 of 52 non-unanimous civil-liberties cases. Justices Potter Stewart and Tom Clark generally alternated as the swing Justices for much of this period. But on national-security cases, which dominated much of the era, Justices Felix Frankfurter and John Marshall Harlan II cast the decisive votes.

The national-security cases are emblematic of the early Warren Court. Rather than embrace a "hard" view of the Constitution, the Court made extensive use of constitutional avoidance—permitting the Justices to initially rule in favor of Communists and other subversives while allowing themselves the freedom to change their minds in subsequent cases. Correspondingly, by ruling on statutory

[8] United States v. Darby, 312 U.S. 100 (1941). See Keith Whittington's "Congress Before the Lochner Court" (2005, 821–23) for a brief overview of the significance of the Supreme Court during the *Lochner* era.

grounds, the Court often returned the issue to Congress—so that Congress could either acquiesce to the Court or express its disapproval of the Court's ruling by enacting new legislation.

During its 1956–1957 Term, the Court decided 12 cases involving Communists, ruling against the government in every case. Most significant, on June 17, 1957 ("Red Monday"), the Court handed down four decisions that severely limited Smith Act prosecutions (for the "knowing or willing" "advocacy or teaching" of the "desirability or propriety of overthrowing the Government of the United States").[9] These decisions, while signaling the unconstitutionality of governmental efforts to clamp down on subversives, were decided on statutory grounds. For example, in *Yates v. United States*, the Court (in an opinion by Justice Harlan) concluded that the Smith Act by its terms was limited to "incitement" and did not extend to abstract advocacy.[10]

Congress responded with a vengeance, coming—as Chief Justice Warren (1977, 313) put it—"dangerously close" to enacting legislation that would have stripped the Supreme Court of appellate jurisdiction in five domestic-security areas. The Court relented, issuing decisions that limited the scope of earlier rulings and otherwise permitted the government to prosecute cases against subversives. The fact that the Court did this after the *defeat* of proposed jurisdiction-stripping measures was significant, prompting the *New York Times*, for example, to complain that "[w]hat Senator Jenner [the principal sponsor of court-stripping legislation] was unable to achieve [in Congress,] the Supreme Court has now virtually accomplished on its own" (A Regrettable Decision 1960).

No doubt, a Justice truly committed to the policy goals of the 1956–1957 Term's civil-liberties decisions would have continued to risk possible legislative backlash. This explains the willingness of Chief Justice Warren and Justices Black, Douglas, and Brennan to oppose the Court's retreat—often filing vociferous dissents. In particular, the 1960 Court had reason to think that Congress would acquiesce to pro-civil-liberties rulings. Earlier Court-curbing proposals had failed, and the Court controversy was not a major factor in the 1958 elections. More significant, "the Congress became more liberal. Seven Republican Senators who had battled the Court, including Jenner … had left due either to retirement or electoral defeat" (Murphy 1962, 237–38).

But for Justice Frankfurter (and presumably his ally, Justice Harlan), the hue and cry following the Court's 1956–1957 Term rulings was too much. Not only did Congress seek to slap the Court down, the American Bar Association and Judge Learned Hand launched sharp attacks against the Court. Frankfurter was a pro-government New Dealer who sought to limit judicial intrusions into the legislative process by advancing any number of "judicial restraint" doctrines. His antigovernment decisions were a departure from this norm and, as such, there is reason to think that he was not strongly committed to the civil-liberties agenda championed by Black, Douglas, Warren, and Brennan. By retreating from 1956 to 1957 Term decisions

[9] See 18 U.S.C. § 2385 (2000).

[10] 354 U.S. 298, 318 (1957).

and returning to his typical mode of deferential decisionmaking, he was able to demonstrate his bona fides to Court critics.

To summarize, the Court's retreat from its 1956 to 1957 Term rulings is not a story of a Court acting strategically—by issuing minimalist non-constitutional decisions in an effort to best assess how to advance its pro-civil-liberties agenda. Instead, the Harlan/Frankfurter flip and the vociferous criticism of that flip by pro-civil-liberties Justices illustrates the existence of divergent preferences on an incoherent Court. Frankfurter and Harlan had weak preferences and, as such, were not truly aligned with the Court's four liberals (Warren, Douglas, Black, Brennan). That Frankfurter and Harlan preferred non-constitutional decisions in the 1956–1957 Term speaks to those weak preferences, as does their willingness to change direction in response to anti-Court criticism by Congress, the bar, and respected jurists.

In 1962, Frankfurter stepped down and the Court was transformed. Liberal activist Arthur Goldberg replaced Frankfurter and joined forces with the Court's four liberals. With five Justices now firmly committed to a progressive agenda, there was no need for the Court to make use of constitutional avoidance or otherwise limit its pursuit of its preferred legal-policy vision. Goldberg (and Abe Fortas, the Justice who replaced Goldberg in 1966) agreed with Warren about 90 % of the time, and the intra-agreement rate among the five liberals likewise hovered around 90 %. When Thurgood Marshall joined the Court in 1967 (replacing Tom Clark), the Court moved even farther to the left. Marshall was in the majority 95 % of the time (second only to Brennan, in the majority 98 % of the time), and the intra-agreement rate among "the most cohesive bloc in modern Court history" (Fortas, Warren, Brennan, and Marshall) was 93 % (Heck 1980, 872).

Ideological cohesion within the Warren Court played out in innumerable ways. More than any Court before it, the Warren Court was willing to overturn constitutional precedent. Thirty-two precedents were overturned from 1962 to 1968; 30 of these overrulings advanced liberal outcomes. Likewise, from 1962 to 1968, 66 state statutes were invalidated; 62 of these invalidations advanced liberal outcomes.

The ideological coherence (and corresponding ambitiousness) of the Warren Court is also reflected in the ways in which the Court pursued its policymaking agenda. The Court rewrote constitutional law and, in critical respects, the Court was more ambitious in pursuing its liberal agenda than were Congress and the White House (even during the Johnson administration, when Democrats controlled both Congress and the Presidency). The key to all this was Earl Warren, who, as Bernard Schwartz observed, "strongly believed that the law must draw its vitality from life rather than precedent" and that the Court needed to perform a transforming role, "usually thought of as more appropriate to the legislator than the judge," in order for the Court "to keep step with the twentieth century's frenetic pace of social change" (Schwartz 1993, 275, 263). In particular, Warren and the dominant coalition on the post-1962 Court aggressively pursued the nationalization of political problems and processes, especially equality for the underrepresented (minorities, the poor, the accused, and children). In so doing, the Court opened up areas that had "been thought closed to the exercise of judicial power" (Funston 1977, 314), often "articulating broad rules that went well beyond the particular circumstances of individual cases" (Palmer 1999, 42).

If the hallmark of the first Warren Court was its use of constitutional avoidance in anti-subversive cases, the post-1962 Warren Court demonstrated its willingness to impose a hard view of legal policymaking by embracing prophylactic rules—rules intended to bind lower courts and government officials (even if it meant sometimes prohibiting otherwise constitutional behavior). This bit of constitutional bravado highlights the fundamental differences between pre- and post-1962 Warren Court decisionmaking. The post-1962 Court knew its mind on legal-policy questions and, as such, was willing to bind itself, lower courts, and government officials. Consequently, instead of invoking the avoidance canon when considering the legality of anti-subversive legislation, the post-1962 Warren Court "brought the domestic-security apparatus to a halt" (Powe 2002, 316), declaring unconstitutional federal laws banning Communists from working in defense facilities and limiting the mailing of "communist propaganda."[11] More than that, the post-1962 Court was willing to risk elected-branch disapproval in order to advance its legal-policy agenda.

Miranda v. Arizona[12] is the quintessential example of the post-1962 Warren Court's willingness to run risks and pursue its vision of legal policymaking. Notwithstanding public-opinion polls showing significant opposition to post-1962 Warren Court criminal-procedure decisions and the calls by 27 states (in an amicus brief) for the Court to slow down its criminal-procedure revolution, *Miranda* mandated a specific set of warnings that police must read to criminal suspects. In so doing, the Court required every state to change its interrogation practices. More than that, the decision read like a legislative code, not a constitutional opinion. Correspondingly, in overturning the longstanding totality-of-the-circumstances test governing the admissibility of confessions, the Court gave "disproportionate attention" (Powe 2002, 395) to matters of policy, not law. Among other things, the Court began by announcing a new rule "so specific that there could be no claim that [it] flowed directly from the text of the Constitution" (ibid.). More striking, by embracing a prophylactic rule, the Court concluded that it was appropriate (as a matter of policy) to foreclose some constitutionally permissible interrogations in order to stop unconstitutional interrogations.

The Warren Court's federalization of criminal procedure is a hallmark both of its legal-policy agenda and of the ability of a coherent Court to advance such an agenda. A strong advocate for those who were poorly served by the political process, the Court pursued doctrinal innovations to protect racial minorities, the poor, the accused, juveniles, religious minorities, political dissidents, and underrepresented voters. In so doing, the Court cared about results—not legal niceties (such as adhering to or even citing precedent). Indeed, reflecting its desire to reach the "correct" result even when the "doctrinal tools … were not readily at hand" (Tushnet 1993, 10), the post-1962 Warren Court cited fewer precedents than other Supreme Courts.

---

[11] United States v. Robel, 389 U.S. 258, 263–64 (1967); Lamont v. Postmaster Gen., 381 U.S. 301, 306–07 (1965).

[12] 384 U.S. 436 (1966).

6.5 The Rehnquist Court

The Rehnquist Court (1986–2005) promised but did not deliver a constitutional revolution. With four Justices nominated by Ronald Reagan (and with all four on the Court from 1987 to 2005), the Rehnquist Court seemed destined to embrace Reagan's brand of judicial conservatism. When running for President in 1980 and 1984, Reagan pledged to appoint judges who "share our commitment to judicial restraint" (Republican Party Platform 1984) and reached out to social conservatives by condemning Supreme Court decisions on school prayer, busing, and especially abortion. In particular, Reagan called for the overruling of *Engel v. Vitale*[13] (school prayer) and *Roe v. Wade*[14]—saying that "God should [never] have been expelled from the classroom" and that *Roe* was as divisive and wrong as *Dred Scott v. Sandford*[15] had been (Reagan 1983, 603, 1984, 16–21).

The social-conservative agenda, however, was not the agenda of the Rehnquist Court. By steering a centrist path, the Rehnquist Court avoided controversy and, for the most part, tracked public opinion. Furthermore, with shifting voting alignments and a propensity to divide five to four (doing so in more than 20 % of all cases and in a much higher percentage of controversial cases), the Rehnquist Court's identity was largely defined by the voting predilections of Justices Sandra Day O'Connor and Anthony Kennedy. On abortion and school prayer, O'Connor and Kennedy, citing concerns of stare decisis and the Court's legitimacy, cast key votes to reaffirm the essential holdings of *Roe* and *Engel*. Indeed, "Republican domination of the [Rehnquist] Court" did not result "in the overruling of a single revolutionary Warren Court decision" (Nagel 2006, 24).

This is not to say that the Justices were unwilling to overturn precedent. The Rehnquist Court overturned 44 constitutional precedents. The Court's targets, however, underscore the incoherence of Rehnquist Court decisionmaking. The Court steered neither a clearly liberal nor a clearly conservative path when overturning precedents (reaching liberal results in 41 % and conservative results in 59 % of these cases). More than that, the Rehnquist Court was highly selective in its invocation of stare decisis—taking the doctrine seriously when it backed up the result it preferred and ignoring it when it did not.

In understanding the Rehnquist Court's on-again off-again approach to precedent, I will focus on the competing approaches of Justices Kennedy and O'Connor. For Justice O'Connor, her willingness to sign onto a majority opinion was often contingent on the Court's embracing a view of the law that seemed limited to the case at hand. For Justice Kennedy, it was better to ignore a disfavored precedent than meet it head on. Under either approach, however, Court

[13] Engel v. Vitale, 370 U.S. 421 (1962); Roe v. Wade, 410 U.S. 113 (1973); Dred Scott v. Sandford, 60 U.S. 393 (1856). The Court in *Dred Scott* infamously held that slaves, former slaves, and descendants of slaves could not be citizens and declared that Congress had no power to prohibit slavery in the territories.

[14] 410 U.S. 113 (1973).

[15] 60 U.S. 393 (1856).

decisionmaking was incoherent. Decisions might be fact-specific and nongeneralizable or decisions might fail to discuss relevant precedents in ways that too made them nongeneralizable. To make these points more concrete, I will turn my attention to two emblematic Rehnquist Court privacy decisions—*Washington v. Glucksberg* and *Lawrence v. Texas*.[16]

Glucksberg held that there is no right to physician-assisted suicide. In an opinion written by Chief Justice Rehnquist (for a five-member majority that included Justices Kennedy and O'Connor), the Court purported to apply "[o]ur established method of substantive-due-process analysis."[17] In fact, *Glucksberg* is a mess—filled with omissions, internal inconsistencies, and a general disregard of the precedent it claims to follow. The explanation: The Chief Justice thought it better to sacrifice a clear statement of doctrine in order to secure the votes of Justices Kennedy and O'Connor.

To win over Justice Kennedy, Chief Justice Rehnquist could not favorably cite *Bowers v. Hardwick*.[18] In *Bowers*, the Court concluded that states can criminalize same-sex sodomy and, in so doing, limited the sweep of substantive-due-process protections. Contending that the Court "is most vulnerable and comes nearest to illegitimacy when it deals with judge-made [rights]," *Bowers* confined substantive due process to those rights that are grounded in the nation's legal traditions and practices.[19] In *Glucksberg*, the Court appeared to embrace and extend *Bowers*. It declared that fundamental rights must both be "objectively 'deeply rooted' in this Nation's history and tradition" *and* "implicit in ordered liberty.'"[20]

But Justice Kennedy disapproved of *Bowers*. Not only would he eventually cast the key vote in *Lawrence v. Texas*[21] (overturning *Bowers*), he had written the majority opinion in a decision the previous Term rejecting (on equal-protection grounds) a Colorado law prohibiting the granting of "protected status" to homosexuals.[22] Assuming that Justice Kennedy would not sign on to a decision that strongly backed *Bowers*, the Chief Justice may have thought it better to ignore *Bowers* than to risk losing one of the Justices in his fragile five-member coalition.

For similar reasons, Chief Justice Rehnquist seemed to limit *Glucksberg*'s reach in order to secure Justice O'Connor's vote. In a telling footnote, he suggested that the Court might not follow the *Glucksberg* formula in future challenges to assisted suicide laws. In this way, Chief Justice Rehnquist took into account the views of Justice O'Connor, who, in a concurring opinion, made clear that she would not join a decision that absolutely barred substantive-due-process challenges to assisted-suicide laws. Noting that a mentally competent person experiencing great pain may have a fundamental right to hasten his or her death, Justice O'Connor joined

[16] Washington v. Glucksberg, 521 U.S. 702 (1997); Lawrence v Texas, 539 U.S. 558 (2003).

[17] 521 U.S 702, 720 (1997).

[18] 478 U.S. 186 (1986).

[19] 478 U.S. 186, 194 (1986).

[20] 521 U.S. 702, 720–21 (1997).

[21] 539 U.S. 558 (2003).

[22] Romer v. Evans, 517 U.S. 620 (1996).

Glucksberg insofar as there was "no reason to think the democratic process" would not strike the appropriate balance on the issue.[23]

Six Terms later, in finding a constitutional right to same-sex sodomy, *Lawrence* underscored the irrelevance of *Glucksberg* and, more generally, the fact that Rehnquist Court decisions rarely did more than announce case-specific results. This is evidenced in both Justice Kennedy's five-member majority opinion and Justice O'Connor's concurring opinion. It is telling that Kennedy saw no reason to struggle over apparent inconsistencies between his *Lawrence* decision and the methodology he embraced in *Glucksberg*. The other telling feature of Kennedy's opinion is its sweeping language about the "transcendent dimension" of "liberty," about "freedom extend[ing] beyond spatial bounds."[24] Reflecting both his intense interest in how his decisions are perceived and his "expansive view of courts' role in public life" (Greenburg 2007, 160), Kennedy was far more interested in "throwing down moral thunderbolts" than in following precedent (even his own) (Lazarus 2003).

In sharp contrast, Justice O'Connor's concurring opinion in *Lawrence* broke no doctrinal ground. Reflecting her tendency "to focus on the particulars of the dispute before the Court" and to embrace "rationales on which diverse people can agree" (Sunstein 2006, 1907), Justice O'Connor argued that the Texas law was grounded in an impermissible purpose ("moral disapproval" of gays) and, consequently, there was no need to revisit *Bowers*. In other words, just as she had carved out a palliative-care exception in *Glucksberg*, O'Connor resisted Kennedy's expansive reasoning, preferring, instead, a "flexible," "context-specific" approach (Tushnet 2005, 54).

Glucksberg and *Lawrence* exemplify Rehnquist Court decisionmaking and, with it, the inability of an incoherent Court to cause significant doctrinal shifts. Without a solid coalition of five (or more) ideologically like-minded Justices, the Rehnquist Court did not "make a single move that would radically change or unsettle existing constitutional doctrine" (Friedman 2002, 146). Instead, the confluence of decision-making styles on the Rehnquist Court was a perfect storm for the making of an incoherent Court. Leading (so to speak) the Court was a pragmatic Chief Justice uninterested in an "overarching substantive theory of constitutional interpretation" and willing to sacrifice doctrinal coherence in order to cobble together a five-member majority (Rosen 2005, 79, 87). More significant, two dramatically different swing Justices typically cast the deciding votes in key cases—one of whom was a minimalist (whose fact-specific decisionmaking did not bind her or the other Justices in subsequent cases), the other of whom was quite willing to make expansive statements about doctrine and the judicial role (but felt neither bound by those principles in subsequent cases nor obligated to contemplate precedents at odds with his decisionmaking). This mix of personalities, as the above discussion reveals, was on full display in *Glucksberg* and *Lawrence*.

The Rehnquist Court, while unique in some respects, exemplifies the tendencies of incoherent Courts. Besides the individual preferences of the swing Justices, there are other structural explanations for why an incoherent Court would be less likely to

[23] 521 U.S. 702, 737 (1997) (O'Connor, J., concurring).

[24] Lawrence v. Texas, 539 U.S. 558, 562 (2003).

issue broad opinions or overrule landmark precedents. In order to cobble together a majority coalition, Justices often will compromise their individual preferences regarding the reach of the decision. As a result, the "Justices will often deliberately cloud their opinion to obtain the fifth vote" "so long as the ambiguity is not incompatible with their views" (Kirman 1995, 2099).

On an incoherent Court, there are more closely divided cases and, as a result, more opportunities for Justices in the majority to make compromises in order to hold together a majority coalition. In particular, there are more occasions when Justices will ask the decision-writer to address their concerns through addition or deletion and "tacitly threaten to withhold support if the changes are not made" (Maltzman and Wahlbeck 1996, 581). And when the opinion is being written by a swing Justice, it may be that other members of the majority coalition place fewer demands on the opinion-writer—for fear that the swing Justice will drop out of the majority and file a special concurring opinion. Against this backdrop, it is to be expected that the decisions of incoherent Courts are in tension with each other: The rationales employed are not necessarily embraced by a majority of Justices and are often muddied by compromise, and cases often turn on narrow factual distinctions (because the legal rule is not intended to bind the Court in subsequent cases). This is certainly true of the Rehnquist Court's substantive-due-process decisions, but it is also true in that Court's decisions with respect to religion, race, and its once-vaunted federalism revival.

6.6 The Roberts Court

From its inception in the 2005–2006 Term and at least until the 2012–2013 Term, the Roberts Court has been largely incoherent. Dominated by two blocs of four Justices (a center-left bloc and a conservative bloc), the Roberts Court has often found its critical fifth vote in right-leaning swing Justice Anthony Kennedy. In the 2006–2007 Term, for example, Kennedy was in the majority in each of the Court's twenty-four five-to-four rulings; in the 2009–2010 Term, he was in the majority in 14 of 16 five-to-four rulings. And while Kennedy is somewhat conservative, he is far more liberal than the other four conservatives. In the 2011–2012 Term, for example, Kennedy supplied the critical fifth vote in ten cases—joining the Court's conservatives on five rulings and its liberals on five rulings. In the 2012–2013 term, he was in the majority in 83 % of the Court's divided cases (more than any other Justice) and wrote the Court's five-to-four decision invalidating the Defense of Marriage Act.[25] Perhaps for this reason, the Roberts Court broke little doctrinal ground and overruled only eight precedents in its first 5 years.

At the same time, the early Roberts Court was certainly right-leaning and far more cohesive than the Rehnquist Court (which, as already noted, was defined by two swing Justices with quite different decisionmaking styles). In several significant

[25] United States v. Windsor, 133 S. Ct. 2675 (2013).

cases, Justice Kennedy joined the Court's four conservatives to issue rulings that (while claiming to adhere to precedent) were very hard to square with existing doctrine. A quick tour of some of these rulings suggests that an incoherent Court can reshape doctrine through "underrulings" or "stealth overrulings" (Peters 2008; Friedman 2010)—that is, reinterpretations of past precedents that effectively nullify those rulings (while also allowing a later Court to revive those never-officially-nullified decisions).

Here are four prominent examples of this practice. (1) In *Gonzales v. Carhart*,[26] the Court approved federal partial-birth abortion legislation that largely mirrored previously invalidated state partial-birth legislation. The earlier state law had been invalidated, in part, because it contained no health exception; *Gonzales v. Carhart* deferred to congressional findings that a health exception was unnecessary. (2) In *Federal Election Commission v. Wisconsin Right to Life*,[27] the Court concluded that a ban on corporate or union funding of electioneering communications in the weeks before an election could be constitutionally applied only to ads "susceptible of no reasonable interpretation" other than advocacy,[28] notwithstanding the Court's apparent approval of an outright ban in the 2003 *McConnell v. Federal Election Commission* decision.[29] (3) In *Parents Involved in Community Schools v. Seattle School District No. 1*,[30] a plurality of four Justices concluded that the voluntary integration of public schools violated *Brown v. Board*'s nondiscrimination mandate and that the Supreme Court's 2003 approval of diversity as a compelling government purpose in university admissions did not extend to high schools.[31] (4) In *Florida v. Powell*[32] and *Berghuis v. Thompkins*,[33] the Court concluded that *Miranda v. Arizona* neither compelled police to tell criminal suspects of their rights to have a lawyer present during an interrogation nor required suspects to formally waive their *Miranda* rights.

These decisions back up claims—based on political scientists' measures of whether a Justice is liberal or conservative—that the Roberts Court is the "most conservative since the anti-New Deal court of the 1930s" (Caplan 2012). They also suggest that the Roberts Court (at least through the 2012–2013 term) is not sufficiently cohesive to remake legal doctrine in its own image by overruling significant swaths of precedent or issuing a substantial number of rule-like decisions. In other words, while the replacement of Samuel Alito for Sandra Day O'Connor solidified the Court's conservative base, there is too much ideological space between Anthony Kennedy and the Court's four conservatives for the formation of a coherent group of five conservative Justices.

[26] 550 U.S. 124 (2007).

[27] 551 U.S. 449 (2007).

[28] 551 U.S. 449, 470 (2007).

[29] 540 U.S. 93 (2003).

[30] 551 U.S. 701 (2007).

[31] *Id.* at 740–48.

[32] 559 U.S. 50 (2010).

[33] 130 S. Ct. 2250 (2010).

Consider, for example, *Parents Involved*.[34] Unwilling to join forces with the four conservatives and set out an absolute prohibition against race-conscious admissions schemes, Justice Kennedy said that ending racial isolation is a compelling governmental interest and that race-conscious measures may be explored if race-neutral measures fail. By way of contrast, Justice Kennedy is a First-Amendment absolutist and was willing to declare that the government could not limit independent political expenditures by corporations and unions. That 2010 ruling, *Citizens United v. Federal Election Commission*,[35] overturned the 2003 *McConnell* decision.[36] And while undoubtedly significant, it stands as an exception to the Roberts Court practice of claiming to operate within the boundaries of precedent. Unless and until Justice Kennedy is no longer the Court's swing Justice, the Roberts Court will likely operate as a right-leaning incoherent Court. And while the 2012 reelection of Barack Obama may prove transformative (if the President is able to appoint a fifth liberal), there is no reason to think that either Justice Kennedy or one of the Court's four conservative Justices will voluntarily step aside.

6.7 Conclusion

The past may not be prologue. Although this chapter has highlighted barriers to group formation and the related tendency of the post-New Deal Courts to be incoherent, there is some reason to think that future Supreme Courts will be more coherent. The ideological distance between Justice Kennedy and the Court's conservative and liberal blocs is substantial—reflecting the fact that post-1991 Republican appointees have been strongly conservative and that, since the 1993 retirement of Byron White, Democratic Justices have been liberal. Party polarization has contributed to this development; a Democratic President will not appoint a conservative, a Republican will not appoint a liberal. More telling, neither party is likely to appoint a moderate, for all seven Justices appointed after 1991 are clearly conservative or clearly liberal. In other words, many of the barriers to group formation may give way to groups of ideologically like-minded Justices identified with one or the other political party.

Time, of course, will tell whether the barriers to group formation are sufficiently potent to block the formation of a coherent Court. Justices with strong legal-policy preferences are most interested in advancing those preferences and most willing to join ideologically identifiable groups; Justices with weaker policy preferences are more interested in the exercise of individual power and the cultivation of a reputation as a judicial independent. More to the point, the Court's future as either a coherent or incoherent Court is tied to the question of whether the Court's median Justice(s) are willing to join ranks with both the conservative/Republican bloc and the liberal/Democratic bloc.

---

[34] 551 U.S. 701 (2007).

[35] 558 U.S. 310 (2010).

[36] 540 U.S. 93 (2003).

References

Ackerman B (1999) Taxation and the Constitution. Columbia Law Rev 99(1):1–58
A regrettable decision (1960) New York Times, March 2
Arrow H, McGrath J, Berdahl J (2000) Small groups as complex systems. Sage Publications, Thousand Oaks
Baum L (2006) Judges and their audiences: a perspective on judicial behavior. Princeton University Press, Princeton
Baum L, Devins N (2010) Why the Supreme Court cares about elites, not the American people. Georgetown Law J 98(6):1515–1581
Berger R (1984) The activist legacy of the new deal court. Wash Law Rev 59(4):751–793
Caplan L (2012) "The most conservative Supreme Court", taking note (blog), New York Times, October 1, http://takingnote.blogs.nytimes.com/2012/10/01/the-most-conservative-supreme-court/?ref=affordablecareact
Cushman B (2000) Formalism and realism in Commerce Clause jurisprudence. Univ Chicago Law Rev 67(4):1089–1150
Devins N (2008) Ideological cohesion and precedent (or why the court only cares about precedent when most justices agree with each other). N C Law Rev 86(5):1399–1442
Devins N, Federspiel W (2010) The Supreme Court, social psychology, and group formation. In: The psychology of judicial decision making. Oxford University Press, New York, pp 85–102
Eastland T (1993) The tempting of Justice Kennedy. Am Spectator 26(2):32–37
Epstein L, Jacobi T (2008) Super medians. Stanford Law Rev 61(1):37–99
Epstein L, Knight J (1998) The choices justices make. CQ Press, Washington, DC
Forsyth DR (1999) Group dynamics, 3rd edn. Wadsworth Publishing Co., Belmont
Friedman B (2010) The wages of stealth overruling (with particular attention to *Miranda v. Arizona*). Georgetown Law J 99(1):1–63
Friedman LM (2002) The Rehnquist Court: some more or less historical comments. In: Belsky M (ed) The Rehnquist Court: a retrospective. Oxford University Press, New York, pp 143–158
Funston RY (1977) Constitutional counterrevolution? The Warren Court and the Burger Court: judicial policy making in modern America. Schenkman Publishing Company, Inc., Cambridge, MA
Gillman H (2001) What's law got to do with it? Judicial behavioralists test the 'legal model' of judicial decision making. Law Soc Inq 26(2):465–504
Greenburg JC (2007) Supreme conflict: the inside story of the struggle for control of the United States Supreme Court. Penguin Press, New York
Heck E (1980) Justice Brennan and the heydey of Warren court liberalism. Santa Clara Law Rev 20(3):841–887
Irons PH (1982) The New Deal lawyers. Princeton University Press, Princeton
Kirman I (1995) Standing apart to be a part: the precedential value of Supreme Court concurring opinions. Columbia Law Rev 95(8):2083–2119
Lazarus E (2003) "The pivotal role of justice Anthony Kennedy: why the Supreme Court's romantic may only become more influential over time", Findlaw's Writ, August 3, 2003, http://writ.news.findlaw.com/lazarus/20030807.html
Leary MR (1996) Self-presentation: impression management and interpersonal behavior. Westview Press, Boulder
Maltzman F, Wahlbeck PJ (1996) Strategic policy considerations and voting fluidity on the Burger Court. Am Pol Sci Rev 90(3):581–592
Murphy WF (1962) Congress and the Court: a case study in the American political process. University of Chicago Press, Chicago
Nagel RF (2006) Bowing to precedent. Wkly Stand 11(29):24–28
Palmer B (1999) Issue fluidity and agenda setting on the Warren Court. Pol Res Q 52(1):39–65
Peters CJ (2008) Under-the-table overruling. Wayne Law Rev 54(3):1067–1104
Posner RA (2008) How judges think. Harvard University Press, Cambridge, MA

Powe LA Jr (2002) The Warren Court and American politics. Belknap Press of Harvard University Press, Cambridge, MA
Reagan R (1983) The public papers of the presidents of the United States, book 1. United States Government Printing Office, Washington, DC
Reagan R (1984) Abortion and the conscience of the nation. Thomas Nelson Publishers, Nashville
Republican Party Platform of 1984 (1984) Republican National Convention Committee on Resolutions, Congressional Quarterly Almanac 40/55-B (1984)
Roosevelt F (1938) The public papers and addresses of Franklin D. Roosevelt, volume two, the year of crisis, 1933. Random House, New York
Rosen J (2005) Rehnquist the great? Atl Mon 295(3):79–90
Segal JA, Spaeth HJ (2002) The Supreme Court and the attitudinal model revisited. Cambridge University Press, Cambridge
Schwartz B (1993) A history of the Supreme Court. Oxford University Press, New York
Sunstein CR (2006) Problems with minimalism. Stanford Law Rev 58(6):1899–1918
Tushnet M (1993) The Warren Court as history: an interpretation. In: Tushnet M (ed) The Warren Court in historical and political perspective. University Press of Virginia, Charlottesville, pp 1–35
Tushnet M (2005) A court divided: the Rehnquist Court and the future of constitutional law. W. W. Norton & Co., New York
Urofsky MI (2001) The Warren Court: justices, rulings, and legacy. ABC-CLIO, Santa Barbara
Warren E (1977) The memoirs of Earl Warren. Doubleday & Company, Inc., Garden City
Whittington KE (2005) Congress before the *Lochner* Court. Boston Univ Law Rev 85(3):821–858

Chapter 7
Stare Decisis and the Selection Effect

Frederick Schauer

Abstract This chapter contends that there are significant systemic obstacles to determining whether the Supreme Court actually adheres to stare decisis. Political-science research suggests that precedent exerts relatively little constraint on the Court's decisionmaking. The author contends that this research is unreliable, however, because of the *selection effect*: A strong norm of stare decisis, if it existed, would allow only the closest cases—those where precedent is least constraining—to reach the Court in the first place. Whether the selection effect actually operates in this way, however, depends on whether litigants, lawyers, and lower-court judges believe the Court applies stare decisis. And whether the Court does so is precisely what the empirical studies cannot reveal. As things stand, then, there is no reliable way to know whether the Court really follows precedent. The Court could fill this information gap by conspicuously reaffirming decisions known to be opposed by a majority of Justices, but it rarely has done so. This failure, more than any empirical research, suggests that the Court does not in fact accord much weight to precedent.

7.1 Defining Stare Decisis

Stare decisis is the term used to describe the obligation of a court to follow *its own* previous decisions. And because stare decisis is thus limited to the putative constraints of a court's own previous decisions, it is most accurately understood as a subset of and not congruent with the idea of precedent. The idea of precedent generally is broader, including both vertical precedent, the duty of a court to adhere to the decisions of courts above it on the judicial hierarchy; and horizontal precedent,

F. Schauer (✉)
School of Law, University of Virginia, 580 Massie Road,
Charlottesville, VA 22903, USA
e-mail: schauer@virginia.edu

C.J. Peters (ed.), *Precedent in the United States Supreme Court*, Ius Gentium: Comparative Perspectives on Law and Justice 33, DOI 10.1007/978-94-007-7951-8_7,

the duty of a court to follow its own decisions from some time in the past.[1] When we are talking precisely about stare decisis, therefore, we are referring only to the latter, to horizontal precedent. And when we are discussing precedent in the context of decisionmaking by the Supreme Court of the United States, we are entirely within the domain of horizontal precedent and stare decisis, because vertical precedent has no applicability to courts that sit atop the judicial pyramid.[2]

Specifying the broad outlines of the idea of stare decisis is relatively straightforward, but justifying the practice or the obligation is something else again. Whether it is wise for a legal system to adopt a prescriptive norm of stare decisis is a matter of genuine debate, as was pithily noted by Oliver Wendell Holmes in saying that it was "revolting" for courts to be expected to follow decisions which persist for "no better reason … than that so it was laid down in the time of Henry IV" (Holmes 1897, 469). After all, the bite of a norm of stare decisis takes hold only when some court or judge believes that some previous decision was mistaken (Alexander 1989; Schauer 1987). If the court or judge believes that the previous decision was sound, then a second-order norm of stare decisis will be of no consequence. The first-order substantive norm will be sufficient to secure consistency between the past decision and the present one, and adding an additional obligation to reach the same result is superfluous.[3] But if the current court or judge disagrees with the previous decision, then a norm of stare decisis will give her a reason, albeit not necessarily a conclusive one,[4] to reach a decision she believes to be wrong.

Once we understand that stare decisis is interesting only or at least primarily when it directs judges to make what they think are erroneous decisions—or, alternatively formulated, at least gives them a reason for making such erroneous decisions—we can understand not only why the norm of stare decisis is of relatively recent vintage in the span of the common law's history,[5] but also why it remains controversial to this day. Justice Antonin Scalia (1989, 869; 1997, 139, 149), for example, has been highly skeptical of a norm that requires him, as he sees it, to place some obligation of obedience to previous occupants of the (Supreme Court)

---

[1] On the distinction between vertical and horizontal precedent, see Dobbins (2010), Schauer (2009, 36–37), Kornhauser (1995), and Alexander (1989).

[2] Except, of course, to the extent that so-called apex courts craft their opinions and establish rules in light of how they expect courts below them to understand and interpret those rules on future occasions.

[3] The statement in the text is slightly too simple. A judge may have more or less confidence in her agreement with a prior decision, and agreement may thus be better understood in scalar rather than bimodal terms. And to the extent that this is the case, then internalization (in Hart's (2012) sense) of a norm of stare decisis may supplement agreement with the earlier decision, producing greater confidence in the outcome than would have existed absent the stare decisis norm.

[4] As noted above in note 3, the fact that the obligations of stare decisis are typically understood as short of absolute makes the statement in the text—that stare decisis is interesting or important only when a judge disagrees with the prior decision—a somewhat misleading overstatement. A judge's agreement with a prior decision may be relatively weaker or stronger, and a judge who weakly agrees with a previous decision might have a stronger reason to follow it because of the additional reason of stare decisis than she would have were no such additional reason to be present.

[5] See Lee (1999) and Wise (1975).

judicial role above an oath-enforced obligation to the Constitution itself. And although Justice Scalia has been skeptical of the stare decisis norm, even he, interestingly, has observed that his colleague Justice Clarence Thomas is more skeptical still.[6] Moreover, the extent of academic skepticism about the stare decisis norm appears to be even greater than the judicial. Admittedly, it is common for commentators to complain that Justices who reach results with which the commentators disagree on substantive grounds have failed to follow precedent,[7] but such complaints are highly selective. Indeed, academic criticism of judges for failing to follow precedents with which the commentators disagree is sufficiently rare that it supports the conclusion that few academics in fact subscribe to what stare decisis, properly understood, actually requires. Moreover, there is a large number of academic critiques of the very idea of stare decisis, especially in the constitutional context, that are far less case- or issue-specific.[8]

7.2 Does Stare Decisis Constrain?

The normative debates about stare decisis are thus alive and important, but my goal here is less normative than it is descriptive and conceptual. And as a descriptive matter, especially in the context of the Supreme Court, an important question is whether there actually is, descriptively, a norm of stare decisis that plays a causal role in determining the votes of individual Justices or the outcomes of the Court. And if there is such a norm, just how strong is it?

A generation ago, such empirical questions about the existence and causal effect of a stare decisis norm might have been answered by reference to judicial and extrajudicial statements of the Justices, or by the use of selected anecdotes of votes or decisions that seemingly did, or did not, take a norm of stare decisis seriously.[9] Now,

[6] Ken Foskett quotes Justice Scalia as saying that Justice Thomas "does not believe in *stare decisis*, period" (2004, 281–82) (emphasis in original).

[7] For example, see Dworkin (2007), complaining that the fourth in a line of Supreme Court cases on student speech, *Morse v. Frederick*, 551 U.S. 393 (2007), failed to follow the precedent of the first case, *Tinker v. Des Moines Indep. School Dist.*, 393 U.S. 503 (1969)—even though the second and third cases in the same line (*Bethel School Dist. v. Fraser*, 478 U.S. 675 (1986), and *Hazelwood School Dist. v. Kuhlmeier*, 484 U.S. 260 (1988)) had ruled against students and in favor of restrictions and thus seemed consistent with *Morse*.

[8] The most-explicit arguments against stare decisis in constitutional law come from the political right. See, for example, Paulsen (2005), Lawson (1994), and Cooper (1988). But the systematic rejection of precedential constraint by the (liberal) Warren Court has also been well documented. See Maltz (1980); see also Guardians Ass'n v. Civil Service Comm'n, 463 U.S. 582, 618 (1983) (Marshall, J., dissenting) (rejecting the idea that stare decisis should stand in the way of sound substantive principle).

[9] The statements of the Justices, whether in opinions or extrajudicial, are particularly unhelpful, because the overwhelming number of claims of reliance on precedent are made by Justices in support of outcomes they believe substantively correct. Far more rare but nevertheless more telling are the opinions or votes of Justices known to disagree with the first-order merits of a position that they

however, the situation is different. We have genuine data, mostly generated by political scientists.[10] And although a number of subtly different positions can be identified in the research, the data nevertheless suggest that, at least with respect to the Supreme Court, stare decisis has in actuality played much less of a role in determining the votes of individual Justices than the traditional law-school-based ideology has supposed. Just how much of a role a norm of stare decisis plays is debated, but there appears to be widespread agreement among most of the researchers that various non-doctrinal and non-precedential ideological or political attitudes play at least as large a role, with many concluding that such factors play a significantly larger role than do the decisions of earlier cases. For at least many of the political scientists,[11] it appears as if the Justices, especially but not only in cases of high ideological salience and valence, rely chiefly on their attitudinal policy or moral preferences, which they then proceed to explain—or rationalize[12]—on the basis of carefully selected previous cases that appear to support that outcome. Past decisions, therefore, appear to play a justificatory role but not a causal one, as Legal Realists have claimed at least as far back as Judge Joseph Hutcheson's famous 1929 article on the judicial "hunch" as the temporally primary and causally dominant basis for a judicial decision (Hutcheson 1928–1929).[13]

When we turn to opinions, doctrines, and constitutional rules, however, and focus on Supreme Court output in terms broader than simply outcomes, the research conclusions are more mixed. Some number of political scientists, purporting to identify what they call "jurisprudential regimes," have argued that the data support the conclusion that stare decisis does have an effect on the creation of doctrine, especially on matters such as levels of scrutiny and tests that specify what factors

are, for second-order reasons of stare decisis, supporting. See Schauer (2007); see also Kelman (1985). And for the argument that stare decisis may have indirect effects that are harder to measure but may be more consequential, see Fallon (2001).

[10] See, for example, Bailey and Maltzman (2011), Bartels (2009), Fowler and Jeon (2008), Bailey and Maltzman (2008), Hansford and Spriggs (2006), Segal and Spaeth (2001), Wahlbeck (1997), Segal and Spaeth (1996), and Brenner and Spaeth (1995).

[11] Segal and Spaeth (1996, 2001) and Brenner and Spaeth (1995) are perhaps the most skeptical about the effect of stare decisis, but most are at least more skeptical than the typical law professor or law student, and certainly more skeptical than the public statements of judges and Justices.

[12] "Rationalization" was the term of choice for many of the Legal Realists in arguing that judges typically or often first reached a result on largely non-legal grounds and only thereafter sought to explain, justify, or rationalize that law-independent outcome choice on legal grounds. See Frank (1930) and Hutcheson (1928–1929). On this aspect of and understanding of Legal Realism, see Schauer (2013).

[13] The judicial opinion as an *ex post* rationalization of decisions reached on other grounds is also one of the principal themes in Frank (1930). See also Stumberg (1939, 532); Cohen (1935, 809–12); Cohen (1933, 237); Frank (1933, 910–11); and Llewellyn (1931, 1238–39). Note also the comment attributed to Chief Justice Hughes by Justice Douglas that "[a]t the constitutional level where we work, 90 % of any decision is emotional. The rational part of us supplies the reasons for supporting our predilections" (Douglas 1980, 8). And on the distinction between the logic of decision and the logic of justification, a distinction that provides some philosophical support for the rationality of the Realists' less philosophical observations, see Wasserstrom (1961).

should guide a judicial decision.[14] The conclusions of this research have been challenged,[15] and in addition it is not clear that those who conduct the research have sufficiently distinguished the causal contribution of an internalized stare decisis norm from the decidedly different phenomenon of path dependence.[16] But in any event, even those who conduct the research make clear that the principal import of their findings is with respect to the effect of doctrinal structure on lower courts (Richards and Kritzer 2002),[17] rather than making much of a case against the attitudinalists about stare decisis in the strict sense in the Supreme Court. Thus, with respect to the extent to which the Supreme Court considers itself actually bound by its decisions in earlier cases, apart from what the Justices or commentators might say, the fair conclusion seems to be that a genuinely extant norm of stare decisis, exemplified by a Justice or the Court deciding against what she or he or it is on record (in an opinion or elsewhere) as believing, is roughly as rare as the bulk of the political science research appears to have concluded.

7.3 Explaining the Selection Effect

That stare decisis seems to have a rather limited role in actually determining Supreme Court outcomes should come as little surprise. Unlike the more-creative but far-less-constrained process of reasoning from and decisionmaking on the basis of analogy,[18] decisionmaking on the basis of stare decisis requires that there be a previous decision on roughly the same question.[19] If a previous decision is only in the neighborhood of the current question or issue, it hardly takes even a particularly creative legal mind to be able to distinguish the previous decision and, typically, to locate other decisions that would lend some degree of support for whatever decision the Justice would now prefer to reach. Thus, although we can say that in 2013 the question whether a state's total prohibition of all abortions is constitutionally permissible is the same question that the Supreme Court faced in 1973 in *Roe v. Wade*,[20] it is rare that the Supreme Court decides to revisit exactly the same question it has decided at some point in the past.

---

[14] See Kritzer and Richards (2005) and Richards and Kritzer (2002).

[15] See Lax and Rader (2010).

[16] See Hathaway (2001). Path dependence will certainly make otherwise counterfactually eligible results impossible or undiscoverable, but this is a different phenomenon from that of a judge who actually sees a possible result and feels constrained by a stare decisis norm from reaching it.

[17] See also Cross and Spriggs (2010) and Kritzer and Richards (2003).

[18] On analogical reasoning in law, see Levi (2013), Weinreb (2005), Spellman (2004), Brewer (1996), and Sunstein (1993). For skepticism about the extent to which analogical reasoning, especially in law, is a distinct form of reasoning at all, see Posner (2006), Alexander (1998), and Alexander (1996).

[19] On the often-ignored distinction between precedential and analogical reasoning, see Schauer (2008).

[20] 410 U.S. 113 (1973).

But now we have a window into a real problem. The Supreme Court is, of course, the master of its own docket. In addition the Court has, in recent years, decided, with argument and full opinions, fewer than 80 cases a year, selected from the almost 8,000 per Term that the Court is asked to decide.[21] But now consider these figures in light of the widely analyzed selection effect.[22] The basic idea is uncomplicated: If the law (and the predicted outcome in court) applicable to a dispute is clear, then one side will expect to win and the other to lose. Under such conditions, the rational expected loser will concede, settle, or otherwise choose to refrain from litigation in order to avoid a costly but likely futile courtroom battle.

The corollary of the reluctance of expected losers to litigate is that the array of disputes which are *not* settled prior to litigation or judgment emerges as a non-random and decidedly unrepresentative sample of the full field of legal events. Rather, the disputes that wind up in court are disproportionately those in which two opposing parties holding mutually exclusive positions each think that litigation is worthwhile. And normally this will be so only when the law or the facts are unclear. Because the field of litigated cases thus systematically underrepresents the easy cases and overrepresents the hard ones, generalizing about all applications of law from the unrepresentative set of litigated cases is a serious error.

The selection effect operates throughout the litigation process. Expected losers prior to trial will disproportionately settle or succumb rather than litigate, and thus lawsuits will ordinarily be filed and then tried to judgment only when both parties believe they have genuine chances to win. Similarly, losers at trial will typically not appeal unless they believe there is some likelihood of prevailing on appeal, and the field of appellate decisions thus selects for difficult cases at the edges of law even more than the field of cases tried to verdict. Indeed, although the selection-effect literature treats the dispute as the starting point of the legal process, in fact selection takes hold even earlier. When the law is clear, a dispute will typically not even arise, and the very fact of a dispute is itself law-dependent. Because I would prefer to pay my taxes later than April 15th (or not at all), the Internal Revenue Service and I have

---

[21] In the Court's 2010 Term, for example, it considered 7,868 petitions for certiorari or other form of review, granted review in 90 of those cases, and ultimately decided 75 with full signed opinions and after briefing and argument. See The Statistics (2011, 369). In the 2011 Term, a total of 7,685 petitions was considered, and again there were 75 final dispositions with full signed opinions after briefing and oral argument (The Statistics 2012).

[22] The scholarship on the selection effect is vast, the canonical modern source being George L. Priest & Benjamin Klein's "The Selection of Disputes for Litigation" (1984). The Priest and Klein hypothesis about the nature of the disputes that are settled or litigated has spawned a substantial literature, much of it focused on challenging or supporting Priest and Klein's claim that the selection effect will incline towards a 50 % win rate for plaintiffs in the cases that do not settle and thus wind up being tried to judgment. See, for example, Revesz (2000), Shavell (1996), Kessler et al. (1996), Waldfogel (1995), Hilton (1993), Eisenberg (1990), Wittman (1985), Priest (1985), and Bebchuk (1984). That question is theoretically and empirically important, but for purposes of this chapter all that is needed is the core insight that the cases that go to trial are a non-random and disproportionately indeterminate sample of legal events. On this basic point, useful analyses include Taha (2010), Kastellec and Lax (2008), Lederman (1999), Schauer (1988), and Posner (1986, Sect. 21).

opposing preferences. But the law is so clear (at least in my case) that it would not occur to me that I had a "dispute" with the IRS. Only when parties with opposing preferences can each make a non-preposterous reference to a legal or other norm would the conflict of preferences even ripen into a "dispute" in the first place.

The lesson to be drawn from the selection effect is now apparent. Litigation and appeal disproportionately select for events in which the law is vague, multivocal, or otherwise indeterminate, or in which there are opposing defensible accounts of the facts. Consequently, drawing conclusions about law in general from this skewed and unrepresentative class of legal events—the hard cases—exaggerates law's indeterminacy (Schauer 1985). And most importantly in the current context, most genuinely easy cases will not be litigated, and if litigated will not be appealed, and if appealed will not generate petitions for certiorari (that is, for review by the Supreme Court), and if the subject of such a petition will see that petition denied. Thus, if there existed a strong norm of stare decisis, litigants who identified a previous decision on point would recognize that they would clearly win or clearly lose were the case to get to the Supreme Court.[23] And the selection effect tells us that most of those who anticipated clearly losing would opt out of the litigation or appeal process long before their probably hopeless case came to the Supreme Court. As a result, the kinds of cases that would seemingly be controlled by the stare decisis norm would not reach the Court at all. If there were clear Supreme Court precedent, and if it was to be expected that the Court would follow that precedent, then events controlled by that precedent would disproportionately not give rise to disputes, and if disputed would disproportionately not generate litigation, because one side to the litigation would know to a high likelihood that its position would not prevail. And so on up the appellate ladder, culminating in the Supreme Court itself.

7.4 Selection's Influence on Stare Decisis

Given the operation of the selection effect, and its impact on disputes seemingly settled by the decisions of prior cases, the empirical results produced by political scientists and others should come as little surprise. When we combine the selection effect with the Supreme Court's virtual total control of its own docket, we can understand why the Supreme Court will rarely even see the easy cases. Those cases will not be litigated, or not be appealed, or not be the basis for a petition for certiorari. Thus the cases the Supreme Court sees will be those selected, either explicitly by the Court or implicitly by the selection effect, precisely because of their difficulty.

[23] It is important to acknowledge that much of the force of the selection effect may not apply to many criminal cases. Because most criminal defendants and most habeas corpus petitioners proceed *in forma pauperis* and thus at no cost to themselves (even apart from the fact that the time expended on litigation may be a consumption item and not a cost for those who are incarcerated), the normal disincentives to pursue likely hopeless litigation, appeal, and post-conviction remedies will often be absent.

And thus, if we have a group of 70–100 cases, say, selected precisely because there is no law on the question they present, or because there is law on both sides of the question, we would be astonished to discover that stare decisis had much of a role to play. Stare decisis in particular, and (formal) law more generally, could hardly be expected to be very important in the decision of a group of cases selected precisely because, in part, of their legal indeterminacy. Law simply will not matter very much for cases chosen just because the law could not straightforwardly decide the questions they raised.

The selection effect therefore ensures that, even if there is a strong norm of stare decisis, examination of Supreme Court cases will not identify it. If a strong stare decisis norm exists, the cases controlled by it will not be disputed, or litigated, or appealed, or selected by the Supreme Court for decision. The selection effect will keep those cases that are controlled by stare decisis out of court and thus out of even consideration for certiorari. Looking only at Supreme Court decisions to examine whether stare decisis exists thus constitutes a classic case of selecting for the dependent variable—looking only at the instances caused (or, in this case, not caused) by some state of affairs, and ignoring the ones in which the hypothesized relationship does not exist. As a result, the existing empirical research on stare decisis in the Supreme Court is unable systematically to tell us whether, in the event that cases controlled by a norm of stare decisis did happen to reach the Court, the prior decision, and thus the norm of stare decisis, would in fact control.

7.5 Hiding Stare Decisis's (Potential) Effect

But matters are even more complex than this. We have just concluded that if there is a norm of stare decisis, its effect will not appear in the population of Supreme Court decisions. But suppose that there is no norm of stare decisis. Suppose that the views of Justice Thomas and, to a lesser extent, Justice Scalia prevailed, and that a majority of the Supreme Court did not believe that there was an obligation of fidelity to prior decisions just because of their existence. This would not be an absurd possibility, either descriptively or normatively. Stare decisis is itself a comparatively new component of common-law decisionmaking,[24] and the common law proceeded apace for centuries before a norm of stare decisis was introduced. Moreover, although precedential constraint is an increasingly important dimension of judicial decisionmaking in the civil-law world, for a very long time, precedent in any form, vertical or horizontal, was a relatively unimportant part of legal systems in which the code was understood to be far more important than any particular court's interpretation of it.[25]

The absence of a norm of stare decisis would not, therefore, mean the absence of law. Were there no stare decisis norm, Supreme Court Justices would, we can hope,

---

[24] See note 5 and accompanying text.

[25] See Fon and Parisi (2006) and Shoenberger (2009).

apply their best judgment to whatever they believed to be the legitimate sources of constitutional (or, for that matter, statutory) law. These sources might, depending on the particular constitutional or interpretive theories of particular Justices, include one or more of, among others, the meaning of the text as that text would now be understood, or the meaning of the text as it was understood at the time of its writing, or the original intentions of the drafters or ratifiers, or the best moral and pragmatic understanding of the text in light of current conditions and problems, or something else. But a law-based but precedent-independent approach to legal adjudication and interpretation could, in theory, exist, and such an approach would be—again in theory, and to emphasize—a substantially law-based approach to constitutional and statutory interpretation in which stare decisis played no role.

If we had such a system—if stare decisis were not understood, descriptively or normatively, as a component of Supreme Court decisionmaking—then what would we learn about the role of stare decisis from an inspection of actual Supreme Court decisions? The answer here is more obvious: If there is no norm of stare decisis on the Supreme Court, then an examination of Supreme Court cases will, not surprisingly, reveal that stare decisis is not a factor in explaining Supreme Court decisions. Assuming a sufficiently rigorous analysis that would exclude spurious correlation and look for the causal effect of prior decisions on current outcomes, we would expect that the absence of a norm of stare decisis would be revealed by a study of the cases the Supreme Court actually decides. If there is no norm of stare decisis, we are extraordinary unlikely to find one.

7.6 The Empirical Gap

This conclusion of the previous section—that if there were no norm of stare decisis, we would be extremely unlikely to discover one by examining the array of Supreme Court decisions—is indeed obvious, but combining that conclusion with the conclusion of the preceding section is slightly less so. That is, if there is no norm of stare decisis, then examining Supreme Court cases will not identify stare decisis as a factor in explaining Supreme Court outcomes. But if there *is* a norm of stare decisis, and if it is known (or signaled by the Court) that there is such a norm, then the selection effect will keep the disputes controlled by that norm off the Supreme Court's docket, and examining the outcomes of the cases that are on the docket will again fail to locate a stare decisis norm. In other words, stare decisis will not appear as a factor in explaining Supreme Court outcomes if it is (or would be) a factor in those decisions, and it will not appear as a factor if it is not a factor.

It would be tempting to conclude on the basis of the foregoing that the search for stare decisis on the Supreme Court is destined to be a futile one. And thus that the topic of stare decisis on and for the Supreme Court is a topic of little interest and even less significance. But that conclusion would be too quick, and the balance of this paper will be dedicated to exploring why that is so.

The basic point is a simple one. Stare decisis might be significant even if the selection effect assures that cases in which stare decisis might matter will rarely come before the Court, and that is because stare decisis, if it is in effect, will play a role in determining which cases are litigated or appealed in the first place. In other words, an effective norm of stare decisis will influence which differences of opinion or conflicts of preferences will become disputes, which disputes are litigated, which first-stage litigation outcomes are appealed, and which appeals are the subject of petitions for certiorari.

Stare decisis would have this effect, however, only if the parties to disputes were aware of the existence of the stare decisis norm. That is, parties to disputes whose claims would be futile with a stare decisis norm in place, but not without, would only refrain from litigation if they knew that what might otherwise be a plausible case was rendered implausible by, and only by, the application of an actually existing stare decisis norm. This dynamic would be most obvious at the point at which a losing party in a state supreme court or in a United States Circuit Court was deciding whether to petition for certiorari. Such decisions involve a calculation of the likelihood of success, and although a strong stare decisis norm will still not be absolute,[26] the careful calculation will take account of the way in which a decision contrary to an earlier precedent will be less likely than the same decision would be absent the precedent.

But now the problem should be apparent. If a majority of the Justices of the Supreme Court internalize and apply a norm of stare decisis, then this will affect the decisions of disputants to litigate, and of litigants to pursue their cases to trial, and, if unsuccessful there, to appeal. But this dynamic will operate only if the aforesaid disputants and litigants are actually aware of the norm of stare decisis. And if the analysis in the foregoing sections is correct, there will be no systematic way in which those disputants and litigants will know that such a norm of stare decisis exists, because the cases the Court actually takes and decides will not be ones in which a norm of stare decisis, even if it existed, will affect the outcome.

7.7 Signaling Stare Decisis

To recapitulate: Analyzing the role of stare decisis in the Supreme Court through the lens of the selection effect reveals two related problems. First, because cases in which stare decisis might have controlled the outcome will systematically be grossly underrepresented in the cases that actually come before the Court, there appears to be no reliable way, at least short of subjecting the Justices to a polygraph examination,

---

[26] This need not be the case. Prior to the House of Lords's Practice Statement of 1966, even the highest courts in Great Britain were prohibited from reversing their own precedents. See Practice Statement (Judicial Precedent), [1966] 1 W.L.R. 1234 (H.L.); see also Blom-Cooper (2009, 782). After 1966, however, there remain no courts in common-law jurisdictions that do not have the power to reverse precedents that they themselves have created, even though any meaningful norm of stare decisis will make such an action more difficult—will require a stronger justification than would have been necessary to reach the same outcome in the absence of the earlier decision.

to determine whether stare decisis is in fact a norm internalized by a majority of Justices at any particular time. And second, and relatedly, if there is an internalized stare decisis norm, the Court has no effective way of signaling that fact to lawyers and prospective litigants.

At least as to the second problem, it is possible to imagine a remedy. *If* the Court, or a majority of its members, have actually internalized a norm of stare decisis, then they could signal this by selecting at the certiorari stage and then deciding cases in which the stare decisis norm would be both apparent and outcome-determinative. The Court could, for example, go out of its way to apply previously announced doctrines with which a majority of the current Court was known to disagree.[27] Or dissenters in earlier cases could relinquish the practice of persistent dissent, becoming part of the majority to apply a rule or doctrine at whose origin they dissented. Or Justices might even, in extra-judicial statements, announce their willingness to recognize the precedential effect of cases that had earlier attracted their disagreement. In these and other ways, a Court that accepted stare decisis but recognized the difficulty of signaling that fact in light of the selection effect could overcome the barriers the selection effect creates, and make clear that challenges to existing doctrines would not be looked upon favorably, even by Justices who disagreed with those doctrines.

We know, of course, that none of this is likely to take place. And because there is no reason to believe that the Justices are unaware of the ways in which they could adopt any of the foregoing strategies or otherwise signal allegiance to a stare decisis norm, the very fact that they seem unwilling to do so encourages the inference that perhaps stare decisis makes as little difference as the political science research appears to suggest. Such an inference is far from conclusive, of course, but it adds further weight to the conclusion that the Supreme Court's talk of stare decisis is not much more than talk.

References

Alexander L (1989) Constrained by precedent. South Calif Law Rev 63(1):1–64
Alexander L (1996) Bad beginnings. Univ Pa Law Rev 145(1):57–87
Alexander L (1998) The banality of legal reasoning. Notre Dame Law Rev 73(3):517–533
Bailey MA, Maltzman F (2008) Does legal doctrine matter? Unpacking law and policy preferences on the U.S. Supreme Court. Am Pol Sci Rev 102(3):369–384
Bailey MA, Maltzman F (2011) The constrained court: law, politics, and the decisions justices make. Princeton University Press, Princeton
Bartels BL (2009) The constraining capacity of legal doctrine on the U.S. Supreme Court. Am Pol Sci Rev 103(3):474–495
Bebchuk LA (1984) Litigation and settlement under imperfect information. Rand J Econ 15(3):404–415
Blom-Cooper L (2009) 1966 and all that: the story of the practice statement. In: Blom-Cooper L, Dickson B, Drewy G (eds) The judicial House of Lords. Oxford University Press, New York, pp 1876–2009

[27] Dickerson v. United States, 530 U.S. 428 (2000), might be such a case, although judicial supremacy issues make the case a far from perfect example.

Brenner S, Spaeth HJ (1995) Stare indecisis: the alteration of precedent on the Supreme Court, 1946–1992. Cambridge University Press, Cambridge
Brewer S (1996) Exemplary reasoning: semantics, pragmatics, and the rational force of legal argument by analogy. Harv Law Rev 109(5):923–1028
Cohen FS (1933) Ethical systems and legal ideals. Harcourt: Brace, New York
Cohen FS (1935) Transcendental nonsense and the functional approach. Columbia Law Rev 35(6):809–849
Cooper CS (1988) Stare decisis: precedent and principle in constitutional adjudication. Cornell Law Rev 73(2):401–410
Cross FB, Spriggs JF II (2010) The most important (and best) Supreme Court opinions and justices. Emory Law Rev 60(2):407–502
Dobbins JC (2010) Structure and precedent. Mich Law Rev 108(8):1453–1496
Douglas WO (1980) The Court years, 1939–1975. Random House, New York
Dworkin R (2007) The Supreme Court phalanx. N Y Rev Books 54(14):92–101
Eisenberg T (1990) Testing the selection effect: a new theoretical framework with empirical tests. J Legal Stud 19(2):337–358
Fallon RH Jr (2001) Stare decisis and the Constitution: an essay on constitutional methodology. N Y Univ Law Rev 76(2):570–597
Fon V, Parisi F (2006) Judicial precedents in civil law systems: a dynamic analysis. Int Rev Law and Econ 26(4):519–535
Foskett K (2004) Judging Thomas: the life and times of Clarence Thomas. Harper Collins Publishers, New York
Fowler JH, Jeon S (2008) The authority of Supreme Court precedent. Soc Netw 30(1):16–30
Frank J (1930) Law and the modern mind. Brentano's, New York
Frank J (1933) Why not a clinical lawyer-school. Univ Pa Law Rev 81(8):907–923
Hansford TG, Spriggs JF II (2006) The politics of precedent on the U.S. Supreme Court. Princeton University Press, Princeton
Hart HLA (2012) The concept of law, 3rd edn. Oxford University Press, Oxford
Hathaway OA (2001) Path dependence in the law: the course and pattern of legal change in a common law system. Iowa Law Rev 86(2):601–665
Hilton KN (1993) Asymmetric information and the selection of disputes for litigation. J Legal Stud 22(1):187–210
Holmes OW (1897) The path of the law. Harv Law Rev 10(8):457–478
Hutcheson JC (1928–1929) The judgment intuitive: the function of the 'hunch' in judicial decision. Cornell Law Q 14(3):274–288
Kastellec JP, Lax JR (2008) Case selection and the study of judicial politics. J Empirical Leg Stud 5(3):407–446
Kelman M (1985) The forked path of dissent. Supreme Court Rev 1985:227–298
Kessler D, Meites T, Miller G (1996) Explaining deviations from the fifty-percent rule: a multimodal approach to the selection of cases for litigation. J Legal Stud 25(1):233–259
Kornhauser LA (1995) Adjudication by a resource-constrained team: hierarchy and precedent in a judicial system. South Calif Law Rev 68(6):1605–1629
Kritzer HM, Richards MJ (2003) Jurisprudential regimes and Supreme Court decisionmaking: the *Lemon* regime and Establishment Clause cases. Law Soc Rev 37(4):827–840
Kritzer HM, Richards MJ (2005) The influence of law in the Supreme Court's search-and-seizure jurisprudence. Am Polit Res 33(1):33–55
Lawson G (1994) The constitutional case against precedent. Harv J Law Publ Policy 17(1):23–33
Lax JR, Rader KT (2010) Legal constraints on Supreme Court decision making: do jurisprudential regimes exist? J Polit 72(2):273–284
Lederman L (1999) Which cases go to trial?: An empirical study of predictors of failure to settle. Case West Reserv Law Rev 49(2):315–358
Lee TR (1999) Stare decisis in historical perspective: from the founding era to the Rehnquist Court. Vanderbilt Law Rev 52(3):647–735
Levi EH (2013) An introduction to legal reasoning, 2nd edn. University of Chicago Press, Chicago
Llewellyn K (1931) Some realism about Realism—responding to Dean Pound. Harv Law Rev 44(8):1222–1264

Maltz EM (1980) Some thoughts on the death of stare decisis in constitutional law. Wis Law Rev 1980(3):467–496
Paulsen MS (2005) The intrinsically corrupting influence of precedent. Constitutional Comment 22(2):289–298
Posner RA (1986) Economic analysis of law, 3rd edn. Little, Brown & Co., Boston
Posner RA (2006) Reasoning by analogy. Cornell Law Rev 91(3):761–774
Priest GL (1985) Reexamining the selection hypothesis: learning from Wittman's mistakes. J Legal Stud 14(1):215–243
Priest GL, Klein B (1984) The selection of disputes for litigation. J Legal Stud 13(1):1–55
Revesz RL (2000) Litigation and settlement in the federal appellate courts: impact of panel selection procedures on ideologically divided courts. J Legal Stud 29(2):685–710
Richards MJ, Kritzer HM (2002) Jurisprudential regimes in Supreme Court decision making. Am Polit Sci Rev 96(2):305–320
Scalia A (1989) Originalism: the lesser evil. Univ Cincinnati Law Rev 57(3):849–865
Scalia A (1997) Response. In: Scalia A (ed) A matter of interpretation: federal courts and the law. Princeton University Press, Princeton
Schauer F (1985) Easy cases. South Calif Law Rev 58(1):399–440
Schauer F (1987) Precedent. Stanford Law Rev 39(3):571–605
Schauer F (1988) Judging in a corner of the law. South Calif Law Rev 61(6):1717–1733
Schauer F (2007) Has precedent ever really mattered in the Supreme Court? Ga State Univ Law Rev 24(2):381–401
Schauer F (2008) Why precedent in law (and elsewhere) is not totally (or even substantially) about analogy. Perspect Psychol Sci 3(6):454–460
Schauer F (2009) Thinking like a lawyer: a new introduction to legal reasoning. Harvard University Press, Cambridge
Schauer F (2013) Legal realism untamed. Tex Law Rev 91(4):749–780
Segal JA, Spaeth HJ (1996) The influence of stare decisis on the votes of United States Supreme Court justices. Am J Polit Sci 40(4):971–1003
Segal JA, Spaeth HJ (2001) Majority rule or minority will: adherence to precedent on the United States Supreme Court. Cambridge University Press, New York
Shavell S (1996) Any frequency of plaintiff victory at trial is possible. J Legal Stud 25(2):493–501
Shoenberger A (2009) Change in the European civil law systems: infiltration of the Anglo-American case law system of precedent into the civil law system. Loyola Law Rev 55(1):5–21
Spellman BA (2004) Reflections of a recovering lawyer: how becoming a cognitive psychologist—and (in particular) studying analogical and causal reasoning—changed my views about the field of psychology and law. Chicago-Kent Law Rev 79(3):1187–1214
Stumberg GW (1939) May's law of crimes. By Kenneth C. Sears and Henry Weihofen. Tex Law Rev 17(4):531–532
Sunstein CR (1993) On analogical reasoning. Harv Law Rev 106(3):741–791
Taha AE (2010) Judge shopping: testing whether Judges' political orientations affect case filings. Univ Cincinnati Law Rev 78(3):1007–1042
The Statistics (2011) The Supreme Court, 2010 Term: the statistics. Harv Law Rev 125(1):362–377
The Statistics (2012) The Supreme Court, 2011 Term: the statistics. Harv Law Rev 126(1):388–403
Wahlbeck PJ (1997) The life of the law: judicial politics and legal change. J Polit 59(3):778–802
Waldfogel J (1995) The selection hypothesis and the relationship between trial and plaintiff victory. J Polit Economy 103(2):229–260
Wasserstrom RA (1961) The judicial decision: toward a theory of legal justification. Stanford University Press, Stanford
Weinreb LL (2005) Legal reason: the use of analogy in legal argument. Cambridge University Press, New York
Wise EM (1975) The doctrine of stare decisis. Wayne Law Rev 21(4):1043–1060
Wittman D (1985) Is the selection of cases for trial biased? J Legal Stud 14(1):185–214

Chapter 8
Methodological Stare Decisis and Constitutional Interpretation

Chad M. Oldfather

Abstract This chapter assesses the Supreme Court's reluctance to give stare decisis effect to its methodologies of constitutional interpretation. While the Court claims to presumptively follow the substantive results of its prior constitutional decisions, it has never considered itself bound by the interpretive approaches (e.g., originalism, textualism, or "living constitutionalism") used to reach those decisions. The author suggests an explanation for this somewhat mysterious state of affairs. A rule of methodological stare decisis would require the Court to employ the same interpretive method in a huge category of cases (e.g., all cases involving the Constitution), which would generate unpredictable results in many cases the Court could not reasonably anticipate, thus aggravating the drawbacks of stare decisis. At the same time, the usual benefits of stare decisis (such as predictability and stability) would not be very well served by methodological stare decisis. In contrast, the Court can reasonably follow precedent regarding constitutional "decision rules"—methods for implementing the Constitution, such as tiers of scrutiny—because those rules are relatively determinate and can be contained within narrowly defined areas of substantive doctrine.

8.1 Introduction

Imagine that the Supreme Court decides a case, *A v. B*, which requires it to interpret the Constitution. In doing so the Court issues an opinion that justifies the decision in terms of a particular interpretive methodology. Sometime later, a differently composed version of the Court faces the case of *C v. D*, which raises a

C.M. Oldfather (✉)
Law School, Marquette University, 1215 W. Michigan St.,
Milwaukee, WI 53233, USA
e-mail: chad.oldfather@marquette.edu

C.J. Peters (ed.), *Precedent in the United States Supreme Court*, Ius Gentium: Comparative Perspectives on Law and Justice 33, DOI 10.1007/978-94-007-7951-8_8,

variant of the same constitutional issue. A majority of this later Court would not have reached the same result in *A v. B* but has nonetheless concluded that it should follow its precedent.

Under current practice, the second Court's obligation is to the substantive holding of *A v. B* and not to its interpretive methodology. Put differently, the Court must honor what its predecessor held—the application of a right or structural feature of the Constitution to a given factual setting—rather than the manner in which its predecessor determined the meaning of the constitutional provision at issue. And while the distinction between substance and methodology will not always be free from ambiguity, it is meaningful nonetheless to speak of a difference between, for example, the individual right to bear arms outlined in *District of Columbia v. Heller*[1] and the originalist methodology that decision used to get there, or the privacy right of *Griswold v. Connecticut*[2] and the penumbral reasoning in which Justice Douglas's opinion for the Court grounded it. In both cases the Court could adhere to the substance of its prior decisions without continuing to honor their methodological choices. Indeed, that is precisely what it has done in the context of the right to privacy.

As unremarkable as this might be, as a descriptive matter it ought to be at least slightly puzzling. Deciding according to precedent entails, on one account, "deciding on the basis of what was done when the same matter had to be resolved in the past" (Duxbury 2008, 1). This idea seems expansive enough to include methodology, to involve what might be described as "deciding how to decide on the basis of how it was done when a similar matter had to be resolved in the past." Yet for all the heat that methodological clashes generate, no one has advocated in favor of giving stare decisis effect to methodology in constitutional cases.[3]

When the issue is framed in that way, an easy answer suggests itself. None of the Justices has advocated in favor of methodological stare decisis because none of them wishes to commit to someone else's preferred methodology. Each, perhaps, would be in favor of making a methodological commitment if it were a commitment to the approach that he or she favors, but not any other.

On reflection, however, this easy answer is unsatisfactory. After all, stare decisis as applied to substantive holdings also entails a commitment to be bound by someone else's preferences. Indeed, on most accounts of the doctrine the only context in which it does any work is where a court disagrees with its predecessor's conclusions. It must be, then, that there is something different about the nature of how stare decisis would operate in the methodological context that makes it less attractive than its substantive counterpart.

---

[1] 554 U.S. 570 (2008). The Court in *Heller* concluded that the Second Amendment creates an individual right to possess firearms for, among other things, self defense in the home.

[2] 381 U.S. 479 (1965). The Court in *Griswold* grounded a right to purchase and use contraceptives in a "zone of privacy" created out of penumbras emanating from many of the rights expressly protected in the Bill of Rights.

[3] "Although methodological disputes grow heated in some cases, it is striking that in the domain of constitutional adjudication, the justices have seldom exhibited much interest in attempting to bind themselves or each other, in advance, to the kind of general interpretive approaches that academic theorists champion" (Fallon 2009, 1013).

The question is not simply of academic interest. An emerging body of literature takes up the somewhat analogous question of whether courts ought to give stare decisis effect to statutory interpretation methodology (Gluck 2010; Foster 2008; Bandy 2011; Connors 2008). As that literature reveals, some state courts have experimented with giving precedential effect to statutory interpretation methodology, and some continue to do so. Of the four academic pieces that squarely address the question, three advocate in favor of the practice. Moreover, each suggests that the case for methodological stare decisis might transfer to constitutional interpretation, though each author is careful to acknowledge that the situations are not identical.

There are a number of ways one could approach the question of whether to give stare decisis effect to constitutional methodology. One might undertake a formalist analysis of the question, in which, for example, one posits that the very nature of the "judicial power" entails a conception of precedent that extends so far as to embrace interpretive methods, or that it requires resort to a single, specific theory of interpretation. Or one could contend that the doctrine of precedent extends only to matters of law, and that whatever interpretive methodology is, it is not "law."[4]

The issues in play here ultimately go to the heart of constitutional interpretation. The formulation and application of doctrines of precedent and interpretive methodologies alike implicate some of the larger issues of constitutional and judicial legitimacy. As the Court put it in *Planned Parenthood v. Casey*, "The Court must take care to speak and act in ways that allow people to accept its decisions on the terms the Court claims for them, as grounded truly in principle."[5] Frequent overruling, it further noted, "would overtax the country's belief in the Court's good faith."[6] Full consideration of the relationship between stare decisis and methodology thus requires grappling with some of the most fundamental issues of constitutional theory.

This chapter's goal is more modest. It is to take a first step in the process of unpacking the various considerations that might inform the decision whether to give precedential effect to constitutional methodology, with a focus on the justifications for and mechanisms of stare decisis, generally considered.

---

[4] The argument might run something like this: The type of reasoning involved in selecting a methodology is distinct from the type of reasoning involved in resolving a substantive legal question, in that the latter typically involves the application and manipulation of a variety of authorities and types of reasoning in the context of resolving a dispute over the content of a legal standard. Those authorities are generally regarded as providing imprecise guidance, and are backed up by a cluster of procedures and norms of the sort identified by Karl Llewellyn (1960, 19–51) in his catalog of "major steadying factors" in appellate adjudication. This, taken as a whole, constitutes judicial reasoning, the sort of thing that becomes engrained via a process that begins in law school and continues through practice, and is thereby something to which judges may legitimately claim some expertise. The choice of an interpretive methodology, in contrast, is prior to or at least separate from all of that. In its most important aspects it entails political reasoning rather than legal reasoning, and therefore it is not the sort of thing that can be verifiably better or worse in the way that we might say that legal reasoning can be.

[5] 505 U.S. 833, 865 (1992).

[6] *Id.* at 866.

8.2 An Example

It may be helpful to begin with a more-developed example. Consider the line of cases starting with *Crawford v. Washington*,[7] which concerns the applicability of the Confrontation Clause[8] to hearsay statements made by witnesses who are unavailable to testify at trial. Prior to *Crawford*, the admissibility of such statements was governed by the test set forth in *Ohio v. Roberts*,[9] pursuant to which they could be admitted so long as they bore "adequate 'indicia of reliability.'"[10] *Crawford* marked a major change in course, replacing *Roberts*'s nonoriginalist approach with a thoroughly originalist one.

Justice Scalia wrote the opinion for the Court in *Crawford*. In his characterization, the petitioner argued that *Roberts* should be reconsidered because it "strays from the original meaning of the Confrontation Clause."[11] With that introduction, the Court proceeded directly to an historical inquiry into the Clause's original meaning. That inquiry, the Court concluded, "supports two inferences about the meaning of the Sixth Amendment."[12] First, that the Confrontation Clause extends to out-of-court statements, primarily what the Court labeled "testimonial hearsay." Second, "that the Framers would not have allowed admission of testimonial statements of a witness who did not appear at trial unless he was unavailable to testify, and the defendant had had a prior opportunity for cross-examination."[13]

Two things are notable about the analysis for present purposes. First, the Court went out of its way to characterize the results in its past cases as "largely consistent with these two principles."[14] In a sense, then—a sense that is consistent with the classic understanding of the operation of stare decisis (Pound 1941, 7–8)—the Court implicitly characterized its decision as of a piece with its precedents. Second, the Court noted that, while "the results of our decisions have generally been faithful to the original meaning of the Confrontation Clause, the same cannot be said of our rationales."[15] The *Roberts* test, it concluded, was in some respects too broad and in others too narrow when compared with the original meaning. The particulars of the comparison are not as significant as the open acknowledgement of the methodological shift.

Significantly, the Court's discussion did not address stare decisis at all. Because, it maintained, "the test we announce is an empirically accurate

---

[7] 541 U.S. 36 (2004).

[8] "In all criminal prosecutions, the accused shall enjoy the right … to be confronted with the witnesses against him" (U.S. Const., amend. VI).

[9] 448 U.S. 56 (1980).

[10] *Id.* at 66.

[11] 541 U.S. at 42.

[12] *Id.* at 50.

[13] *Id.* at 53.

[14] *Id.* at 57.

[15] *Id.* at 60.

explanation of the results our cases have reached,"[16] it would not have felt compelled to do so based on any sense that its resolution of *Crawford* would have required the overruling of a prior case. In substantive terms, all or nearly all of its holdings stood. And while it was compelled to acknowledge the differences between its rationale and that of *Roberts*, it apparently found nothing about a change in rationale that required consideration of whether the doctrine of precedent ought to give it pause. This is so despite the fact that *Crawford* differed from *Roberts* not only with respect to the rule it adopted for determining whether the Confrontation Clause bars the admission of hearsay, but also with respect to the very mode of analysis by which it approached the larger task of determining the meaning and application of the Confrontation Clause in this context. Indeed, the fact that Justices Stevens, Souter, Ginsburg, and Breyer (none of whom typically resort to originalist methodology) all joined Justice Scalia's thoroughly originalist analysis underscores the point that no one thought the decision was conclusively resolving any larger methodological disputes.

This conclusion is supported by the subsequent cases in the *Crawford* line. For a time, the Court was willing to follow Justice Scalia's originalist lead. He wrote the majority opinions in the Court's next three cases concerning the Confrontation Clause. Each of them—*Davis v. Washington*,[17] *Giles v. California*,[18] and *Melendez-Diaz v. Massachusetts*[19]—draws on the same sorts of historical sources as *Crawford*. Some 7 years after *Crawford*, Justice Scalia finally found himself in the minority on a Confrontation Clause issue. As Justice Sotomayor's opinion for the Court characterized it, the issue in *Michigan v. Bryant* [20] required the Court to consider how an exception first identified in *Davis* applied in a new context.[21] Nothing in the *Bryant* opinion suggests a change of course. Indeed, the Court expressly claims to be following *Crawford* and the cases that followed it.[22]

The doctrinal particulars of the Court's analysis are not significant for our purposes. What is significant is that, methodologically, *Bryant* departed from the approach of its immediate predecessors. In considering how to address the new context presented, the Court made no effort to further explore the original understanding of the Confrontation Clause, or even to reflect on how the historical sources relied on in its past opinions would inform such an inquiry. Instead, the Court engaged in a common-law-type analysis in which the Court used its past decisions as the primary

[16] *Id.* at 59 n.9.

[17] 547 U.S. 813 (2006).

[18] 554 U.S. 353 (2008).

[19] 129 S. Ct. 2527 (2009).

[20] 131 S. Ct. 1143 (2011).

[21] *Id.* at 1156.

[22] Part II of the Court's opinion traces the history of the recent development of the Court's Confrontation Clause jurisprudence, beginning with *Crawford*'s overruling of *Roberts* and ending with the Court's statement of how the issue presented in *Bryant* differed from those in previous cases. *Id.* at 1152–56. Throughout, the Court treats the cases in the *Crawford* line as authority that it is following.

source of raw material. More significant still, for present purposes, is the fact that Justice Sotomayor's opinion in no way suggested that this methodological change of pace is at all remarkable.

To underscore the point, consider the separate opinions of Justices Thomas and Scalia in *Bryant*. Justice Thomas, concurring in the judgment, issued a brief opinion outlining his view that the Court ought to have "consider[ed] the extent to which the interrogation resemble[d] those historical practices that the Confrontation Clause addressed."[23] Justice Scalia, in dissent, ended the opening paragraph of his opinion with a claim of continued adherence "to the Confrontation Clause that the People adopted."[24] His analysis paid considerably more attention to history than did the majority's, and characterized the majority opinion as "a revisionist narrative in which reliability continues to guide our Confrontation Clause jurisprudence."[25] He ultimately accused the majority of clandestinely attempting "to resurrect *Roberts* by a thousand unprincipled distinctions without ever explicitly overruling *Crawford*."[26] This, because "honestly overruling *Crawford* would destroy the illusion of judicial minimalism and restraint. And it would force the Court to explain how the Justices' preference comports with the meaning of the Confrontation Clause that the People adopted—or to confess that only the Justices' preference really matters."[27]

Consider what is absent from this exchange. As we saw, the majority felt no need to justify its departure from the originalist methodology of *Crawford*. Just as significantly, Justice Scalia took the majority to task primarily for what he regarded as its departure from the holdings of the *Crawford* line of cases. He did not argue that the majority ought to have regarded itself as bound by *Crawford*'s originalism, and referenced methodology only obliquely in chastising the majority for what he regarded as its covert return to the substance of *Roberts*. To be sure, it is not possible to completely disentangle substance and method, for it may be that the only way for the Court to have remained true, in Justice Scalia's mind, to the substantive commitment to *Crawford* would have been for it to have undertaken an originalist analysis. But a bare argument that the majority was wrong for failing to be originalist is not the same as an argument that the majority was wrong because it failed to follow the methodology of an on-point precedent. Moreover, Justice Scalia's analysis implicitly leaves open the possibility that he would have accepted an opinion that reached his preferred conclusion even if it did not use originalist methods to do so. It is not the sort of discussion one would expect to see in a world of methodological stare decisis.

A commitment to methodological stare decisis as a value independent of substantive stare decisis would entail a different sort of argument. It would have

[23] *Id.* at 1167 (Thomas, J., concurring in the judgment).

[24] *Id.* at 1168 (Scalia, J., dissenting).

[25] *Id.* at 1174.

[26] *Id.* at 1175.

[27] *Id.*

required the conscious consideration in *Crawford* of whether it was appropriate to depart from the methodology of *Roberts* and its predecessors, and a conscious consideration in *Bryant* of whether it was appropriate to depart from the originalism of *Crawford*. Put differently, it would have involved the suggestion that the *Bryant* majority ought to have addressed expressly its departure from *Crawford*'s methodological choice.[28]

Nothing turns on the specifics of this example. *Crawford* is unique only in presenting these issues in a relatively stark form. Apart from that, it is simply a recent illustration of an entirely common feature of the Court's jurisprudence.

8.3 The Justifications for and Processes of Stare Decisis

That stare decisis applies in the context of constitutional law is, of course, one of the assumptions that underlies this volume. As Harry Jones (1983, 13) noted 30 years ago, "American constitutional law is essentially *case law*, a system in which the decision of the Supreme Court and other courts are guided and structured by precedent." More recently, Andrew Wistrich (2012, 760) remarked, "In the realm of constitutional law, common law precedents are more dog than tail." At least in its substantive dimensions, then, one would expect the justifications for the doctrine to track those in the common-law context.

8.3.1 Justifications

The question of how the practice of stare decisis is justified turns out to have a variety of answers, and a relatively large literature explores these justifications as well as the mechanisms by which stare decisis operates. This section seeks to briefly summarize the justifications so as to set the stage for further consideration of how those justifications apply to interpretive methodology. Among the justifications offered, four stand out. These include: (1) that stare decisis facilitates the like treatment of like cases; (2) that it enhances predictability and thereby allows those who must comply with the law to better anticipate the future; (3) that it strengthens decisionmaking by allowing courts to avoid considering each case from first principles and by creating "an aura of similarity among decisionmakers even where none may exist," which may in turn strengthen external credibility; and

[28] The more recent Confrontation Clause case of *Williams v. Illinois*, 132 S. Ct. 2221 (2012), also shows the Court's lack of concern for the maintenance of methodological consistency. Of the four opinions in the case, only Justice Thomas's concurrence engaged in any deep way with materials bearing on the original understanding of the Confrontation Clause. *Id.* at 2255. For the first time in this line of cases, Justice Scalia did not write an opinion, and joined Justice Kagan's dissent instead.

(4) that it furthers stability (Schauer 1987, 600). These justifications of course shape the mechanisms by which stare decisis is implemented, and will also provide the basis for an assessment of the viability and appropriateness of the doctrine's application to methodology.

8.3.1.1 Treating Like Cases Alike

The argument that precedent is necessary to ensure that like cases are treated alike has both deontological and consequentialist versions. The deontological strand stems from the notion of formal justice, which is taken in turn to mandate, as a good in its own right, the equivalent treatment of like cases (Duxbury 2008, 170).[29] Consequentialist justifications, in contrast, do not regard equivalent treatment as inherently valuable, but instead tie the practice to rule-of-law and other justice-related values, including impartiality, consistency, and the satisfaction of parties' reliance interests (Duxbury 2008, 171; Peters 1996, 2039–40). The suggestion, of course, is that adherence to past cases will further all these interests. The doctrine of precedent provides judges with an external metric by which to make decisions, and the consistent adherence to this metric in turn facilitates reliance. Importantly for present purposes, both sets of justifications presuppose some criteria by which to determine which cases are alike and therefore due like treatment (Schauer 1987, 596).

8.3.1.2 Predictability

Arguments from predictability focus on the interests of the parties to whom the underlying standards are addressed. For those who must comply with the law, it is important to be able to know that courts will consistently apply legal materials. Moreover, courts that do so "not only provide us with important information for the purposes of organizing our individual affairs but also make it more likely that citizens generally will navigate the legal system with confidence" (Duxbury 2008, 162). This predictability is not an unalloyed good, for, since precedent functions as a rule ("if set of facts *x*, then result *y*") and can thereby be both over- and underinclusive, any given application of precedent may come at the price of a decision that is unjust under a more global view of a given case (Schauer 1987, 597–98). Thus the force of the argument from predictability varies from one context to another, depending on factors such as the expected frequency and magnitude of suboptimal results.

---

[29] For a critique of the deontological justifications, see Peters (1996).

8.3.1.3 Strengthened Decisionmaking

There are two components to the argument that stare decisis leads to strengthened decisionmaking. The first is tied to efficiency. When a decisionmaker finds that it can rely on precedent, it need not expend the resources necessary to work through the problem in as deep a manner as would be the case were it considering the question anew (Schauer 1987, 599). A key element of this process is the assumption—inherent in the very mechanism of stare decisis—that the prior decision is likely to have been correct (Schauer 1994, 49–50). Standing behind that assumption is the doctrine's push toward the following of decisions that the current court would disagree with, such that it need not scrutinize the assumption of correctness in each case. Unless a past decision strikes the court as potentially wrong on its face, it need not entertain the possibility.

The second component arises from the effects of stare decisis on perceptions of the decisionmaking institution. Reliance on precedent may "create an aura of similarity among decisionmakers even where none may exist. Using a system of precedent to standardize decisions subordinates dissimilarity among decisionmakers, both in appearance and in practice" (Schauer 1987, 600). This, in turn, may strengthen credibility with external constituencies who will now perceive that courts are deciding according to law rather than personal preference.

8.3.1.4 Stability

Finally, there is the suggestion that a regime of stare decisis facilitates stability. When courts regard themselves as bound by past decisions, and act in a manner consistent with that conception, the natural effect is some degree of doctrinal stability. This sort of rootedness inhibits doctrinal volatility, leading to a regime in which law remains relatively constant. From certain perspectives, that constancy is a good in its own right. It also contributes to the mechanisms identified in the preceding arguments (Schauer 1987, 602). Such stability is, of course, not without cost, for it impedes flexibility and may cause a lag in law's ability to update itself in a changing world.

There are other downsides to a regime of stare decisis. Adherence to precedent can generate bad, or at least suboptimal, decisions in two respects. The first occurs if the precedent being followed was wrongly decided. In that situation adherence to the past case not only compounds a past error, but also helps to perpetuate that error by providing firmer grounding for its application in future cases. The second is more localized, and stems from the sense in which precedent functions as a rule of decision, isolating certain criteria as the exclusive basis for adjudication. This reductionism leads, as is the case with nearly all rules, to over- and underinclusiveness by precluding the decisionmaker from accounting for all the factors that might ultimately bear on a just resolution.

8.3.2 Processes

Although there are different conceptions of the specific mechanisms by which precedent works (Alexander 1989), it is possible to make some general observations about the processes by which courts apply the results of past cases to the disputes presently before them. Two aspects of those processes merit attention for purposes of the analysis here: the need for some method for determining which past cases properly serve as precedent for a given dispute; and a court's need in dealing with precedent to be mindful not only of past cases' implications for the present dispute, but also of the present dispute's implications for those in the future.

In order for a system of precedent to work, of course, judges must have some basis on which to determine which cases provide authoritative guidance for the resolution of a present dispute. Notably, each of the asserted benefits of precedent assumes the existence of criteria by which to determine when a given case is within the scope of a particular precedent. This is easiest to appreciate in connection with the maxim that like cases be treated alike, which presupposes some way of determining when cases are alike (Schauer 1987). The difficulty arises from the fact that the relationship, or lack of relationship, between any two cases can be assessed at a number of different levels of abstraction. Karl Llewellyn identified two doctrines of precedent—the "strict view," in which past cases are characterized as relating only to "redheaded Walpoles in pale magenta Buick cars," and the "loose view," which regards a past case as having decided all points put before it, "[n]o matter how broad the statement, no matter how unnecessary on the facts, or the procedural issues" (Llewellyn 1930, 63–69). In reality, though, Llewellyn simply identified the ends of a continuum. To pick briefly at one element of his illustration, the past case might be regarded as applying to cars, American cars, Buicks, or those of unusual coloring, and that breakdown undoubtedly fails to exhaust the list of characterizations that we might think appropriate depending on precisely what is at stake.

Determining the precedential scope of a past case, then, requires resort to some criteria for identifying which aspects of the case bear on the question of whether it has anything useful to say about the matter presently before the court. These "rules of relevance" and the "categories of assimilation" they produce are not self-defining, but instead "are contingent upon both time and culture" (Schauer 1987, 578). The color of a car, especially if it is magenta, might matter more in a world in which Henry Ford will sell a Model T in any color a customer wants—so long as it is black—than it would today. That it is an American car, in contrast, might matter more today when that is no longer the sort of thing that goes without saying.

Crucially, a regime of stare decisis serves its various justifications differently depending on the breadth of the relevant categories of assimilation—that is, on whether "likeness" is determined by reference to categories that are relatively large or narrow. The higher the level of generality at which similarity is assessed, the broader the scope of constraint imposed by the doctrine (Schauer 1987, 596). Regarding our past case as applying to American cars brings more present cases within its scope than if we regard it as applying only to Buicks, or magenta cars, or magenta Buicks. A narrower characterization similarly lessens the contribution that our past case makes to predictability, lessens the work that it does in facilitating decisionmaking, and gives it a smaller role in securing the stability of the precedential edifice. In each respect, this is simply because a narrower characterization occupies a smaller portion of the legal topography.

As Frederick Schauer has demonstrated, the need for criteria by which to determine similarity is also tied to the second procedural component identified above, namely the need for a court operating within a regime of stare decisis to be mindful of the likelihood that its present decision will serve as precedent in subsequent cases. Schauer (1987, 572) calls this the "forward-looking aspect of precedent." The consequence is that adherence to the doctrine of stare decisis has a constraining effect even where no past decisions provide authority in a case. This is because the court must account for the fact that it, and other future courts, will be bound by its present decision:

> If the future must treat what we do now as presumptively binding, then our current decision must judge not only what is best for now, but also how the current decision will affect the decision of other and future assimilable cases. Thus, the current decisionmaker must also take into account what would be best for some different but assimilable events yet to occur. The decisionmaker must then decide on the basis of what is best for *all* of the cases falling within the appropriate category of assimilation. (Schauer 1987, 589)

A final, important aspect of the mechanisms of stare decisis bears noting. It is that precedent, in Justice Brandeis's formulation, "is not a universal, inexorable command."[30] Even where a court has concluded that a present case falls within the precedential scope of a past decision, such that it cannot be distinguished away, the court retains the ability to conclude that the past case was sufficiently mistaken that it should be overruled. In constitutional cases, this dynamic is typically justified in terms of the difficulty of amending the Constitution. But overrulings occur, perhaps even just as frequently, in nonconstitutional areas, too. "The doctrine of precedent, in short, is not what a philosopher would call a categorical imperative but a rule of imperfect obligation" (Jones 1983, 24).

8.4 Methodological Stare Decisis

The goal in this section of the chapter is to examine the case for methodological stare decisis. Although the focus is on assessing the case for methodological stare decisis in constitutional interpretation, it will be helpful if we open by briefly considering the arguments made in favor of giving precedential effect to statutory-interpretation methodology. As the analysis will reveal, the arguments for methodological stare decisis are, in the constitutional context, stronger with respect to the determination of decision rules than they are for operative propositions

---

[30] Washington v. W.C. Dawson & Co., 264 U.S. 219, 238 (1924) (Brandeis, J., dissenting).

(more on that distinction below), and the case for both is weaker than the case for methodological stare decisis as applied to statutory interpretation.

8.4.1 Methodological Stare Decisis and Statutory Interpretation

As noted at the outset, the most-developed arguments for methodological stare decisis have concerned statutory interpretation. To a degree, this follows from the understanding that substantive statutory-interpretation decisions are entitled to strong stare decisis effect due to the relative positions of courts and legislatures in the lawmaking enterprise (Connors 2008, 683). Legislatures are able to amend statutes in response to disfavored judicial interpretations. A legislature's failure to amend a statute in light of a judicial interpretation is at least suggestive of its agreement with the interpretation, and therefore provides a strong reason for adherence to it. Those arguing in favor of methodological stare decisis advance a related set of reasons.

In broad form, the arguments offered in support of statutory methodological stare decisis track the more general justifications for precedent. (Although its advocates often speak in terms of stare decisis, as does this chapter, it would be more appropriate to regard them as a distinct variety of rule-consequentialist argument.) In the most-developed of these efforts, Sydney Foster argues that the application of stare decisis to methods of statutory interpretation would serve two primary ends. First, it would further rule-of-law values by limiting judicial discretion and thereby making law more predictable. Second, it would enhance interbranch coordination by giving Congress a fixed set of background rules to legislate against. This, in turn, would make it easier for Congress to foresee how proposed language would be interpreted, and thereby to effectuate its intent (Foster 2008, 1887–89).

As Foster points out, these benefits of methodological stare decisis are distinct from the benefits of stare decisis applied substantively. Yet, she contends, a regime of statutory methodological stare decisis also would produce the same set of benefits that are attributed to substantive stare decisis. It would enhance predictability for private parties in the same way it would for Congress, and this in turn would facilitate the creation of, and honor the existence of, reliance interests. With greater methodological certainty would come fewer disputed interpretive issues and thus less litigation, coupled with more-determinate, and thus more-predictable, substantive law (Foster 2008, 1894; Connors 2008, 709–10). In turn, Foster contends, methodological stare decisis would promote rule-of-law values by treating like parties alike and, further, by fostering the perception that interpretation is a law-governed activity.

This is not mere academic theorizing. Abbe Gluck studied statutory interpretation cases in five states and found that courts in four of them had adopted a consistent methodology. Each adopted a version of what she calls "modified textualism," an approach that "ranks interpretive tools in a clear order—textual analysis, then legislative history, then default judicial presumptions" (2010, 1758). Although malleability may be part of this methodology's appeal, Gluck found evidence that it provides actual constraint. Of course, the fact that methodological consistency has worked for statutory interpretation at the state level does not mean its logic transfers to the federal courts, much less that it would transfer to interpretation of the Constitution. It suggests, however, that the concept as applied to the Constitution is not simply hypothetical.

8.4.2 Methodological Stare Decisis and Constitutional Interpretation

Consideration of whether to give stare decisis effect to constitutional-interpretation methodology requires us first to confront the question of precisely what methodology might mean in the constitutional context. As Michael Gerhardt has noted, there are many senses in which the Court adheres to past practices that would fall within a broad definition of methodology. These include various norms and traditions ranging from the preference for avoiding constitutional issues to the issuance of opinions of the Court rather than seriatim opinions of each Justice (Gerhardt 2008, 3). There is even, in a very broad sense, consistent agreement on the identity of proper sources of decisional guidance, or at least on what sources are clearly improper. That is, while the Justices do not agree on the list of materials that can properly be consulted, they do seem to agree that coin flips, comic books, and the Canadian Constitution, to name just a few possibilities, do not typically provide useful insight into the meaning of the U.S. Constitution.

8.4.2.1 Decision Rules and Operative Propositions

There is another sense in which the Court seems to give stare decisis effect to methodological decisions. Much of constitutional doctrine consists of the adoption and refinement of tests by which courts are to assess whether the Constitution has been violated. The familiar tiered-scrutiny framework, for example, could easily be conceived of as embodying a methodology, and one that has been more or less consistently embraced by the Court. Within this framework as it operates under the Equal Protection Clause, laws that draw distinctions among groups of people will be subjected to differing levels of scrutiny—which involve different sorts of analysis—depending on the nature of the classification. Thus, for example, a court faced with a law that includes racial classifications must subject it to strict scrutiny, meaning that the court must ask whether the classification is necessary to achieve a compelling governmental purpose. A law that does not draw the sorts of distinctions that invite heightened scrutiny, in contrast, must merely satisfy the rational-basis test, meaning the court asks whether it is rationally related to a legitimate governmental purpose.

Whether we wish to lump them under the heading of methodology or not, these sorts of processes, as we will see, present a different problem, and they do not seem to be what advocates of statutory methodological stare decisis have in mind when referring to the potential transportability of their arguments to the constitutional context. Put differently, instead of referring to the processes of implementing the Constitution, these advocates are referring to the processes of determining constitutional meaning. That will be our primary focus as well.

In navigating this divide between constitutional implementation and constitutional meaning, it is useful to invoke Mitchell Berman's distinction between operative propositions and decision rules. The distinction stems from the recognition that there is a difference between constitutional meaning and the ways in which courts determine it, on the one hand, and the constitutional doctrine by which courts implement that meaning, on the other. Berman (2004, 9) sets it up as follows: "[L]et us call constitutional doctrines that represent the judiciary's understanding of the proper meaning of a constitutional power, right, duty, or other sort of provision 'constitutional operative propositions'; doctrines that direct courts how to decide whether a constitutional operative provision is satisfied [are] 'constitutional decision rules.'"

> An example will help. The Fourteenth Amendment provides that "[n]o state shall … deny to any person within its jurisdiction the equal protection of the laws." The courts are called upon, in the process of adjudication, to determine what this provision means. In performing that task, the courts may rely on any number of interpretive considerations, including such "modalities" as text, history, precedent, structure, moral judgment, and the like. Suppose the federal judiciary interprets the provision to mean that government may not classify individuals in ways not reasonably designed to promote a legitimate state interest. Such, then, is the constitutional operative provision. But that is not the whole of judge-made constitutional doctrine. A court cannot implement this operative proposition without some sort of procedure (perhaps implicit) for determining whether *to adjudge* the operative provision satisfied when, as will always be the case, the court lacks unmediated access to the true fact of the matter. It needs, that is to say, a constitutional decision rule. (Berman 2004, 9–10)

That decision rule could be simply a requirement that anyone raising an equal protection challenge establish by a preponderance of the evidence that the challenged classification is not reasonably designed to promote a legitimate state interest. But the Court also could tie its decision rule to a different sort of determination, such as whether certain sorts of classifications (e.g., racial) are apparent on the face of a challenged regulation.

Decision rules, then, are a product of judges' epistemic uncertainty rather than of the "meaning" of the Constitution. That is, they are tools designed to account for the fact that judges lack complete information in any given case, which creates the possibility of erroneous determinations regarding whether an operative proposition is satisfied. Under the Equal Protection Clause, the Court has adopted the tiered-scrutiny framework as its set of decision rules. The greater scrutiny given to laws that make certain sorts of classifications, primarily those based on race or gender, represents a judgment concerning the nature of the interests at stake as well as courts' (in)ability to uncover the true motivation for a law. To return to Berman's example, a decision rule tied to facially race-based classifications may be driven, at least in part, by a sense that a simple "preponderance of the evidence" decision rule would lead to the underenforcement of the Equal Protection Clause in that context, due to courts' inability to determine when a classification was truly meant to advance a legitimate interest.

Decision rules can certainly be described as methodological, in the sense that they provide a method by which courts implement the Constitution. But it is important to recognize that they are distinct from the interpretive methodologies that courts employ in determining constitutional meaning. Decision rules are crafted based on a host of factors that are distinct from (if often related to) the substance of the operative proposition they serve, including not only the minimization of errors overall, but also consideration of whether the nature of the interests involved counsels in favor of skewing such errors as will inevitably occur in favor of a particular set of parties. (One might say, for example, that the rational-basis test skews errors in favor of the government, while strict scrutiny skews them in favor of challengers to governmental action.)

The line of cases with which we opened provides us with another example. *Crawford* itself was primarily concerned with determining the meaning of the Sixth Amendment as applied to hearsay, and the Court's conclusion that the Confrontation Clause is concerned with testimonial hearsay is probably best regarded as the establishment of an operative proposition. The cases subsequent to *Crawford* involved, to a greater degree, the development of mechanisms for the implementation of the operative proposition. They continued to refine the operative proposition—the meaning of testimonial hearsay—but also increasingly focused on decision rules, such as by identifying the perspectives and information that courts can properly take into account in determining whether a given statement is testimonial.

As these examples suggest, and as Berman (2004) acknowledges, the distinction between operative propositions and decision rules may be easier to grasp conceptually than it is to apply to any particular body of doctrine. Thus, "whether a given piece of doctrine is an operative proposition depends on one's account of constitutional meaning, which in part depends upon one's theory of constitutional interpretation. Because there exist different plausible theories of proper constitutional interpretation, there exist different plausible conceptions of constitutional meaning" (74). As he notes, for example (76), categorizing something like the tiered-scrutiny framework as a set of decision rules seems natural under an originalist or textualist framework, but is less clear if one takes, for example, a common-law approach to constitutional interpretation, according to which one might view a level of scrutiny as part of the contemporary meaning of a given provision.

Even so, while the line between operative propositions and decision rules might be difficult to locate in any given instance, Berman's is a helpful account, and it is easy to appreciate that the processes of formulating the two components of constitutional law will differ. The bulk of constitutional theory—the familiar debates over originalism, living constitutionalism, political-process theory, and so forth—concerns the process of divining constitutional meaning (that is, operative propositions), and involves to a great degree debate over which sources can properly be considered in the course of such inquiry. The formulation of decision rules, in contrast, tends to involve a more limited, and uniform, set of considerations. Berman outlines "six analytically distinct factors or families of factors that might appeal to a judge considering whether, and how, to form a constitutional decision rule," considerations he labels "*adjudicatory*, *deterrent*, *protective*, *fiscal*, *institutional*, and *substantive*" (Berman 2004, 93). These types of considerations are largely distinct from those that factor into the determination of operative propositions,[31] and the resulting analysis is largely instrumental in nature. This is so regardless of the degree to which the process of deriving the meaning of the constitutional provision involves instrumental considerations.

8.4.2.2 Stare Decisis and Constitutional Methodology

The question of whether to give stare decisis effect to interpretive methodology boils down to whether to systematically privilege one meta-rule of constitutional adjudication (stare decisis) over another (a methodological choice) in situations where the two conflict. On most accounts, the Constitution does not provide its own answer to this query. The selection and application of a method of interpretation thus involves consideration of a cluster of pragmatic and prudential factors, just as the question of whether to give stare decisis effect to a past decision turns on such judgments.

As the authors developing the arguments for methodological stare decisis in the statutory context recognize, while some of their reasoning might transfer to constitutional interpretation, the two situations present different dynamics. The largest difference is the one that underlies the difference in the precedential effect given to substantive holdings in the two contexts, namely that it is considerably easier to change a statute than to change the Constitution. "[W]hile statutory interpretation doctrine is capable of influencing how statutes are drafted, constitutional interpretation doctrine is not capable of influencing how constitutional provisions are drafted, with the exception of subsequently adopted constitutional amendments" (Foster 2008, 1872). The preceding section's discussion suggests another wrinkle, namely that the analysis is likely to be different for decision rules and operative propositions.

Operative Propositions

One can easily imagine an argument, grounded in the standard justifications for precedent, in favor of giving stare decisis effect to the processes by which operative propositions are established. To apply the same methodology to two cases, each of which turns on the meaning of the Constitution, is to treat those two cases alike, at least along one dimension. And it perhaps leads to enhanced predictability, again at

[31] Though, as noted above, this distinction is much more apparent when the methodology for discerning the operative proposition is textualist or originalist in nature.

a very broad level, in the sense that prospective litigants can have a sense of the types of arguments that they must make in support of their position. One might also imagine that the decisionmaking process will be strengthened, at least in the sense that the court need not devote its resources, intellectual or otherwise, to taking up anew in each case the question of what types of arguments and information it ought to consider in undertaking its analysis.

Compelling as this may at first sound, it weakens under scrutiny. Consider first the question of treating like cases alike. There is undoubtedly a sense in which methodological stare decisis would further the goal of treating like cases alike. But this is to engage "likeness" at a relatively high level of generality, and one that does not come with natural limits. If constitutional Case 1 is decided under Methodology A, then treating constitutional Case 2—a like case in that it turns on the interpretation of the Constitution—alike would, on this view, require the application of Methodology A to Case 2, and indeed to all other constitutional cases.

We may not, however, think it appropriate to define either like cases or like treatment in this way (Schauer 1987, 578). The point can be appreciated by consideration of an originalist analysis. Imagine a provision in the Bill of Rights that, as a matter of original understanding, protects conduct A against government infringement, but not conduct B. Assume further that, from the perspective of the Framers' generation, cases involving those two types of conduct are not like cases, and need not be treated in like fashion. From our contemporary vantage point, however, the distinction between conduct A and B is immaterial, such that we would consider them to be like cases. (Perhaps the differential treatment of men and women that was a common feature of the Framers' era but is considerably less characteristic of ours falls into this category.) The problem arises because interpretive methodology and the operation of stare decisis are not independent of one another. Instead, methodological choices can influence perceptions of what categories of assimilation are appropriate. The logic of at least some methodologies could produce categories that compel like treatment according to features of the cases that would not otherwise factor into an analysis of similarity. To say that the operative scope of the right involved in the two cases is to be determined via the same methodology, then, is to say that they will be treated alike along a dimension that ignores the features of the cases that we would normally take into account in determining whether they are alike.

Crawford provides another example. The "testimonial hearsay" formulation generated by the Court's originalism, we can imagine, accurately represents the line that the Framers wished to draw given their concerns and given the resources and characteristics of the criminal justice system of their time. We might further imagine that they would wish to use the same line to accommodate their concerns were they presented with today's criminal justice system. Addressing all cases involving hearsay under *Crawford*'s originalist analysis, then, would be to treat them alike both methodologically and, on one view (the Framers'), substantively. But that, too, might overlook the features that we might regard as providing the appropriate grounds for judging likeness (which might turn on things that have changed considerably since the Framers' time, such as the nature of the criminal-justice system or the ability to summon the police quickly by dialing 9-1-1), as the fracturing of the *Crawford* coalition in subsequent cases suggests.

But the problem may be even larger than these examples reveal. The difficulty is that there is no natural cutoff point for the application of the categories of assimilation. Proponents of theories of constitutional interpretation do not, by and large, consider their theories to be applicable only to portions of the Constitution. If one is an adherent of originalism, or common-law constitutionalism, or what have you, one has adopted the position that the entire Constitution ought to be interpreted in a manner consistent with that theory. Implicit in that is a conclusion that the appropriate category of assimilation turns solely on whether a case concerns the Constitution. If so, it must be resolved by resort to the same methodology as past cases. To be sure, this may be overstating the point a bit. Proponents of eclectic or pragmatic theories of interpretation, for example, might claim to have avoided this difficulty. But those theories, too, operate globally insofar as they would preclude resort to unified theories.

Alternatively, it might be possible to narrow the categories somewhat—to maintain, for example, that different methodologies are appropriate depending on whether a case involves the "rights" provisions of the Constitution versus the "powers" provisions, or to slice things even more narrowly. The point remains, though, that any effort to give precedential effect to methodological choices would create pressure to rely on categories of assimilation that are broader than what reference to underlying substantive doctrine is likely to generate.

Another way to appreciate the point is to consider the forward-looking aspects of precedent. The way this dynamic normally works is as follows. A court deciding a case in which it knows that it is setting precedent must account in its decisional process for the fact that it is doing so. It must consider the best result in the case before it, but it must also anticipate the sorts of future cases in which its present decision will operate as precedent and attempt to craft a rule that will best address those cases as well. This is a perilous process, and one that can misfire if the case before the court is in some way not representative of the relevant range of cases (Oldfather 2009, 338–50).

But now imagine the situation of the court that is faced with the prospect of binding itself to a methodology. Unless the range of cases in which it regards itself as doing so is roughly coextensive with the range of cases to which the substantive rule generated in the case would apply, the court's powers of imagination must be even greater, because (assuming the methodology is somewhat determinate in application) it will be committing itself to results in a set of cases that may bear little substantive similarity to the case before it.[32]

[32] This concern motivated Justice O'Connor's one-paragraph partial concurrence in *Michael H. v. Gerald D.*, 491 U.S. 110, 132 (1989), which marks one of the few times concern about something akin to methodological stare decisis has appeared in an opinion. In it, she declined to join Justice Scalia's preferred approach to due-process analysis, noting, "I would not foreclose the unanticipated by the prior imposition of a single mode of historical analysis."

The tensions created by the pull toward broad categories of assimilation generate further tensions given the noncategorical nature of precedent as typically applied. A court can often overrule a substantive precedent with little or no spillover effect. A decision to reverse course on, say, the way hearsay is treated under the Confrontation Clause does not have inevitable implications beyond the doctrine's reach. And this is entirely consistent with a regime of stare decisis more generally.

Consider, though, how this would work in a world of methodological stare decisis. Suppose that the application of a particular methodology will necessarily lead to an unpalatable substantive result—we can use the easy example of an originalist approach to the legality of paper money[33]—or that overruling an undesirable substantive precedent would be inconsistent with adherence to the established, precedential methodology. Overruling the precedent or departing from the methodology would create greater uncertainty about the continuing validity of the larger regime of methodological stare decisis. What this suggests, then, is that maintenance of a regime of methodological stare decisis would likely require that it be, contra Brandeis, an inexorable command, or something approaching one, for the simple reason that too-frequent departures from the established methodology would undercut its precedential force. At the same time, the necessary breadth of the associated categories of assimilation would provide more frequent cause for courts to want to depart. These pressures might well doom an attempted regime to failure. This is so, again, because it is difficult to come up with categories of assimilation that do not extend across substantive boundaries. Perhaps, as noted above, it would be possible to formulate different regimes of methodological stare decisis for, say, rights provisions and structural provisions. Even those, however, would not be as flexible or accommodating as substantive stare decisis, simply because the rationales would apply too bluntly and too broadly across a wide swath of cases.

Contemplation of the implications of methodological stare decisis with respect to the remaining justifications for precedent yields similar conclusions. Consider the role of precedent in fostering predictability. At the level of determining operative propositions, any gains in predictability are likely to be somewhat illusory. The fact that citizens and governmental actors are able to know with certainty what methodology courts will apply to constitutional questions does not mean they will be able to confidently determine what conduct is permissible. This could be a product of the underdeterminacy of at least some methodologies. But even a methodology that is highly determinate in application may not lead to easily predictable results. Even if one were to posit that, for example, originalism is a determinate means to constitutional implementation, that provides only some help in any actor's effort to determine how the Constitution applies to her situation. It is one thing to know that a court will look to the standards of 1789 in resolving the question of how the

[33] In the *Legal Tender Cases*, 79 U.S. 457 (1870), the Court reversed its prior holding that paper money violated the Constitution. Most scholars regard the constitutionality of paper money as clearly inconsistent with original understanding (Monaghan 1988, 744). See also Larry Alexander's engagement with the *Legal Tender Cases* in Chap. 3 of this volume.

Constitution applies to one's conduct. It is another thing entirely to know what the standards of 1789 were, the determination of which requires a process that would be at best difficult for, and perhaps even inaccessible to, most of those required to conform their conduct to the standard. Because of the costs of implementation, greater methodological predictability does not necessarily or even likely entail greater predictability in terms of the content of operative propositions.

So, too, with strengthened decisionmaking and stability. In the usual situation in which precedent applies, a court relying on it "may justifiably 'relax,' in the sense of engaging in less scrutiny of the case" (Schauer 1987, 599). The court applying the precedent may assume that the prior court went through the work of considering what future cases might look like and crafted a rule in a manner that was mindful of the potential for variations such as the one before the second court. The process does not work so smoothly when the question concerns the prior court's choice of methodology. The only saved decisional costs would be those involved in choosing a methodology. But such savings are unlikely to be substantial. To be sure, new Justices on a Supreme Court that adhered to a consistent methodology would be spared the effort of developing their own constitutional vision, at least to the extent they had not brought one with them. But that is in an important if not complete sense a one-time cost, a decision that is made at the wholesale level of a judicial career rather than the retail level of case-by-case adjudication. Individual Justices' methodological preferences may evolve over the course of their careers, but they are not up for reconsideration with each new decision.

Stability perhaps presents more of a mixed bag. Regardless of whether a regime of methodological stare decisis would be sustainable over the long term, its adoption would for some period of time imperil rather than foster stability. Absent some way to restrict the categories of assimilation, its application would require remaking significant swaths of law. As the switch to originalist methodology in the context of the Confrontation Clause demonstrates, the change can be dramatic. Over time, of course, a world of fixed methodological commitments would reach a new equilibrium, and the absence of methodological variance would engender a sort of stability. It might not, however, be the sort of ground-level stability promised by substantive stare decisis, for the reasons identified in the predictability discussion above. Moreover, if I am correct in suggesting that methodological stare decisis is inherently unsustainable, then, of course, efforts to implement it would generate substantial uncertainty.

Decision Rules

The analysis changes considerably when we turn our attention to decision rules. Recall the reason for skepticism regarding whether methodological stare decisis, as applied to the determination of operative propositions, would lead to like cases being treated alike. Focusing on methodology as the locus of like treatment entails assessing the similarity of cases according to their amenability to methodology. This creates pressure to gauge likeness at a broad level—such as by treating all cases involving constitutional interpretation to the same methodology—and overlooks the more situationally relevant features of cases that we naturally take into account in determining which are alike. Relatedly, a court applying a given methodology to the process of determining the scope of an operative proposition has little sense of just how broad the precedential scope of its decision might end up being. Consider for example a case concerning a novel application of substantive due process doctrine. At least in the early stages of a regime of methodological stare decisis, the deciding court would be unable to know whether its methodological choices bearing on the formulation of operative principles would bind all future constitutional claims, all substantive due process claims, only some subset of these claims, or some differently defined category of cases. The logic of such a system would create pressure for broadly drawn categories of assimilation, generating wide swaths of similar methodological treatment that would not guarantee like treatment according to other, more natural metrics.

Adherence to decision rules, which embody the processes or methodologies by which operative propositions are implemented, does not create the same dangers. The Court can consistently follow the methodological choices embodied in decision rules because it, and everyone else, will be readily able to anticipate their scope of application. Decision rules are formulated in such a way as to apply within the limited substantive domain described by the operative proposition they implement, and to lead to results within that limited domain that accord more comfortably with a modern notion of what it means to treat like cases alike. This is simply because basing likeness on the factors triggering the applicability of operative propositions better reflects our expectations concerning similarity. Thus, to return once more to *Crawford*, the methodologies that the Court develops for lower courts to use in implementing the "testimonial hearsay" standard are by their nature limited to the narrow doctrinal confines of the relationship between the Confrontation Clause and hearsay. There is no danger of their leading to inadvertent mischief in the law of takings or the dormant Commerce Clause. The Court may conclude (and indeed arguably has concluded) that not all cases that logically fall within history's definition of testimonial hearsay should be treated the same way. But so long as in acting on that conclusion it tinkers only with the decision rules by which lower courts determine what constitutes testimonial hearsay, a decision not to adhere to precedent does not threaten the continued maintenance of decision rules in other domains.

As with the notion of treating like cases alike, the analyses of the latter three justifications for precedent soften when we move from operative propositions to decision rules. Here again, this is because the problems presented by categories of assimilation largely fall away. It is no longer a matter of "we must follow this methodology because this, too, is a question of constitutional interpretation," but rather of "… because this, too, is a question of substantive due process," or separation of powers, or congressional authority, or justiciability, and so on. Precedent can thereby function in a manner similar to its operation in the common law.

Moreover, the analysis takes on the cast of common-law reasoning in another sense. Part of what differentiates common-law judging from constitutional adjudication, as practiced at the level of determining operative propositions, is that in the latter context there is very little consensus on the premises underlying the enterprise (Posner 2008, 277). Constitutional theory proposes judicial orientations ranging from those in which the Court's job is no more or less than to discern meaning and apply the written Constitution as it was understood at the Framing, to those in which we owe the document no fidelity whatsoever. And while Justices tend not to adhere to either extreme, their positions nonetheless stake out a wide range in between, and further vary as to how courts should approach topics like federalism, separation of powers, and the protection of individual rights. Disagreements can arise at any level of abstraction, from the point of application to first principles.

Decision rules do not involve this dynamic. The fixing of an operative proposition significantly narrows, if it does not settle entirely, the permissible aims of the enterprise. Once *Crawford* determines that the Confrontation Clause is concerned with testimonial hearsay, the universe of potential approaches to the application of the Confrontation Clause is narrowed considerably. Thus, where the substance of an operative provision has been fixed, reasoning about decision rules looks much more like common-law reasoning. And as with common-law reasoning, it is much more realistic to speak of predictability, decisional efficiency, and stability as benefits of adhering to past decisions.

8.5 Conclusion

Ultimately, the product of this analysis is likely related to why, for example, Justice Scalia (1989) is a self-proclaimed "faint-hearted originalist." He is willing to follow his methodology only so far, and the boundaries within which he is willing to follow it are defined by the same sorts of substantive, on-the-ground facts that drive judges' formulation of categories of assimilation. As Richard Fallon (2009, 1014) has put the point, the reason we do not see Justices settling on a methodology is that

> the justices might believe that although they are bound by tacit norms of constitutional adjudication, their tacit knowledge defies accurate expression in propositional form. Specifically, the justices might believe that although one or another constitutional theory comes closest to describing accurately the normative constraints to which they are subject, none does so perfectly, and that the tacit norms of constitutional adjudication thus actually constrain them from adopting any theory that might diverge from those tacit norms in possibly unforeseeable future cases.

At the end of the day, perhaps the answer is that doing justice in a given case requires consideration of a host of factors, and the appropriate weights to be given them are not constant. Adherence to a consistent methodology privileges one component of the mix—a component that turns primarily on considerations of the proper role of the judiciary in the constitutional scheme—over all others. It is to take a very judge-centric view of the constitutional scheme, even when the methodology at issue is one that purports to minimize the power of judges, for it presupposes that the most important thing in the resolution of a constitutional dispute is to define the role of the judiciary.

References

Alexander L (1989) Constrained by precedent. South Calif Law Rev 63(1):1–63

Bandy J (2011) Interpretive freedom: a necessary component of Article III judging. Duke Law J 61(3):651–691

Berman M (2004) Constitutional decision rules. Va Law Rev 90(1):1–168

Connors JW (2008) Treating like subdecisions alike: the scope of stare decisis as applied to judicial methodology. Columbia Law Rev 108(3):681–715

Duxbury N (2008) The nature and authority of precedent. Cambridge University Press, New York

Fallon R (2009) Constitutional constraints. Calif Law Rev 97(4):975–1037

Foster S (2008) Should courts give stare decisis effect to statutory interpretation methodology? Georgetown Law J 96(6):1863–1911

Gerhardt M (2008) The power of precedent. Oxford University Press, New York

Gluck A (2010) The states as laboratories of statutory interpretation: methodological consensus and the new modified textualism. Yale Law J 119(8):1750–1862

Jones HW (1983) Precedent and policy in constitutional law. Pace Law Rev 4(1):11–27

Llewellyn KN (1930) The bramble bush: some lectures on law and its study. Columbia University School of Law, New York

Llewellyn KN (1960) The common law tradition: deciding appeals. Little, Brown, and Co., Boston

Monaghan HP (1988) Stare decisis and constitutional adjudication. Columbia Law Rev 88(4):723–773

Oldfather CM (2009) Universal de novo review. George Wash Law Rev 77(2):308–365

Peters CJ (1996) Foolish consistency: on equality, integrity, and justice in stare decisis. Yale Law J 105(8):2031–2115

Posner R (2008) How judges think. Harvard University Press, Cambridge, MA

Pound R (1941) What of stare decisis? Fordham Law Rev 10(1):1–13

Scalia A (1989) Originalism: the lesser evil. Univ Cincinnati Law Rev 57(3):849–865

Schauer F (1987) Precedent. Stanford Law Rev 39(3):571–605

Schauer F (1994) Precedent and the necessary externality of constitutional norms. Harv J Law Publ Policy 17(1):45–55

Wistrich AJ (2012) The evolving temporality of lawmaking. Conn Law Rev 44(3):737–826

Chapter 9
Constitutional Method and the Path of Precedent

Randy J. Kozel

Abstract This chapter argues that methodologies of constitutional interpretation and questions of constitutional stare decisis are inextricably connected, such that courts cannot commit to a complete theory of stare decisis without also committing to a theory of interpretation. The author contends that while some components of the stare decisis inquiry are independent of interpretive theories, others—in particular the questions of whether and to what extent following an incorrect precedent is harmful—depend for their answers on which interpretive methodology one adopts. The author traces this dependent relationship to the existence of divergent normative underpinnings for various interpretive theories. And he suggests that the fact of methodological pluralism on the U.S. Supreme Court, and indeed within the jurisprudence of individual Justices, is likely to frustrate the development of a coherent, comprehensive approach to stare decisis in constitutional cases.

9.1 Introduction

Text is what starts the engine of American constitutional law, but precedent is what really makes it hum. Legal briefs and judicial opinions are awash in efforts to marshal, characterize, and distinguish prior opinions. And even novel arguments are consistently framed to suggest that what seems like a break from the past is actually an enhancement of continuity.

This is an abridged version of a longer article, "Settled Versus Right: Constitutional Method and the Path of Precedent," published originally in the *Texas Law Review* (Kozel 2013).

R.J. Kozel (✉)
Law School, University of Notre Dame, 2118 Eck Hall of Law,
Notre Dame, IN 46556, USA
e-mail: rkozel@nd.edu

C.J. Peters (ed.), *Precedent in the United States Supreme Court*, Ius Gentium: Comparative Perspectives on Law and Justice 33, DOI 10.1007/978-94-007-7951-8_9,

The pervasiveness of precedent is equaled by the controversy it engenders. In its most robust form, the invocation of precedent can lead a court to issue a ruling that runs counter to what its decision would otherwise be. The prospect is far from hypothetical. Some of the most significant decisions in the modern constitutional canon have emphasized the propriety of deferring to precedent notwithstanding doubts about a decision's substantive merits.[1] It is little wonder that the Supreme Court's approach to precedent—often referred to by the Latinate shorthand, stare decisis—drips with political valence and serves as a flashpoint during the vetting of every would-be Justice.

The prevailing wisdom among Supreme Court Justices and academic commentators alike is that precedent has a critical role to play in shaping the trajectory of constitutional law. Yet disagreement abounds over how to develop a theory of precedent that lends itself to principled application. Within the American legal system, no constitutional precedent is beyond judicial revocability, and the Supreme Court occasionally overrules its past decisions. At other times, however, the existence of an applicable precedent leads the Justices to embrace a constitutional interpretation despite reservations about its soundness.[2] Justice Brandeis famously described the overarching tension as between the law's being "settled" and its being "settled right,"[3] though it is perhaps more illuminating to restate the dichotomy in terms of "settled and wrong" versus "unsettled and right."

My initial goal in this chapter is to link the conceptual ambiguity that surrounds theories of precedent to their estrangement from interpretive method. Judicial opinions and scholarly commentary have yielded well-theorized accounts of certain consequences of departing from precedent, including the disruption of settled expectations. But even an exhaustive analysis of those effects would be inadequate, because they deal only with the importance of leaving the law *settled*. Before determining whether to retain or reject a flawed precedent, there must also be an inquiry into the importance of getting the law *right*—in other words, of replacing a flawed constitutional rule with a better one. Conducting that latter assessment is enmeshed with the process of selecting a method of constitutional interpretation.

Precedents are neither good nor bad; it is interpretive method that makes them so.[4] The urgency of rectifying a misapplication of the law will look very different as between an originalist who takes her touchstone as the Constitution's original public meaning and a living constitutionalist who accepts the primacy of contemporary understandings and mores. Further, multiple perspectives commonly emerge *within* interpretive schools as the result of varying normative premises. For example, some proponents of originalism defend that approach on consequentialist grounds,

---

[1] See, for example, Planned Parenthood of Se. Pa. v. Casey, 505 U.S. 833, 861 (1992). See also "Stare Decisis and the Constitution: An Essay on Constitutional Methodology" (Fallon 2001).

[2] See, for example, Dickerson v. United States, 530 U.S. 428, 443 (2000); *Casey*, 505 U.S. at 853, 861; Dep't of Revenue of Ky. v. Davis, 553 U.S. 328, 359–60 (Scalia, J., concurring in part).

[3] Burnet v. Coronado Oil & Gas Co., 285 U.S. 393, 406 (1932) (Brandeis, J., dissenting).

[4] With apologies to William Shakespeare, who wrote in *Hamlet* that "there is nothing either good or bad, but thinking makes it so." (1988, act 2, scene 2, lines 250–52).

while others describe it as reflecting the role of popular sovereignty in legitimating judicial review.[5] Their respective normative premises lead the consequentialist and popular-sovereigntist strands of originalism to adopt divergent views regarding the severity of constitutional errors. This phenomenon is not unique to originalism; it applies across constitutional theories. The perceived benefit of deviating from precedent is always derivative of one's interpretive method and normative priors.

This interdependence can be useful in organizing the various ramifications of precedent according to their relationship with constitutional method. Considerations such as the disruptiveness of overruling a settled rule are *independent* of method. They are amenable to meaningful discussion outside the context of any particular interpretive philosophy. By contrast, the substantive harms caused by the ongoing retention of a flawed precedent are *dependent* effects; they generate their content only upon being situated within a broader interpretive framework. If one believes that the First Amendment prohibits discrimination against corporate speakers, a coherent theory of precedent requires an apparatus for gauging how harmful it would be to retain the contrary rule. So, too, if one believes that the Constitution protects a right of intimate conduct between people of the same gender, that it lacks any right to nontherapeutic abortions, or that it forbids the utilization of race-conscious admissions in higher education. The determinants of precedential durability include the costs of perpetuating an erroneous rule. Those costs, in turn, stem from methodological and normative commitments.

What, then, of contemporary constitutional practice? As Chad Oldfather discusses in Chap. 8 of this volume, the Supreme Court has resisted the adoption of any unified strategy for resolving constitutional disputes. The Court occasionally ascribes controlling significance to the Constitution's original meaning, as in its recent discussion of the Second Amendment's right to bear arms.[6] In other cases original meaning is a non-factor, leaving room for theoretical, prudential, or doctrinal considerations to move to the forefront. The inconsistency is partly the product of the Court's status as a multiparty institution whose members exhibit varying jurisprudential sympathies. It also reflects the conscious choices of some individual Justices to resist adoption of a single theory of interpretation. These institutional and individual considerations have converged to establish the Court's approach to constitutional interpretation as fundamentally *pluralistic*.

Even if one is initially inclined to accept interpretive pluralism as a valid approach to adjudication, I am going to suggest that when viewed alongside the U.S. Supreme Court's prevailing approach to stare decisis, pluralism is a doctrinal dead-end. Evaluating the severity of a given constitutional mistake requires invoking a particular interpretive method and a corresponding set of normative premises. Without those anchors, the value of constitutional accuracy is left undefined. Rejecting all interpretive theories in favor of pluralism undermines efforts to compare the costs

---

[5] Compare "Reconciling Originalism and Precedent" (McGinnis and Rappaport 2009, 804–05) with "Originalism, Popular Sovereignty, and Reverse Stare Decisis" (Lash 2007, 1446–47).

[6] See District of Columbia v. Heller, 554 U.S. 570 (2008).

and benefits of precedential continuity, because pluralism affords no metric by which to gauge the relative importance of interpreting the Constitution correctly.

Before closing this Introduction, I offer two notes on terminology. First, for purposes of what follows, I use the concept of an "interpretive method" to refer to any consistent and overarching strategy for determining the meaning of the U.S. Constitution. Second, I am using the concepts of accuracy, rightness, and error as something like terms of art. I employ them in reference to the interpretations that a jurist would have voted to implement in the absence of contrary precedent. I acknowledge the argument that some revisions of the law that are preferred by subsequent judges may reflect the empowerment of new coalitions with new judicial philosophies more so than the identification and eradication of genuine "error." I also recognize the prospect that, according to some interpretive theories, the resolution of constitutional disputes must take into account the effects of overruling an applicable precedent, such that the best interpretation of the Constitution may vary over time with the accretion of precedent. On that account, precedent might be perceived as constitutive of law, the implication being that it is not quite accurate to say that any given precedent is "right" or "wrong." But even for adherents of such an approach, circumstances will arise in which a judge believes that existing precedent ought to be revised or replaced. The pivotal question remains unchanged: When should deference to precedent dissuade a decisionmaker from pursuing the result that she would otherwise view as preferable? Indeed, an important part of my project is exploring the path a judge must travel before concluding that a given constitutional ruling is warranted despite the fact that the same ruling would be incorrect if certain precedents were not on the books.

9.2 Precedent's Place in Constitutional Discourse

Given the underlying nuance that can sometimes be obscured by terms like "precedent" and "stare decisis," it is worthwhile to take a moment to describe the diverse functions of precedent in modern constitutional discourse.

The bluntest function of precedent is *hierarchical control*.[7] A court of superior rank issues an opinion interpreting the Constitution. Thereafter, inferior courts face a binding obligation to treat that interpretation as controlling. The obligation persists even if an inferior court views the precedent as incorrect or reasonably predicts that the superior court itself is no longer likely to follow it.[8] Within American constitutional law, the rule of hierarchical precedent—also called vertical precedent—is indefeasible and absolute.

A court's prior decisions can also exert influence on future adjudicators by means of *persuasion*: Though the later court is not required to follow the opinion in question, it is free to study the opinion's reasoning, thereby benefiting from the analytical

[7] See generally Caminker (1994).

[8] See Agostini v. Felton, 521 U.S. 203, 237 (1997).

work already done by other judges. Likewise, the later court can examine whether its predecessors' empirical assumptions and projections have been borne out over time. Unlike hierarchical control, the persuasive function of precedent does not portray the mere issuance of a precedent as carrying independent significance. Sooner or later, a court that looks to precedent in a persuasive fashion must gauge the soundness of the precedent's reasoning. As Justice Scalia has noted, "[i]f one has been persuaded by another, so that one's judgment accords with the other's, there is no room for deferral—only for agreement."[9] The consultation of precedents for persuasive purposes continues to be useful in helping later courts to understand and evaluate competing arguments. Notwithstanding this utility, however, the persuasive function of precedent never requires a court to issue a ruling whose substantive merit it doubts.

What initially appears to be a persuasive invocation of precedent often reveals itself as something different—an exercise in *stage-setting*. In constitutional disputes, as in other forms of litigation, judges (like the attorneys who litigate before them) utilize precedents as a means of framing and bolstering their arguments. The implication is not necessarily that the reviewing court believes that it *must* follow the precedents. Nor is it that the precedents warrant consideration due solely to the persuasiveness of their reasoning. Instead, the very existence of the precedents is used to suggest that the subsequent court's ruling represents an unremarkable application of established principles. Though the prior decisions may not have spoken to the precise question under review, they are depicted as setting the doctrinal stage and suggesting the appropriate result by analogy or modest extension.

Like the persuasive function of precedent, the use of precedent for stage-setting is non-constraining. A court that describes past decisions as consistent with its holding does not necessarily indicate that its ruling would have been different but for the existence of precedent. To the contrary, the court might well agree with the decisions' rationales. Stage-setting influences the superstructure of judicial rhetoric and reason-giving. It may even supply an element of "lawyerly authenticity" (Calabresi 2005, 329). But it does not affect the bottom line by requiring a judge to accept a constitutional interpretation that she disfavors on the merits.

Between the poles of absolute constraint and no constraint are those functions of precedent that affect the substance of judicial rulings without imposing an inexorable duty to reaffirm existing law. For starters, respect for precedent can promote incrementalism and continuity by acting as a *braking* mechanism that encourages judges to be moderate and gradual in their decisionmaking. The underlying theory, which is deeply embedded in the common-law tradition, is that it is generally preferable for courts to make changes at the margins and exert pressure on the forward trajectory of the law rather than overhauling what was previously settled. Respect for precedent assists in this mission by encouraging judges to seek out plausible bases of distinguishing past decisions instead of abandoning them outright.

The motivation for a court's incrementalism may be the belief, often associated with the political philosophy of Edmund Burke, that caution is prudent because

[9] Kasten v. Saint-Gobain Performance Plastics Corp., 131 S. Ct. 1325, 1340 (2011) (Scalia, J., dissenting).

"new departures are likely to have unanticipated adverse consequences" (Sunstein 2006, 402). Alternatively, incrementalism may reflect the intuition that change will tend to be less disruptive and controversial when it is achieved gradually over time. In either case, incrementalism differs from persuasion and stage-setting through its ability to make a tangible impact on the subsequent court's decision. A judge who is inclined to announce a dramatic legal change but who adopts the incrementalist mindset will be deterred by the prospect of overruling numerous precedents. As a compromise, the judge will articulate the appropriate rule to govern cases like the one at bar without going further by sweeping away multiple decisions or extending the law in revolutionary new ways. A commitment to incrementalism accordingly carries the potential to affect the scope of judicial decisions. Note, however, that incrementalism still permits the reviewing court to reach whatever result it deems appropriate in the case at hand, even if that means overruling an applicable precedent. The incrementalist mindset is a technique for mediating change, not preventing it.

The role of precedent undergoes a metamorphosis when a court endorses a constitutional decision whose intrinsic soundness it doubts in an effort to maintain consistency with its past self. In such a case, the court treats precedent as *self-binding*: The litigated dispute would have had a different outcome but for the precedent's existence. The explanation is not that the subsequent court has come to agree with the precedent's reasoning due to its irresistible logic and persuasiveness. What is meaningful about the precedent is its issuance at some prior time. That temporal priority converts the precedent into a "fundamental restraint" on the subsequent court's power to effectuate its own understanding of the Constitution's content.[10] By contemplating the perpetuation of dubious or suboptimal interpretations, the self-binding function of precedent raises serious challenges grounded in both constitutional structure and the nature of the judicial process.

The province in which constitutional precedent plays a genuinely constraining role can be defined as the set of cases in which a court deems itself bound to accept a rule that it concludes or suspects is substantively erroneous. The subsequent court may surmise that the applicable precedent was unsound from the beginning, or it may believe the rule has been undermined by the passage of time. Either way, the subsequent court is put in the position of announcing a result that it currently believes to reflect a likely misapplication of the Constitution.

The self-binding function of precedent is complicated by the U.S. Supreme Court's characterization of stare decisis in terms of discretion rather than compulsion. As a matter of horizontal constraint—that is, the constraint exerted by precedents issued by the presently deciding court as opposed to a superior tribunal—the Court treats its precedents as only presumptively self-binding, not absolutely so. To guide the inquiry into whether a dubious precedent should be retained, the Court has enumerated an array of factors including reliance expectations,

[10] United States v. Lopez, 514 U.S. 549, 574 (1995) (Kennedy, J., concurring).

workability, evolving factual contexts, and jurisprudential coherence.[11] All the while, the Justices have been unequivocal in preserving their general prerogative to overrule precedents under appropriate circumstances.

The dynamics of horizontal self-binding lead to the "overwhelming question"[12] posed by any theory of constitutional precedent: When should a court willfully perpetuate a reading of the Constitution that it would reject but for the existence of precedent?

9.3 Independent Effects of Constitutional Precedent

Certain implications of following precedent are amenable to preliminary scrutiny without regard to interpretive method. Those elements, which I call the *independent* effects of precedent, are examined in the sections that follow.

9.3.1 Independent Benefits of Continuity

9.3.1.1 Expectations and Disruption

The protection of settled expectations is among the most prevalent justifications for deferring to precedent.[13] When a court issues an opinion, stakeholders modify their behaviors in response. Judicial delineation of the applicable rules affects commercial activities such as the formation of contracts, allocation of investments, and organization of business operations. It influences governmental decisions such as the crafting of legislation designed to foster democratic objectives within lawful bounds. It even affects societal understandings regarding the content of the legal backdrop against which citizens arrange their lives.

When the judiciary reverses course and announces a new rule, it introduces a potentially dramatic source of disruption. Commercial structures that seemed ingenious under the old regime become problematic or even prohibited. Hard-fought and extensively researched legislation is invalidated, with the lawmakers sent back

[11] For a leading formulation of the components of the doctrine of stare decisis, see *Casey*, 505 U.S. at 854–55.

[12] The term, though obviously not the context, is from T.S. Eliot's *The Love Song of J. Alfred Prufrock* (1998).

[13] See, for example, Walton v. Arizona, 497 U.S. 639, 673 (1990) (Scalia, J., concurring in part and concurring in the judgment) ("The doctrine [of stare decisis] exists for the purpose of introducing certainty and stability into the law and protecting the expectations of individuals and institutions that have acted in reliance on existing rules."); cf. Stephen Breyer's (2011, 2024) "Making Our Democracy Work: The Yale Lectures," in which Justice Breyer states: "When the Court considers the work of past Courts, the key concept is *stare decisis* while the key attitude recognizes the importance of *reliance*" (emphasis in original).

to the drawing board for another sapping of public resources. And widespread understandings about the legal backdrop—as well as corresponding assumptions about the stability and reliability of the legal equilibrium—are challenged, sometimes marginally but sometimes substantially.

By retaining a precedent despite its dubious merits, a court can prevent these disturbances from coming to pass. That makes the avoidance of disruption a principal benefit of precedential continuity. Such avoidance is also an *independent* benefit. The unsettling effects of adjudicative change reflect the degree to which stakeholders would be required to adapt their behaviors and understandings to a revised legal order. There remain differences of opinion regarding the quantum of evidence required to prove those effects. In addition, there are significant debates about the types of disruption that should be relevant for purposes of stare decisis. For example, some scholars contend that the disruption of societal understandings caused by a judicial overruling—famously invoked in *Planned Parenthood v. Casey* with respect to abortion rights[14]—is too "inchoate" to serve as a valid component of stare decisis doctrine.[15] Others suggest that a full accounting of the costs of legal change must include this kind of intangible, systemic reaction to precedent.[16] Quite apart from these debates, interpretive method is unnecessary to determine the degree to which adjudicative change would upset expectations and require forward-looking adjustments. Normative choices remain crucial to the level of significance that is ultimately ascribed to settled expectations. The extent of disruption, however, does not fluctuate depending on one's general theory of constitutional interpretation.

9.3.1.2 Rule of Law

Intertwined with the avoidance of disruption is the efficacy of stare decisis in promoting the rule of law. The rule of law requires that "people in positions of authority" operate within a "constraining framework" of publicly-available rules rather than indulging "their own preferences or ideology" (Waldron 2012, 3). It is sometimes described (usefully, I think) in contradistinction to its converse, the rule of individuals. Commitment to the rule of law may be driven by the perceived consequentialist benefits of enhanced stability and order, or by the belief that "reciprocity and procedural fairness" in the imposition and enforcement of legal requirements are "valuable for [their] own sake" (Finnis 2011, 274).

One way in which adherence to precedent advances the rule of law is by fostering a sense of uniformity, consistency, and reliability. Part of the value is tangible, allowing for better forecasting and more efficient planning. The other part is intangible. In law as in life, the benefits of fidelity to precedent include psychological

---

[14] See 505 U.S. at 856.

[15] Cf. Barnett (2005, 266). Larry Alexander reaches a similar conclusion in Chap. 3 of this volume.

[16] See Nelson (2001, 63) and Lee (1999, 702).

comfort; predictability simply makes us "feel better" (Schauer 1987, 598).[17] That feeling extends to attitudes about the constancy of the legal regime and the stability of the legal order.

The knowledge that a decision will serve as a precedent in future litigation can also promote the rule of law by encouraging judges to view individual cases as reflecting recurring problems that require generalizable, forward-looking solutions. The resulting norm of "generality" reduces the hazards of case- or party-specific idiosyncrasy in the adjudication of disputes (Waldron 2012, 19–20). Similarly, the infusion of precedent with durability that outlasts the tenure of the issuing judges facilitates both the reality and the appearance of decisionmaking that is driven by considerations beyond individual personalities. This ideal of impersonal adjudication resounds in then-Judge Cardozo's (1921, 150) caution against allowing the decisions of courts to ebb and flow with the "weekly changes in [their] composition," as well as Hamilton's (1826) famous depiction of precedent as a safeguard against the exercise of "arbitrary discretion."

These rule-of-law benefits of following precedent arise independently of interpretive method. There are, of course, plausible reasons to be skeptical about the ability of precedent to enhance predictability, generate confidence in the legal regime, contribute to the norm of generality, or reduce the impact of individual idiosyncrasies. Among other things, a critic might contend that the discretionary nature of constitutional stare decisis introduces its own layer of unpredictability and exacerbates the effects of judicial personality. These are serious claims, but interpretive method makes no difference to their validity. The relevance of method only arises later, when a court weighs the rule-of-law implications of continuity against the value of rectifying a constitutional mistake or anachronism.

9.3.1.3 Decisional Economy and Resource Conservation

The costliness of a decisionmaking process depends in part on the number of issues that require determination. By limiting the matters that are open for debate in the course of litigation, the doctrine of stare decisis can enhance adjudicative economy.

These efficiency-enhancing properties are most evident in the context of hierarchical precedent. Given their unconditional obligation to follow the decisions of superior tribunals, inferior federal courts are spared from expending the resources needed to reach their own conclusions. Of course, some of the resources that are saved must be redeployed to sorting through, analogizing from, and distinguishing the array of potentially relevant precedents. Moreover, in cases where the Supreme Court is considering whether to abide by its own precedent, the lingering possibility of overruling may prevent the Court from entirely disregarding the precedent's merits and effects. Nevertheless, efficiency benefits arise even in the horizontal context

[17] Schauer (1987, 598) states: "Predictability thus often has value even when we cannot quantify it."

from the choices of litigants to feature certain arguments and ignore others on the (sensible) theory that many previously-decided issues are highly unlikely to be revisited.

Within a typology that classifies the benefits of precedential continuity based on their connection with interpretive method, efficiency represents another independent consideration. Judicial efficiency is an established concept relating to the amounts of time and energy that are necessary to resolve a case. The doctrinal implications of efficiency considerations—that is, their power to affect the final stare decisis calculus—depend upon methodological choices, but their composition does not.

9.3.2 Independent Costs of Continuity

9.3.2.1 Workability

Judicial decisions that have proved cumbersome in operation are commonly singled out as prime candidates for reconsideration.[18] The retention of such precedents imposes costs on the legal system: When a decision is difficult for subsequent courts to understand and apply, the efficiency of decisionmaking is hindered. Unworkable precedents can also breed uncertainty by reducing the ability of litigants, attorneys, and other stakeholders to plan their behaviors and forecast litigation outcomes.

A precedent's workability is an independent consideration that is determined based on its clarity of exposition and practical operation. It is true that different jurists will evince different tolerances for what degree of clumsiness renders a precedent so unworkable as to warrant revision. They likewise will apply their respective tests differently to concrete sets of facts. But the metrics by which workability is assessed need not be bound up with methodological choices. The question whether a precedent's retention is likely to breed uncertainty and hinder judicial administration can be answered *ex ante*, prior to any methodological election.

9.3.2.2 Jurisprudential Coherence

The steady accumulation of legal doctrine makes it inevitable that discrete bodies of precedent occasionally will come into apparent conflict. One line of cases protects corporations' constitutional right to participate in political referenda, while another denies them the right to speak in support of political candidates. One line upholds the power of a state to criminalize sexual conduct between people of the same gender, while another suggests a competing sphere of personal privacy in which

[18] See, for example, Montejo v. Louisiana, 556 U.S. 778, 792 (2009) ("[T]he fact that a decision has proved 'unworkable' is a traditional ground for overruling it.").

governmental influence is severely constrained. The examples are legion, and they will continue to proliferate as overlapping lines of constitutional precedent become more robust and nuanced. The doctrine of stare decisis has taken notice.

If a reviewing court allows two or more competing lines of precedent to coexist, it risks exacting a toll on jurisprudential coherence. Lower courts and stakeholders may find it difficult to determine which doctrinal strand is relevant to a given course of conduct. The likely results include inefficiencies caused by the need for extensive analysis as well as uncertainty among stakeholding parties about how to organize their affairs. Incoherence also threatens systemic impacts by reducing the rationality, both actual and apparent, of the legal order.

Notwithstanding the significance of these effects, interpretive method once again is inapposite to their composition. Competing precedents can be difficult for stakeholders to square regardless of the methodological approaches those precedents embody. As for the systemic costs of incoherence, they arise from dissonance between judicial decisions irrespective of underlying methodological preferences.

9.3.2.3 Rule of Law (Redux)

I previously discussed the rule-of-law benefits that can arise from the preservation of settled precedent. There is also a second aspect to the relationship between precedent and the rule of law—one that cuts in the opposite direction. Entrenching erroneous decisions for the sake of continuity can impair the soundness of the legal regime. Behaviors that should create one set of constitutional ramifications instead yield a very different set. Litigants who would have been victorious if the Constitution were applied correctly are forced to endure losses in service of the greater good.

Excessive deference to flawed constitutional precedents can also threaten to create systemic concerns for the rule of law. In the worst-case scenario, society is forced to endure pervasive misapplications of its most important document. The ability to agitate for legal changes through reasoned argumentation becomes seriously impaired. The prospects for "growth and reexamination" are gradually "chok[ed] off" by reams of ossified precedents (Stone 1988, 69). And the nation's constitutional culture suffers as the polity lapses into resignation due to its perception of constitutional law as defying realistic efforts at improvement.

I am not suggesting that anything approaching this bleak picture actually obtains in practice. My point is simply that it is too facile to describe precedent and the rule of law as engaged in a common and mutually reinforcing enterprise. It may be true that, on balance, the rule of law is better served by having a doctrine of constitutional stare decisis than it would be without one. Yet it does not follow that the retention of erroneous precedents is entirely positive from the standpoint of the rule of law. In any event, the most important point for present purposes is that the rule-of-law implications of precedent are independent effects of continuity. They maintain the same shape regardless of the interpretive method that one prefers.

9.4 Building the Bridge to Constitutional Method

The independent effects of precedential continuity are critical to assessing the ramifications of adjudicative change. They reflect the value of allowing the law to remain settled by focusing attention on considerations such as expectations and disruption. And some of them—including the benefits that overruling a flawed precedent can create for the rule of law, jurisprudential coherence, and doctrinal workability—begin to capture the countervailing benefits of interpreting the law in a sound and rational manner.

But the value of interpretive accuracy also has another dimension: The benefits that would arise directly from the replacement of the flawed rule with the proper one. This *substantive* dimension of accuracy reflects the proximate consequences of implementing the optimal constitutional interpretation instead of deferring to an erroneous precedent.

9.4.1 Interpretive Method and the Value of Accuracy

The substantive impacts of improving upon a flawed constitutional rule are twofold: the elimination of harms that would otherwise result from the flawed precedent's continued operation, and the generation of affirmative benefits that arise from implementing the correct rule. Neither component can be analyzed in the abstract. The value of correcting an erroneous decision is a fundamentally *dependent* aspect of the inquiry into precedent: It requires the integration of interpretive method and underlying normative premises.[19]

It warrants emphasizing that my objective is not to align myself with any particular movement in constitutional theory. Nor is it to propose my own, alternative constitutional methodology. Rather, I aim to demonstrate that *whatever* one's interpretive theory of choice, it is inextricably linked to the proper treatment of constitutional precedents.

9.4.1.1 The Originalist Perspective

Begin by considering one of the most resonant and provocative methodologies in modern constitutional discourse: originalism. The originalist school is founded on the belief that the linguistic meaning of constitutional terms was "fixed at the time [the terms were] adopted" (Solum 2011, 12). Over the past three decades, debate has swirled around the question of which determinants of original meaning should predominate. An early version of originalism emphasized the primacy

[19] I use the concept of "interpretive" method to indicate both the discernment of the Constitution's meaning and the conversion of that meaning into legal doctrine.

of the subjective intentions of the Constitution's Framers (Kesavan and Paulsen 2003, 1134–35). Other jurists and scholars sought to shift the analytical focus from the Framers' intent to the objective public meaning of the Constitution's text (Solum 2011, 22–24). And the debates over the intricacies of originalist method continue apace.

The debates within the originalist school extend beyond identifying the proper referents of original meaning. The deep theoretical justifications for originalism also vary significantly among the philosophy's adherents. One version of originalism is especially useful in illustrating the connection between interpretive method and constitutional precedent. That version, which we might call *structural* originalism in light of its connection with the Constitution's nature, text, and design, is often associated with commentators such as Gary Lawson (1994).[20] Lawson (1994, 26) justifies his support for originalism by reference to the implicit lesson of *Marbury v. Madison*[21] that judicial review of enacted legislation is authorized only because the Constitution itself is "hierarchically superior to all other claimed sources of law." The same principle, Lawson argues, forecloses deference to judicial precedents that misconstrue the Constitution; a judge who believes that the Constitution's original meaning dictates a certain result may never depart from that result for reasons of stare decisis. Along with Lawson, Michael Paulsen has advocated a vision of structural originalism at odds with constitutional stare decisis. In Paulsen's (2005, 289) words, deference to erroneous precedents "undermines—even refutes—the premises that are supposed to justify originalism."

For a jurist who follows commentators like Lawson and Paulsen in emphasizing the Constitution's inexorable superiority over its judicial gloss, flawed precedents must be overruled regardless of the resulting disruption. Once one adopts a method that treats a certain category of precedents as *ultra vires* and illegitimate, no weighing of countervailing considerations is necessary. The flawed precedents by definition are too harmful to tolerate, and they accordingly must be abandoned. On the rationale of the structural originalists, then, all erroneous precedents are situated identically.

9.4.1.2 The Living-Constitutionalist Perspective

Compare the structural originalist position to an interpretive method that supplants original meaning with factors such as contemporary understandings, mores, and policy judgments. In modern parlance such approaches are often grouped under the heading of living constitutionalism.[22]

---

[20] Cf. "Mostly Unconstitutional: The Case Against Precedent Revisited" (2007), in which Lawson slightly revises his prior approach to accept the use of constitutional precedent if the precedent "is the best available evidence of the right answer to constitutional questions."

[21] 5 U.S. (1 Cranch) 137 (1803).

[22] Cf. Strauss (2010, 1), in which the author states that "[a] 'living constitution' is one that evolves, changes over time, and adapts to new circumstances, without being formally amended."

Among the most influential advocates of living constitutionalism is David Strauss, who has articulated a common-law approach to constitutional interpretation. The common-law constitutionalist's point of departure is "rational traditionalism," which regards past practice as significant for reasons of humility and restraint (Strauss 1996, 891). This rational traditionalism is paired with a principle of "conventionalism" that promotes "allegiance to the text of the Constitution … as a way of avoiding costly and risky disputes and of expressing respect for fellow citizens" (911). Precedent, however, is neither infallible nor obligatory. While there is significant value in tradition and convention, the need remains for constitutional evolution toward a legal order that is morally sound. The virtues of fidelity to the past can be overcome by a subsequent court's "[m]oral or policy judgments" (902). Whether a flawed precedent should be overruled accordingly depends in large part on its substance: The judge must ask how confident she is that a "practice is wrong" and how severe the practical consequences of that wrongness are likely to be (895).

For the living constitutionalist like Strauss, a precedent's consistency or inconsistency with the Constitution's original meaning cannot resolve whether the precedent was decided correctly or incorrectly. Moreover, even if one concludes based on a combination of text, tradition, and policy that a given precedent represents a misapplication of the Constitution, it does not necessarily follow that the precedent is so harmful as to warrant overruling. The perseverance of the precedent might be taken as evincing an "accumulated practical wisdom" that strengthens its claim to continued retention (Strauss 2010, 96). At the same time, even longstanding precedents may become vulnerable based on their implications for morality and policy (Strauss 1996, 895).[23]

The contrast with structural originalism is stark. Because structural originalism treats all decisions that deviate from original meaning as irreparably and dispositively flawed, there is no need for distinguishing among erroneous precedents to decide which should be retained and which should be overruled. From the perspective of living constitutionalism, by comparison, drawing those distinctions is vital. Some erroneous precedents are indeed too harmful to tolerate, but others should endure. The value of constitutional accuracy can vary depending on the nature of a given constitutional mistake. The question becomes whether the substantive "stakes" of perpetuating the error are "high enough" to justify a reversal of course (Strauss 1996, 897).

9.4.1.3 Synthesis

Comparing the originalist and living-constitutionalist methodologies begins to uncover the problem with posing the abstract query of whether stare decisis supports the retention of a dubious decision. The question is unanswerable until one's theory of precedent is situated within a broader vision of constitutional interpretation. For

[23] Cf. Fallon (2001, 584). Fallon argues: "An entrenched precedent that is normatively reprehensible should be viewed as vulnerable in a way that a more attractive practice is not."

adherents of structural originalism, the calculus is simple. If a given constitutional precedent is incorrect, it must be overruled—just like every other precedent that deviates from the original meaning of the Constitution's text. The fate of a flawed precedent is less certain on the living-constitutionalist account. There must first be an evaluation of the harmfulness likely to attend the precedent's retention, which depends in part on the severity of the individual and social costs it imposes.

The fact that living constitutionalism entails a more complex approach to precedent than does structural originalism is not necessarily a weakness. Demanding the rectification of every mistaken precedent, as the structural originalist position requires, arguably reflects insufficient regard for the importance of legal stability. It might follow that the living-constitutionalist approach to precedent is superior despite its thorniness in application. Alternatively, one may be persuaded by the structural originalist argument that, practical consequences aside, the Constitution does not permit the privileging of case law over original meaning. In that event, the structural originalist view is justified in treating constitutional accuracy as paramount. The more foundational point is that whatever the precedent under review, the perceived value of accuracy will vary, often substantially, from one interpretive method to another. Constitutional methodologies and theories of precedent must go hand-in-hand.

9.4.2 *From Interpretive Method to Normative Premises*

No one is born an originalist. Nor is anyone born a living constitutionalist. We arrive at our methodological philosophies through normative choices, explicit or implicit, about the manner in which the Constitution ought to be interpreted (Lash 2007, 1439).

The role of normative premises adds another layer to the relationship between precedent and constitutional method. I claimed in the previous section that it is impossible to determine the value of rectifying an erroneous constitutional rule without drawing on a specified interpretive method. This section contends that while the integration of method is necessary, it is not sufficient. A single interpretive philosophy may spring from any number of distinct ideological commitments. Even within a particular school such as originalism or living constitutionalism, there are vast differences in normative underpinnings that can dramatically alter the perceived gravity of constitutional mistakes.

9.4.2.1 Divergent Strands of Originalism

As we have seen, some originalists base their interpretive philosophy on considerations of constitutional structure. In their view, the Constitution's status as the "supreme Law of the Land,"[24] which is the lynchpin of judicial review as pioneered

[24] U.S. Const. art. VI, cl. 2.

in *Marbury*, forecloses deference to flawed constitutional precedents. Judges take an oath to support the Constitution and are "bound by the text as law" (Kesavan and Paulsen 2003, 1127–28).[25] Erroneous precedents are beyond toleration; they must yield to the Constitution itself.

Structuralist arguments are but one path to originalism. Other commentators champion the originalist approach for reasons that are overtly consequentialist. Prominent among them are John McGinnis and Michael Rappaport, who emphasize the presumptive societal benefits of implementing the Constitution's supermajoritarian dictates.[26] The essence of their position is that fidelity to original meaning is desirable because the Constitution was "enacted in accordance with a supermajoritarian process that generally produces beneficial provisions" (2009, 804–05). McGinnis and Rappaport (831–34) also cite other consequentialist advantages of originalism in the form of legal clarity, predictability, and the channeling of efforts at revision through the formal amendment process.

The consequentialist strand of originalism makes it necessary to distinguish among erroneous precedents in a way that structural originalism does not contemplate. Implicit in the consequentialist approach is the suggestion that the most harmful constitutional mistakes are those that remain politically divisive and defy supermajoritarian consensus.[27] The converse is also true. Thus, irrespective of whether a case like *Brown v. Board of Education*[28] was decided correctly from the perspective of original meaning, its continued retention is unproblematic because its principles enjoy such widespread public support (McGinnis and Rappaport 2009, 837–38). This rationale illuminates a central difference between consequentialist originalism and its structuralist cousin, the latter of which recognizes no possibility that an erroneous precedent could legitimately be reaffirmed due to its popular acceptance. The juxtaposition of consequentialist and structuralist originalism also illustrates that just as there is no "universal" theory of constitutional precedent, there likewise is no "originalist" theory of constitutional precedent. Before the principles of stare decisis can be coherently applied, there must be a deeper inquiry into the normative premises that support the various formulations of originalism. Some originalists will defer to a particular type of precedent, while others will not.

The crucial role of normative premises is underscored by introducing a third version of originalism, this one driven by notions of popular sovereignty. Among the ablest proponents of popular–sovereignty originalism is Kurt Lash. Lash (2007, 1444–45) defends the centrality of "the right of a political majority to determine policy in a democratic government" and the unique ability of constitutional rules to embody "the will of the people." On the popular-sovereigntist account,

---

[25] See also U.S. Const. art. VI, cl. 3.

[26] See, for example, McGinnis and Rappaport (2010, 1695).

[27] Cf. McGinnis and Rappaport (2009, 837), advocating favorable treatment of "entrenched precedents" that "are so strongly supported that they would be enacted by constitutional amendment if they were overturned by the courts."

[28] 347 U.S. 483 (1954).

the value of rectifying a mistaken precedent depends on the extent of its intrusion into the democratic process. The most troubling situations are those in which the Supreme Court has incorrectly recognized a constitutional right, thereby preventing a political majority from responding through anything short of constitutional amendment. Other constitutional mistakes are less severe in their intensity because, for example, their flaw is the failure to protect a constitutional right rather than the entrenchment of a right that should not exist (1443). In those cases, there is the prospect of majoritarian correction through the ordinary legislative process (1465). The availability of a majoritarian solution weakens the need for judicial overruling as a safeguard of popular sovereignty (1443).

While popular-sovereignty originalism resembles consequentialist originalism at the most basic level by recognizing a legitimate province for the reaffirmance of erroneous precedents, the types of precedents that may be retained will vary between the two approaches in accordance with their respective normative baselines. The broader takeaway is that the normative underpinnings that drive one's acceptance of originalism factor heavily into the treatment of constitutional precedent.

9.4.2.2 Divergent Strands of Living Constitutionalism

The necessity of grounding a theory of precedent in an underlying set of normative premises extends beyond originalism. Living constitutionalism faces the same obligation, and for precisely the same reasons.

Like originalists, living constitutionalists subscribe to varying belief sets. The strand of living constitutionalism articulated by David Strauss (2010, 38, 45; 1996, 895) acknowledges that deviations from settled law can be justified for compelling reasons of "fairness and social policy," but it nevertheless places a premium on maintaining continuity over time through the adoption of a common-law approach. Other living constitutionalists are less tethered to gradual progression and more receptive to judicial innovations that advance the "constitutional frontier" (Driver 2011, 398). While common-law constitutionalism emphasizes the virtues of incremental change, the "frontier"-minded approach is motivated in part by an institutional judgment about the utility and propriety of Supreme Court leadership in pursuit of social progress.

These distinct normative priorities lead to distinct theories of precedent: A constitutional lawyer who sympathizes with the frontier-minded approach will be more inclined than a common-law constitutionalist to perceive bold judicial innovations as justifiable even when they disrupt settled expectations and destabilize the political order. Thus, just as different strands of originalism can yield differing appraisals of the importance of implementing the Constitution correctly, so too can the various versions of living constitutionalism, or of any other interpretive method. To be complete, a theory of constitutional precedent must account for both interpretive method and the underlying premises that inform it.

9.5 Constitutional Practice and the Problem of Pluralism

The previous section contended that the modern doctrine of stare decisis is fundamentally derivative. I argued that for the doctrine to achieve coherence, the value of rectifying a mistaken precedent must be situated within an interpretive and normative framework. This section examines the implications of those preconditions for constitutional practice at the U.S. Supreme Court. I will suggest that recognizing the link between precedent and interpretive method poses a serious threat to theory-free, pluralistic approaches to judging.

9.5.1 The Primacy of Independent Effects

In applying the doctrine of stare decisis, the Supreme Court regularly focuses on independent effects of precedential continuity, including the disruption that is likely to result from an overruling and the degree to which a precedent appears inconsistent with other lines of cases. Where the independent costs of overruling are great, the dubious precedent is likely to be retained.[29] Where the independent effects are more equivocal, overruling becomes palatable.[30] Under either scenario, the substantive value of implementing a correct constitutional interpretation—and, at the same time, eradicating an incorrect one—plays a limited role.

At first glance, this practice seems puzzling. The conception of stare decisis as incorporating both the value of settlement and the value of accuracy—recall Justice Brandeis's classic dichotomy—precludes fixating on the independent effects of precedential continuity without also considering the direct, substantive consequences of perpetuating a constitutional mistake. Surely it would matter to some Justices whether the effect of a flawed precedent was, say, to validate the lawfulness of racial segregation in public accommodations as opposed to limiting the authority of states to impose tax-collection obligations on out-of-state retailers. The importance of getting the law right can look very different from case to case and context to context.

Yet there remains within the jurisprudence a notable lack of attention to the substantive ramifications of interpretive accuracy. This phenomenon extends to even the most high-profile applications of stare decisis. In *Casey*, for example, the Court emphasized considerations of reliance and institutional legitimacy as warranting the reaffirmance of *Roe*.[31] Pursuant to the Court's own descriptions of the doctrine of stare decisis, its inquiry also should have included a weighing of those considerations against the substantive value of interpreting the Constitution

[29] See, for example, Dickerson v. United States, 530 U.S. 428, 443–44 (2000); *Casey*, 505 U.S. at 860; Quill Corp. v. North Dakota, 504 U.S. 298, 317 (1992).

[30] See, for example, Citizens United v. Federal Election Commission, 130 S. Ct. 876, 913 (2010) ("No serious reliance interests are at stake."); Lawrence v. Texas, 539 U.S. 558, 577 (2003); Payne v. Tennessee, 501 U.S. 808, 828–30 (1991).

[31] See *Casey*, 505 U.S. at 855–56, 861–69.

correctly. On that latter score, the Court said precious little. It made brief reference to the "consequences" of abortion and the possibility that, "depending on one's beliefs," the resulting harms may include the unjust termination of human life.[32] But it went no further, implying that because the costs of renouncing *Roe* were significant, there was no need to dwell on the substantive impacts of retaining it.

It would be an overstatement to claim that the Court *never* mentions the substantive effects of reaffirming erroneous precedents. To take a recent example, in *Citizens United v. Federal Election Commission* the Court noted that a ban on independent expenditures by corporations in support of political candidates would impoverish the marketplace of ideas[33] and validate the insidious exercise of governmental "censorship to control thought."[34] Other opinions likewise reveal the Justices' view that there is significant value in affording expressive liberties the full protection they are due under the Constitution.[35] Similar sentiments can be glimpsed in areas such as the Fourth Amendment's prohibition against unlawful searches.[36] The Court has also noted the potential consequences of over-protecting certain rights, as in its recognition that application of the *Miranda* rules could result in the exclusion of voluntary statements and allow "a guilty defendant [to] go free."[37] And in the statutory context, the Court has acknowledged—without passing judgment on—the argument that erroneous precedents are most in need of overruling when they have proven "inconsistent with the sense of justice or with the social welfare."[38]

These statements suggest an enduring role for the substantive value of accuracy within the stare decisis calculus. Still, the Court's treatment of substantive accuracy tends to be cursory and undeveloped. A tossed-off, abstract reference to the ramifications of a given constitutional mistake—along the lines of "failing to safeguard free speech is bad" or "protecting against unlawful searches is good"—is no substitute for careful scrutiny of its severity. More is needed in order to discharge the Court's self-imposed obligation of comparing the costs of upsetting the law against the benefits of interpretive accuracy.

9.5.2 Institutional Pluralism

Ours is not an originalist Supreme Court. To be sure, the Court often refers to the Constitution's original meaning in explaining its decisions, and originalism occasionally takes center stage. A recent example comes from *District of Columbia v.*

[32] *Id.* at 852.

[33] *Citizens United*, 130 S. Ct. at 912.

[34] *Id.* at 908.

[35] See Federal Election Commission v. Wisconsin Right to Life, 551 U.S. 449, 500 (2007) (Scalia, J, concurring in part and concurring in the judgment).

[36] See Arizona v. Gant, 556 U.S. 332, 349 (2009).

[37] *Dickerson*, 530 U.S. at 444.

[38] Patterson v. McClean Credit Union, 491 U.S. 164, 174 (1989) (quoting Runyon v. McCrary, 427 U.S. 160, 191 (1976) (Stevens, J., concurring) (quoting Cardozo 1921, 149) (internal quotation marks omitted)).

Heller, in which the Court adopted a predominantly originalist focus in determining whether the Second Amendment protects an individual right to possess firearms.[39] But at other times, the Court resolves constitutional questions with little or no attention to original meaning. Depending on the case, factors such as text, history, precedent, justice, political philosophy, and government policy might drive the analysis. The Court has not hazarded an overarching theory to explain the fluctuating relevance of the various considerations. As a result, though there is a predictable array of modalities of constitutional reasoning, their impact on judicial opinions defies explanation by any single organizing principle.

This state of affairs might be taken to suggest that the Court's constitutional jurisprudence embraces the precepts of *pragmatism*. Some leading advocates of legal pragmatism tend to describe it as akin to an anti-theory, encompassing all potential sources of constitutional meaning without being beholden to rigid rules of decision.[40] The pragmatists' benchmark is the achievement of constitutional outcomes that yield the best "results for society" (Farber 1988, 1353). But as examples like *Heller* indicate, the Court sometimes depicts social policy as subordinate or inapposite in resolving thorny constitutional questions. That practice distances its approach from genuine pragmatism, which acknowledges the potential importance of factors like "original intent" but does not allow them to become "decisive" (1353). At most, the Court's constitutionalism is intermittently pragmatic, just as it is intermittently originalist.

The best description of the Court's interpretive approach is not pragmatic but *pluralistic*. It is defined by the absence of any consistent methodological commitment, including even a commitment to pragmatic resolution of disputes. The Court emphasizes various interpretive modalities from case to case—and often within the same case—without suggesting "that the different methods are reducible to one master method," much less furnishing a passkey for undertaking such a decryption (Griffin 1994, 1757).

The prevalence of pluralism owes in part to the Court's composition of different individuals appointed by different Presidents and espousing different judicial philosophies. The institutional dynamics of the Court as a multimember body reduce the probability of methodological consensus. To take just one example, Justice Thomas is especially attentive to the Constitution's original public meaning. His colleagues are, to varying degrees, more inclined to reject originalist prescriptions in light of factors including precedent and social policy. That sort of methodological diversity makes it less likely that five or more Justices will endorse originalism—or, for that matter, any other unified theory of constitutional interpretation.

9.5.3 Individual Pluralism

Practically speaking, judicial decisions are not made by the Supreme Court. They are made by the Justices who comprise it. A second layer of interpretive pluralism

[39] 554 U.S. 570, 576, 605 (2008).

[40] See, for example, Posner (1998, 9) and Farber (1988, 1332).

emerges from the views of the Court's individual members. The validity of adjudicating constitutional disputes through application of a "grand theory" (Tushnet 1988, 1) continues to be a matter of extensive debate. Judge J. Harvie Wilkinson (2012, 4) recently authored an important book that criticizes leading constitutional theories as "competing schools of liberal and conservative judicial activism," while Judge Richard Posner (1998) has expressed similar dissatisfaction with constitutional theory. And commentators like Cass Sunstein (1996, 20–21) advocate the resolution of constitutional disputes through "incompletely theorized agreements" precisely to avoid disagreements over "first principles."

Sympathy for these arguments reaches all the way to the Supreme Court. The experience of John Roberts is a case in point. During his confirmation hearings in 2005, then-Judge Roberts disavowed allegiance to any single theory of constitutional law.[41] He explained that rather than drawing on abstract theory, he favors "bottom up" judging.[42] He elaborated in a response to Senator Orrin Hatch:

> If the phrase in the Constitution says two-thirds of the Senate, everybody's a literalist when they interpret that. Other phrases in the Constitution are broader[, such as] "unreasonable searches and seizures." You can look at that wording all day and it's not going to give you much progress in deciding whether a particular search is reasonable or not. You have to begin looking at the cases and the precedents, what the Framers had in mind when they drafted that provision.
>
> So, yes, it depends on the nature of the case before you I think.[43]

It is worth pausing to note that despite Chief Justice Roberts's protestations, his vision bears some hallmarks of a bona fide theory of constitutional interpretation. First, the Constitution's specific textual commands must be interpreted literally. Second, when the Constitution sets forth broad standards, respect for the document requires resort to other interpretive techniques. On these points, the Chief Justice is in accord with theories such as Jack Balkin's (2011, 6) "living originalism," which embraces a similar distinction between "determinate rule[s]" and broad standards.

Despite these tendencies in the direction of grand theory, Chief Justice Roberts established himself as a theory-skeptic through his attitude toward methodological consistency. The Chief Justice made no pretense of consulting a unified principle to guide the weighing of relevant factors across different types of cases. Constitutional text will control in some cases, history in others, and precedent in still others.[44] Determining which modality will govern is done on a case-by-case basis. Therein lies the true significance of the "bottom up" descriptor: It reflects the Chief Justice's adoption of interpretive pluralism.

---

[41] See Confirmation Hearing on the Nomination of John G. Roberts, Jr., to Be Chief Justice of the United States, 109th Cong. 159 (2005) (hereafter Roberts Confirmation Hearing). At the hearing, then-Judge Roberts said, "I have said that I do not have an overarching judicial philosophy that I bring to every case, and I think that's true." As Gerhardt (2008, 193) notes, "John Roberts avoided controversy by rejecting fidelity to any particular theory of constitutional interpretation."

[42] Roberts Confirmation Hearing at 159.

[43] *Id.*

[44] See *id.* Then-Judge Roberts explained, "[T]he approaches do vary, and I don't have an overarching view" (182).

The example of Chief Justice Roberts illustrates that the Court's pluralism is not solely the product of its multimember composition. It is also the result of individual choice. Nor is the Chief Justice alone in his pluralism. Five years after the Chief's confirmation, Justice Kagan offered her own endorsement of a "case-by-case" approach to interpretive method.[45] For case-by-case Justices, methodological diversity is an individual phenomenon as much as an institutional one. Even if the Court were made up of nine John Robertses or nine Elena Kagans, its interpretive method would remain variable, sometimes proceeding in accord with philosophies such as originalism or living constitutionalism and sometimes heading off in other directions.

9.5.4 Theories of Precedent in Pluralism's Wake

The preceding sections have sought to establish a pair of related propositions. First, in conducting its analyses of precedent, the Supreme Court commonly fails to engage with the direct, substantive impact of implementing the correct constitutional rule. Second, the interpretive approach of both the Court as an institution and some of its individual members is deeply pluralistic, eschewing any commitment to a consistent constitutional method.

Placing these propositions side by side suggests a solution to the puzzle of why the independent effects of precedent dominate the Court's stare decisis jurisprudence. I have contended that integration of a definitive interpretive method, as informed by an underlying set of normative premises, is necessary to assess the value of rectifying a flawed precedent. If that claim is correct, forsaking interpretive theory in favor of pluralism should preclude a full inquiry into the importance of getting the law right. The interpretive pluralist's natural response would be to focus on the *independent* effects of precedential continuity, which do not require the integration of interpretive method. And that is just what the Court tends to do. While this reaction is understandable, it is nevertheless unsatisfactory. By giving short shrift to the substantive dimension of constitutional accuracy, the Court subverts its articulated doctrine of stare decisis.

So how is a Supreme Court Justice to proceed when she is confronted by a constitutional precedent that she views as on-point but incorrect? The most straightforward situation is that involving a Justice who is committed to a defined interpretive philosophy. Such a philosophy furnishes a metric for the Justice to utilize in appraising the severity of constitutional errors. For example, Justice Stephen Breyer (2010, 75) has advocated a paramount focus on ensuring that fundamental

[45] See Confirmation Hearing on the Nomination of Elena Kagan to Be an Associate Justice of the Supreme Court of the United States, 111th Cong. 81 (2010) ("I think in general judges should look to a variety of sources when they interpret the Constitution, and which take precedence in a particular case is really a kind of case-by-case thing.").

constitutional values are borne out in practice.[46] To him, the severity of a constitutional mistake depends on its pragmatic effects. Thus, the primary reason for overruling a case like *Plessy v. Ferguson* was that it "worked incalculable harm" and fell short of promoting equal accommodations—let alone equal respect—for people of all races (150). But Justice Breyer also emphasizes the need for a "thumb on the scale in the direction of stability," suggesting that constitutional mistakes with less dire consequences than *Plessy* often will be innocuous enough to tolerate (153). Justice Thomas, by comparison, commonly takes the position that erroneous precedents should be repudiated.[47] His opinions provide some reason to suspect that he views many deviations from the Constitution's original public meaning as deeply problematic.

A trickier situation is the one exemplified by Justice Scalia's jurisprudence. Justice Scalia is not properly described as a bottom-up judge in the style of Chief Justice Roberts or Justice Kagan. To the contrary, he has taken great care to articulate an overarching interpretive philosophy of originalism to guide his constitutional decisions. At the same time, Justice Scalia has noted that he occasionally will depart from original meaning based on the presumptive benefits of preserving settled law.[48] The result is what he calls a "faint-hearted" version of originalism (Scalia 1989, 864).[49]

As I have suggested with respect to popular-sovereigntist originalism and consequentialist originalism, it is possible for originalist theories to permit the retention of flawed precedents in certain circumstances while remaining theoretically coherent. The *sine qua non* is the invocation of normative premises that provide a principled basis for assessing the degree of harm threatened by the perpetuation of a given constitutional mistake. The crucial question in evaluating Justice Scalia's treatment of precedent is whether he consults a defined normative baseline that can explain both (a) his general preference for original meaning and (b) his view that the importance of correcting constitutional mistakes can sometimes be overridden. If he does act with reference to such a baseline, there is no inherent reason why his precedent-tolerating approach to originalism is untenable.

Finally, we come to those who resist constitutional theory in favor of interpretive pluralism. By disavowing any consistent interpretive method, the pluralists find themselves at odds with the enterprise of constitutional stare decisis. Without a theory for assessing the substantive dimensions of constitutional errors, they lack

[46] Justice Breyer (2010, 75) believes that "the Court should regard the Constitution as containing unwavering values that must be applied flexibly to ever-changing circumstances."

[47] See, for example, McDonald v. City of Chicago, 13 S. Ct. 3020, 3063 (2010) (Thomas, J., concurring in part and concurring in the judgment); Morse v. Frederick, 551 U.S. 393, 410 (2007) (Thomas, J., concurring); Van Orden v. Perry, 545 U.S. 677, 692–93 (2005) (Thomas, J., concurring).

[48] Justice Scalia explains that "*stare decisis* is not *part of* [his] originalist philosophy; it is a pragmatic *exception* to it" (1997, 140) (emphases in original).

[49] Justice Scalia (1997, 138–39) also states, "Originalism, like any other theory of interpretation put into practice in an ongoing system of law, must accommodate the doctrine of *stare decisis*; it cannot remake the world anew".

the tools to appraise the value of constitutional accuracy in any given case. The problem cannot be cured through "bottom up" judging that treats precedent as among an array of relevant factors. Even on an eclectic approach to constitutionalism in which multiple considerations are relevant to the treatment of precedent, there must be some theory for determining how the considerations work together and what happens when they diverge. In the absence of such a theory, the invocation of self-binding precedent is provisionally unsound: unsound because it resists attempts at principled application, but provisionally so because, as explained below, potential solutions are available.

There is admittedly an element of, if not paradox, at least irony in the conclusion that interpretive pluralism cannot be squared with deference to constitutional precedent. Strong deference to precedent might be seen as a response to the very existence of methodological diversity, which increases the probability that a given Justice will perceive certain precedents as mistaken simply because she adheres to an interpretive method that differs from that of her predecessors. The doctrine of stare decisis responds by establishing a presumption of deference notwithstanding the proliferation of diverse interpretive methods. It thereby reduces the destabilizing effects of intertemporal diversity among successive waves of Justices.[50] Yet the conflict between interpretive pluralism and constitutional precedent persists. It may be true that deference to precedent is effective at preserving a stable core within judicial systems characterized by methodological diversity. Nevertheless, the fact remains that without reference to interpretive method, a pluralist has no consistent basis for evaluating the costs of constitutional mistakes.

The incompatibility of stare decisis (as the doctrine is presently articulated by the Court) with pluralistic approaches to interpretation does not extend to every manner in which precedent is invoked. Precedent plays a variety of roles beyond institutional self-binding that are left untouched by the failure to integrate constitutional method. For example, the function of precedent as a means of hierarchical control is not affected, nor is the use of precedent for purposes of persuasion. Only when a Justice describes a precedent as genuinely constraining—that is, as dictating a result that would not obtain but for the precedent's existence—does pluralism become a conceptual obstacle.

9.5.5 Surveying the Potential Solutions

For the interpretive pluralist who wishes to pursue a workable theory of constitutional precedent, three potential options are available: uniform integration of interpretive method across cases; integration of interpretive method on a context-dependent

[50] For a comparable suggestion in the context of statutory stare decisis, see CBOCS West, Inc. v. Humphries, 553 U.S. 442, 457 (2008) ("Principles of *stare decisis* … demand respect for precedent whether judicial methods of interpretation change or stay the same. Were that not so, those principles would fail to achieve the legal stability that they seek and upon which the rule of law depends.").

basis; and adoption of an absolutist approach to precedent. A fourth option would require the intervention of the Supreme Court as an institution: the Court could respond to the challenges created by interpretive pluralism by redesigning the doctrine of stare decisis to exclude the substantive dimensions of constitutional accuracy. Finally, there is the possibility that any dissonance could be overcome through the mechanisms of judicial courtesy and compromise.

9.5.5.1 Uniform Integration

The simplest solution for the pluralist Justice who seeks a coherent approach to constitutional precedent is to undertake the project of constructing a consistent, overarching theory of constitutional interpretation. With such a theory in place, there would be a ready mechanism for assessing the costs of constitutional mistakes. A Justice who devoted herself to a particular interpretive strategy, guided by underlying normative premises, would be well-positioned to fashion a principled theory of precedent. Of course, she would also cease to be an interpretive pluralist.

9.5.5.2 Context-Dependent Integration

Rather than restyling herself as an adherent of one interpretive school or another, our pluralist Justice could articulate a context-dependent set of interpretive methodologies. For instance, originalism might provide the appropriate lens in interpreting the Second Amendment's right to bear arms. In other areas, perhaps including application of the Free Speech Clause, originalism might give way to methodologies such as living constitutionalism or pragmatism. Within each context, the Justice would also articulate a normative justification for her approach, from structuralism or consequentialism in the originalist domains to common-law adjudication or judicial leadership in the domains of living constitutionalism.

The context-dependent approach would not result in any uniform methodological election. Within the contours of a given dispute, however, it would yield an effective apparatus for assigning value to the correction of constitutional mistakes. In a category of cases where structural originalism provided the rule of decision, all constitutional errors would be deemed intolerable; the value of accuracy would trump. By comparison, in categories where common-law constitutionalism reigned supreme, the relevant costs of retaining a flawed precedent would include considerations of justice and social policy.

The central distinction between the context-dependent approach and pure pluralism is the former's commitment to the consistent utilization of predefined methodologies within particular substantive contexts. By furnishing a set of metrics for gauging the intensity of constitutional mistakes, the context-dependent approach addresses the problem of provisional unsoundness. But its success comes at a price—and one that brings the broader vulnerabilities of interpretive pluralism into relief. The context-dependent model entails that in some situations, factors such as policy outcomes will be integral to the severity of a constitutional error. In other situations, policy outcomes will be inapposite. Likewise, a precedent's harmfulness might occasionally be determined by its compatibility with principles of popular sovereignty or supermajoritarian consensus, while in other cases those considerations would have no role to play.

The implications are not different in kind from the implications of interpretive pluralism more generally. After all, pluralism contemplates judicial responsiveness to different indicia of constitutional meaning from case to case and context to context. Yet viewing these consequences through the prism of precedent makes the drawbacks of methodological inconsistency more vivid. The doctrine of stare decisis seeks to promote and accommodate systemic interests in stability, rationality, and the rule of law. Judicial vacillation over the criteria for evaluating the harmfulness of constitutional mistakes is at odds with those norms.

9.5.5.3 Absolutism

If our hypothetical Supreme Court Justice is not prepared to renounce pluralism as her preferred approach to constitutional interpretation, she might consider revising her approach to precedent. Her objective would be to avoid any need for assessing the substantive value of replacing incorrect constitutional rules. There are two forms such a reorientation could take.

Our Justice might resolve that from this day forward she will cease to vote for the overruling of any constitutional precedent. Instead, she will leave the correction of constitutional errors entirely to the Article V amendment process. The Justice would still need to grapple with issues of precedential scope in determining whether a prior decision was, in fact, controlling. But she would be spared the task of making case-by-case determinations about the comparative value of leaving the law settled versus getting the law right.

Relinquishing the judicial power to overrule is strong medicine. So, too, is the pluralistic Justice's second potential option, which is the converse of the first: The Justice could disavow any discretion to reaffirm a constitutional precedent that she views as incorrect. In effect, constitutional stare decisis would be excised from her jurisprudence. All constitutional questions would be resolved based solely on their merits.

9.5.5.4 Doctrinal Redesign

Both absolute deference and zero deference would represent rather severe responses to the incompatibility of pluralism with the doctrine of stare decisis. That severity is not disqualifying, but as a practical matter it does reduce the solutions' appeal. It is thus worth considering whether the Supreme Court might find a more palatable response through some other means.

The tension between stare decisis and pluralism is traceable to the modern doctrine's dual focus on the values of settlement and accuracy. The latter consideration is what necessitates the integration of interpretive method as a means of evaluating the severity of constitutional mistakes. Remove that consideration, and we can circumvent the problem of provisional unsoundness.

The Court might, for example, recast the doctrine of stare decisis as entirely dependent on the disruptive impact of adjudicative change, such that an erroneous precedent would be retained if and only if the disruption likely to accompany its overruling exceeds some predefined threshold. This version of stare decisis could be applied without any integration of interpretive method. Upon concluding that a precedent was mistaken, the Justices would have no need for aligning themselves with interpretive schools like originalism or living constitutionalism. They would simply consider the disruptiveness of reversing course.

In lieu of this disruption-based approach, the Court could resolve the tension between pluralism and precedent by redesigning the doctrine of stare decisis to focus on other independent effects of precedential continuity, such as jurisprudential coherence or workability. The common denominator among the available solutions is disregard for the substantive value of correct interpretation. The direct benefits of replacing a mistaken rule would play no role in the stare decisis analysis. The moment those benefits reentered the fold, the problem of provisional unsoundness would return along with them.

It is not quite correct to say that such a formulation of stare decisis would be *entirely* independent of interpretive method. Even an approach grounded exclusively in the independent effects of precedent would allow deference in some situations, a result that is inconsistent with philosophies such as structural originalism. The independent-effects approach therefore is better described as only thinly method-based. Once a court accepted the threshold proposition that deference to erroneous precedent is constitutionally permissible, it would be free from any obligation to draw distinctions among constitutional errors. The substantive effects of the erroneous precedent would be irrelevant to the precedent's retention or abandonment. Whether a case dealt with abortion rights or criminal procedure, taxation powers or racial discrimination, its direct consequences would be beside the point.

To be sure, such an approach would impose a potentially significant (depending on one's interpretive sympathies) cost by rendering the substantive effects of a precedent inapposite to its durability. And interpretive pluralism would continue to present other challenges for the process of constitutional adjudication; debates and uncertainty over interpretive theory would remain pivotal in making the threshold determination of whether a given precedent was correct or incorrect. Still, grounding the treatment of precedent exclusively in independent considerations such as reliance would prevent the doctrine of stare decisis from being subsumed by disagreements over interpretive theory. In a second-best world in which interpretive and normative pluralism seem unavoidable as a practical matter, perhaps that infusion of independence is enough to justify recasting stare decisis purely in terms of reliance effects, so as to provide the doctrine with an enduring core that transcends changes in judicial personnel and interpretive philosophy. At the very least, the question warrants further exploration.

9.5.5.5 Judicial Compromise

Finally, it is worth considering whether the dissonance between pluralism and stare decisis might be worked out through the simple mechanism of judicial compromise. Different Supreme Court Justices may harbor different views as to what makes an erroneous precedent so harmful as to warrant overruling. But they might find ways to come together around their common ground—for example, by agreeing that the precedent should be retained, even if they disagree over the reason why. Those Justices could then compromise over an opinion that is "shallow" enough to be agreeable to all of them.[51] Alternatively, they might choose to join an opinion that reaches the correct result even if they have quibbles over the way in which the issue of stare decisis is handled.

I see the virtues of both approaches, and I suspect that they occur with some regularity in practice. Yet they provide an incomplete solution to the problem of pluralism. Crafting shallow opinions will tend to reduce the institutional pluralism that results from different Justices' adherence to different methodologies. Of course, it does so at the expense of analytical exposition, which is a trade-off that should give us pause. But more to the point for present purposes, shallow opinion-writing does not solve the problem of individual pluralism. Before he engages with issues of multimember courts and institutional compromise, a jurist must determine, in his own mind, what the proper metric is for assessing the value of getting the law right. Until he undertakes that analysis, shallow opinion-writing will merely paper over a skipped analytical step.

9.5.6 A Dose of Realism?

Might it be that the integration of interpretive method with constitutional precedent is already occurring, *sub rosa* or perhaps even subconsciously, in the Supreme Court's cases?

For example, the Justices might conduct in-depth examinations of the substantive value of accuracy based on their respective philosophical predispositions and normative premises, but then refrain from weaving those examinations into their written opinions. This prospect seems unlikely, as there is no apparent explanation for why the Justices would be inclined to obscure that type of analysis from public view while providing elaborate explanations of their other interpretive moves.

An alternative theory is more plausible. It posits that when the Justices confront dubious precedents, they draw on basic, vaguely-formed intuitions regarding the relative severity of constitutional mistakes. When a Justice declares that she is willing to stand by a precedent for the sake of stare decisis, she is implying that the costs of perpetuating the constitutional mistake are below some internal threshold, even if she does not have a developed theory of interpretation in mind.

---

[51] See generally Sunstein (1996).

It is impossible to know how often this latter scenario reflects the Justices' actual practice. But we can stipulate to its correctness without meaningfully affecting the analysis presented in this chapter. For a Justice whose instincts suggest that a given type of constitutional error is especially harmful, a principled theory of precedent requires unpacking that intuition to test its consistency with the Justice's broader interpretive approach. As we have seen, some approaches to valuing constitutional mistakes are, while superficially plausible, nevertheless irreconcilable with certain interpretive methods. The rule of law demands that personal intuition be transcended rather than indulged.

The Justice who views one constitutional mistake as more harmful than another must explain which normative premises justify her view and whether those premises are consistent with her interpretive method. In the event of an inconsistency, it is incumbent upon the Justice either to overcome her initial intuitions of harmfulness or to adjust her broader theory of constitutional interpretation to take them into account. And in light of the Court's laudable commitment to thorough reason-giving, the appropriate forum for that deliberative process is a written opinion, not the Justice's own mind.

9.6 Conclusion

Contending that a theory of precedent compels a particular result of its own volition runs into a problem of infinite regress, calling to mind Stephen Hawking's (1988, 1) anecdote about "turtles all the way down." Certain factors that are relevant to the choice between retaining and overruling a flawed precedent are amenable to preliminary scrutiny in isolation from interpretive method. But the modern doctrine of stare decisis is founded on the premise that the value of leaving the law settled must ultimately be weighed against the value of getting the law right. Negotiating that tension requires the integration of interpretive method as informed by underlying normative premises. In the absence of such integration, there is no coherent mechanism for defining the value of constitutional accuracy.

References

Balkin JM (2011) Living originalism. Belknap Press of Harvard University Press, Cambridge, MA

Barnett RE (2005) Trumping precedent with original meaning: not as radical as it sounds. Constitutional Comment 22(2):257–270

Breyer S (2010) Making our democracy work: a judge's view. Alfred A. Knopf, New York

Breyer S (2011) Making our democracy work: the Yale lectures. Yale Law J 120(9):1999–2026

Calabresi SG (2005) Text, precedent, and the Constitution: some originalist and normative arguments for overruling *Planned Parenthood of Southeastern Pennsylvania v. Casey*. Constitutional Comment 22(2):311–348

Caminker EH (1994) Why must inferior courts obey superior court precedents? Stanford Law Rev 46(4):817–873

Cardozo BN (1921) The nature of the judicial process. Yale University Press, New Haven
Driver J (2011) The significance of the frontier in American constitutional law. Supreme Court Rev 2011:345–398
Eliot TS (1998) The love song of J. Alfred Prufrock. In: The waste land, Prufrock, and other poems. Dover Publications, Mineola, pp 1–5
Fallon RH Jr (2001) Stare decisis and the Constitution: an essay on constitutional methodology. N Y Univ Law Rev 76(2):570–597
Farber DA (1988) Legal pragmatism and the Constitution. Minn Law Rev 72(6):1331–1378
Finnis J (2011) Natural law and natural rights. Oxford University Press, New York
Gerhardt MJ (2008) The power of precedent. Oxford University Press, New York
Griffin SM (1994) Pluralism in constitutional interpretation. Tex Law Rev 72(7):1753–1769
Hamilton A (1826) Federalist no.78. In: Federalist, on the new constitution. Glazier & Company, Hallowell, pp 432–439
Hawking SW (1988) A brief history of time: from the big bang to black holes. Bantam Books, New York
Kesavan V, Paulsen MS (2003) The interpretive force of the Constitution's secret drafting history. Georgetown Law J 91(6):1113–1214
Kozel RJ (2013) Settled versus right: constitutional method and the path of precedent. Tex Law Rev 91(7):1845–1896
Lash KT (2007) Originalism, popular sovereignty, and reverse stare decisis. Va Law Rev 93(6):1437–1481
Lawson G (1994) The constitutional case against precedent. Harv J Law Publ Policy 17(1):23–33
Lawson G (2007) Mostly unconstitutional: the case against precedent revisited. Ave Maria Law Rev 5(1):1–22
Lee TR (1999) Stare decisis in historical perspective: from the founding era to the Rehnquist Court. Vanderbilt Law Rev 52(3):647–735
McGinnis JO, Rappaport MB (2009) Reconciling originalism and precedent. Northwest Univ Law Rev 103(2):803–856
McGinnis JO, Rappaport MB (2010) Originalism and the good Constitution. Georgetown Law J 98(6):1693–1768
Nelson C (2001) Stare decisis and demonstrably erroneous precedent. Va Law Rev 87(1):1–84
Paulsen MS (2005) The intrinsically corrupting influence of precedent. Constitutional Comment 22(2):289–298
Posner RA (1998) Against constitutional theory. NY Univ Law Rev 73(1):1–22
Scalia A (1997) A matter of interpretation: federal courts and the law. Princeton University Press, Princeton
Scalia A (1989) Originalism: the lesser evil. Univ Cincinnati Law Rev 57(3):849–865
Schauer F (1987) Precedent. Stanford Law Rev 39(3):571–605
Shakespeare W (1988) Hamlet. In: Bevington D, Kastan DS (eds) Four tragedies: Hamlet, Othello, King Lear, Macbeth. Bantam Books, New York, pp 1–274
Solum LB (2011) What is originalism? The evolution of contemporary originalist theory. In: Huscroft G, Miller BW (eds) The challenge of originalism: theories of constitutional interpretation. Cambridge University Press, Cambridge, pp 12–41
Stone GR (1988) Precedent, the amendment process, and evolution in constitutional doctrine. Harv J Law Publ Policy 11(1):67–73
Strauss DA (1996) Common law constitutional interpretation. Univ Chicago Law Rev 63(3):877–935
Strauss DA (2010) The living Constitution. Oxford University Press, New York
Sunstein CR (1996) Foreword: leaving things undecided. Harv Law Rev 110(1):4–101
Sunstein CR (2006) Burkean minimalism. Mich Law Rev 105(2):353–408
Tushnet M (1988) Red, white, and blue: a critical analysis of constitutional law. Harvard University Press, Cambridge, MA
Waldron J (2012) Stare decisis and the rule of law: a layered approach. Mich Law Rev 111(1):1–31
Wilkinson JH III (2012) Cosmic constitutional theory: why Americans are losing their inalienable right to self-governance. Oxford University Press, New York

Chapter 10
Originalism, Stare Decisis, and Constitutional Authority

Christopher J. Peters

Abstract This chapter examines the relationship among three normative questions about American constitutional law: How should the Constitution be interpreted? When may (or should) the Supreme Court overrule its own constitutional precedents? And why is the Constitution binding at all? The author begins by deconstructing the "special difficulty" with stare decisis that proponents of originalist interpretation often perceive. That difficulty, the author contends, can be explained only by reference to some underlying normative theory of constitutional authority—of why the Constitution binds us in the first place. The author then assesses four extant accounts of constitutional authority to determine whether any of them implies both originalism and a distrust of stare decisis. While three such accounts (Values Imposition, Consent, and Moral Guidance) may support originalism and reject stare decisis, none of these accounts is plausible. A fourth account (Dispute Resolution) is more plausible but implies neither strong originalism nor a rejection of stare decisis. Neither originalism nor distrust of precedent, therefore, appears to be supported by a plausible account of constitutional authority.

10.1 Originalism and Stare Decisis: An Introductory Puzzle

"[O]riginalism … seem[s] to have a special difficulty with precedent" (Barnett 2006, 257). This is the diagnosis offered by Randy Barnett, an influential theorist of American constitutional law and a self-professed originalist. It is a diagnosis that is hard to dispute. Over the past quarter century or so, as Barnett proudly (and I think accurately) reports, originalism "has thrived like no other approach to interpretation"

C.J. Peters (✉)
School of Law, University of Baltimore,
1420 North Charles St., Baltimore, MD 21201, USA
e-mail: cpeters@ubalt.edu

C.J. Peters (ed.), *Precedent in the United States Supreme Court*, Ius Gentium: Comparative Perspectives on Law and Justice 33, DOI 10.1007/978-94-007-7951-8_10,

in American constitutional theory and practice (2006, 257). But with its rise has come a vigorous debate within its ranks over the propriety of constitutional stare decisis—the Supreme Court's presumptive deference to its prior constitutional decisions. Some originalists reject stare decisis in all or nearly all cases;[1] others accept it halfheartedly and regretfully;[2] a few attempt explanations, often lengthy and angst-ridden, of why originalism allows for some allegiance to precedent after all.[3] When originalist theorists and judges get together to talk about their ideas, constitutional stare decisis is among their most popular topics.[4]

This is a chapter in a book about constitutional stare decisis, not about originalism or any other type of constitutional interpretation. But I hope to lend support to the insight offered by Randy Kozel in Chap. 9 of this volume that the relationship between the two methodological issues is close and unavoidable. Originalism is a type of answer to a persistent question in American constitutional law and theory: the question of *interpretive methodology*, of how courts (or other interpreters) ought to go about the task of determining constitutional meaning in particular cases. Originalism holds that constitutional meaning should be determined primarily or exclusively by reference to some meaning ("original intent" or "original public meaning") that existed at the time of the Constitution's Framing. For its part, stare decisis requires its own type of methodology: In the form that concerns us here, it insists that the Supreme Court should decide constitutional cases in ways consistent with its prior decisions, even if a current majority of the Court now believes those decisions to be wrong.[5] Originalism's "difficulty with precedent" arises from the fact that the two methodologies sometimes seem to conflict. Deciding a case according to the original intent or original public meaning may require a different result than deciding it consistently with the (nonoriginalist or otherwise incorrect) decision in a prior case.

I will take issue with many originalists, however, to argue that this apparent clash of methodological commands alone cannot explain originalism's "special" difficulty with precedent. It is a clash, after all, that arises under almost any methodology of constitutional interpretation, originalist or not. In order to locate the "special difficulty with precedent" that worries contemporary originalists like Barnett, we have to dig beneath the surface of both originalism and stare decisis to

[1] For example, Gary Lawson (1994, 2007) and Michael Stokes Paulsen (2003, 2005).

[2] Such as Justice Antonin Scalia (1997b, 138–40).

[3] Including John McGinnis and Michael Rappaport (2009b), Kurt Lash (2007), Lee Strang (2006), and Randy Barnett (2006).

[4] Two prominent examples are a symposium published in 2005 in volume 22 of the journal *Constitutional Commentary* and a panel discussion (later published in a book) commemorating the twenty-fifth anniversary of the Federalist Society in 2007 (see Calabresi 2007a, 199–252).

[5] This question is of course distinct from other issues relating to stare decisis in constitutional cases that will not be my focus here. These distinct issues include whether state courts and lower federal courts within the U.S. system must adhere to the Supreme Court's constitutional decisions—the answer is a fairly noncontroversial "yes"—and the extent to which nonjudicial actors (such as state or federal legislators or executive-branch officials) must adhere to the Court's constitutional decisions, to which the plausible answers are more varied and controversial.

uncover what Kozel calls the "normative premises" underlying each practice.[6] Specifically, we have to look to theories of *constitutional authority*: answers to the questions of whether, and on what grounds, those supposedly subject to constitutional law have an obligation to obey it. Only by uncovering the accounts of constitutional authority that might motivate originalism can we understand why, or whether, originalism and stare decisis really do not mix.

I have three primary aims for this chapter. First, I want to bolster the case made by Kozel that constitutional stare decisis cannot be understood or evaluated in a vacuum; its propriety and its implementation can only be assessed alongside the question of how the Constitution ought to be interpreted. Second, picking up the hints dropped by Kozel, I want to demonstrate that answers to questions of constitutional methodology—including how the Constitution should be interpreted and whether erroneous interpretations should be obeyed—ultimately depend on how we answer the foundational question of whether the Constitution has any authority over us at all. And third, I want to suggest, at least as a prima facie matter, that the various accounts of constitutional authority offered or assumed by contemporary originalists cannot in fact explain originalism's "special difficulty" with stare decisis.

I begin in the next section by exploring this supposed "special difficulty" in more depth. I suggest that the difficulty is not so "special"—not unless there are hidden normative motivations underlying originalism that are not apparent on its surface. In Sect. 10.4, using Randy Barnett's provocative defense of originalism as a template, I argue that the normative underpinnings of originalism, or of any interpretative methodology, ultimately must take the form of some account of why the Constitution is authoritative in the first place. Then, in Sects. 10.5, 10.6, and 10.7, I assess the three basic accounts of constitutional authority most often relied upon (often implicitly) by contemporary originalists. Each of these accounts, I contend, turns out to be implausible as a justification of the Constitution's authority, though for reasons that vary widely with each account. In Sect. 10.8, I describe an alternative type of account that might avoid the problems of these others but that is unlikely either to support strong originalism or to condemn stare decisis. Section 10.9 is a brief conclusion.

10.2 Originalism's "Special Difficulty with Precedent"

Originalism, in its currently fashionable version, holds that constitutional meaning should be determined primarily or exclusively by reference to how the text of the Constitution was understood by the public at the time of its Framing.[7] Barnett (2006,

[6] See Kozel's discussion in Chap. 9, Sect. 9.4.2.

[7] Prominent originalists who have endorsed this "original meaning" or "original understanding" approach include Robert Bork (1990), Gary Lawson (1994, 2007), Antonin Scalia (1997a), Michael Stokes Paulsen (2003, 2005), Randy Barnett (2004, 2006), Kurt Lash (2007), John McGinnis and Michael Rappaport (2007, 2009a, b, 2010), and Larry Solum (2008). There are

258–59) offers a syllogism to explain why those who endorse an originalist answer to the question of interpretive methodology also ought to give a skeptical answer to the question of constitutional stare decisis:[8]

(1) Originalism amounts to the claim that the meaning of the Constitution should remain the same until it is properly changed.
(2) None of the three branches of government on whom the written Constitution imposes limits should be able to alter these limitations, either alone or in combination, without properly amending the Constitution in writing.
(3) For this reason, the Supreme Court cannot change the Constitution which it is sworn to uphold and enforce.
(4) Were the Court mistakenly to decide a case that adopts an interpretation that contradicts the original meaning of the text, and this mistake was entrenched by the doctrine of precedent, then the Supreme Court's interpretation of the text would trump its original meaning.
(5) In this manner, the doctrine of precedent is inconsistent with originalism.

Barnett's syllogism, however, turns out to be subtly misleading. Barnett presents the syllogism as a demonstration of the uniqueness of originalism—of why originalism has "a *special* difficulty with precedent" that rival methodologies don't share. But in fact the syllogism points toward something like the opposite conclusion.

Consider Barnett's premise (1): "Originalism amounts to the claim that the meaning of the Constitution should remain the same until it is properly changed." The difficulty with this premise is that almost all extant interpretive methodologies, including nonoriginalist ones, agree that "the meaning of the Constitution should remain the same until it is properly changed."[9] What the various methodologies disagree about is what constitutes "the meaning of the Constitution," and thus what amounts to a "proper change" in that meaning. "Original meaning" originalists define "the meaning of the Constitution" as what the public at the time of the Framing understood its text to mean; "original intent" originalists define constitutional meaning as what (some group of) constitutional Framers intended it to mean; purposivists define constitutional meaning as what best serves the goals that can fairly be attributed to the provision in question; and so on. The operative disagreement is about how to define constitutional meaning, not about whether that meaning should be followed

---

many variations within the general original-meaning approach, most of which are not relevant for present purposes. Over the past generation or so, the search for "original meaning" has supplanted the search for the "original intent" of the Framers as the dominant variant of originalism.

[8] Similar reasoning appears in Lawson (1994, 26–28) and Paulsen (2005, 291).

[9] The possible exceptions are anything-goes pragmatism or straightforward natural-law approaches, which are not properly methods of *interpretation* at all. By pragmatism, I mean the decision of a constitutional case in a way designed to produce the best results, all things considered. Richard Posner endorses something like this approach (Posner 2003). By a natural-law approach, I mean the decision of a constitutional case in a way that accords with certain prepolitical moral values. Arguably neither approach involves *interpretation* of the Constitution, because neither has the goal of identifying the meaning of the Constitution itself (as opposed to the best result or the requirements of natural law). These approaches would be "noninterpretive" in the sense famously described by Thomas Grey (1975, 706–10).

(virtually everyone agrees that it should) or whether "improper" changes in that meaning should be allowed (virtually everyone agrees that they shouldn't).

Barnett obscures this fact when he *equates* originalism with an insistence on adherence to constitutional meaning. Originalism does not "amount to" such an insistence; it shares that insistence with almost every other interpretive methodology. What originalism "amounts to" is a particular type of understanding about what constitutional meaning *is*.

Once we recognize that most interpretive methodologies share with originalism a commitment to identifying and upholding the meaning of the Constitution, we can see that the problem of precedent is not the exclusive province of originalists. If the Supreme Court gets the meaning of the Constitution wrong—as determined by whatever method we adopt for identifying that meaning—then in some sense the Court has "improperly changed" the meaning of the Constitution. Following this incorrect interpretation in subsequent cases would only propagate the improper change, making matters worse. In this respect, as Barnett's fellow originalist Michael Stokes Paulsen (2005, 289–91) suggests, virtually every interpretive methodology has a difficulty with precedent.[10] Originalism is hardly unique in this regard.

And yet it is originalists who do the most hand-wringing about constitutional stare decisis. Why might that be? As Randy Kozel points out in this volume, any theory of constitutional stare decisis must take account of both its benefits and its costs.[11] Do originalists have special reason to fear the costs of stare decisis, or to deny or discount its benefits?

10.2.1 Originalism and the Benefits of Stare Decisis

Let's begin on the benefits side. There is a fairly well-established catalog of "rule of law" advantages that might flow from adherence to precedent—predictability, consistency, judicial economy, and protection of justified reliance chief among them—the

[10] Paulsen (2005, 291) identifies the following exception: "a theory of constitutional interpretation that purports to regard judicial precedents as themselves constitutive of constitutional meaning." Most such theories, however, recognize some determinants of constitutional meaning besides judicial decisionmaking alone. The theory of "common-law constitutionalism" propounded by David Strauss (2010), for example, holds that judicial decisions should be justifiable as interpretations of the constitutional text. In a somewhat different vein, Bruce Ackerman (1991) argues that the "codification" of a legitimate constitutional amendment can be accomplished by "landmark" judicial opinions rather than formal written amendments pursuant to Article V, 289–90; but he insists that these codifying opinions must follow a lengthy process of higher lawmaking that is politics-driven and that resembles the Article V process in all but name, 266–90. Both of these influential views see (some) judicial precedents as "constitutive of constitutional meaning"; but both of them also allow for the possibility of constitutionally erroneous judicial precedent (for Strauss, precedent that is not a justifiable interpretation of the text; for Ackerman, precedent that attempts to amend the Constitution without the discipline of the higher lawmaking process).

[11] See Chap. 9, Sect. 9.3.

desirability of which, as Kozel notes,[12] seems unlikely to vary according to one's theory of interpretation. How important one thinks it is to maintain consistency with a wrongly decided precedent, say, or to protect justified reliance on that precedent does not appear to depend on *why* one thinks the precedent was wrongly decided.

We might think interpretive methodology is relevant, however, in determining whether these rule-of-law values come into play at all. Consider the question whether a person's reliance on a given (wrongly decided) precedent should be thought "justified." Suppose we can identify an interpretive methodology that is both easy to apply and always productive of determinate answers. Anyone with half a brain—or at least a half-decent lawyer—could employ this (mythical) methodology to generate a clear, noncontroversial answer to what the Constitution means in any given case. If such a methodology existed, justifiable reliance on erroneous constitutional decisions would become a thing of the past. It would be easy to identify a constitutional decision as erroneous, and thus any reliance on that decision would be unreasonable. Stare decisis, then, would be unnecessary as a means of protecting justifiable reliance. It also would become unnecessary as a means of promoting predictability, consistency, and judicial economy: All of these benefits could be achieved by simply applying the perfect interpretive method to generate correct constitutional results. Subsequent courts and litigants would not need to rely on stare decisis to control or predict the outcomes of their cases; they could employ the perfect methodology to rely directly on the Constitution itself.

Of course there is no perfectly transparent, perfectly determinate method for interpreting the Constitution. But perhaps originalism comes closer to this unattainable ideal than any of its rivals. If so, then a world in which originalism is the exclusive methodology would be a world in which stare decisis is, if not superfluous, then at least substantially less beneficial than it is in our actual world. We would not need to lean (nearly as much) on precedent to protect reliance, promote predictability, and so forth; originalism would (mostly) do these things for us.

Could this be the basis for originalism's "special difficulty with precedent"? Perhaps originalists distrust precedent because their methodology makes it largely unnecessary. And indeed originalists sometimes claim that their methodology is more determinate than the alternatives. Among the earliest proffered grounds for originalism in its modern era was the constraint of judges (see Scalia 1989; Bork 1990);[13] this rationale implies that originalism is especially capable of imposing

[12] See Chap. 9, Sect. 9.3.1.

[13] The "judicial constraint" rationale is of course not original with modern originalists. Chief Justice Taney famously deployed it in his infamous opinion in *Dred Scott v. Sandford*, 60 U.S. 393, 405, the 1856 decision holding that African slaves, former slaves, and their descendents could never be citizens of the United States and that Congress lacked power to prohibit slavery in the territories:

> It is not the province of the court to decide upon the justice or injustice, the policy or impolicy, of these laws. The decision of that question belonged to the political or law-making power; to those who formed the sovereignty and framed the Constitution. The duty of the court is, to interpret the instrument they have framed, with the best lights we can obtain on the subject, and to administer it as we find it, according to its true intent and meaning when it was adopted.

constraint, by generating answers that are clear and noncontroversial enough to embarrass any judge who fails to reach them.

The difficulty with this hypothesis—that the determinacy of originalism renders stare decisis largely superfluous—is that it finds little support in the realities of constitutional practice. In our actual world, originalist methodology is neither especially transparent nor especially determinate. David Strauss (2007, 218–19) helpfully classifies the troubles here into three categories: "the problem of ascertainability, which is simply the difficulty of doing the historical research needed to figure out what the original understandings were"; "the problem of indeterminacy," that is, the risk that members of the Framing generation had "different understandings about what the words have committed the document to"; and "the problem of translation," or the difficulty in applying the particular understandings of the Framing generation to modern circumstances they could not have foreseen. An originalist interpreter must, first, locate relevant historical evidence regarding what the appropriate collection of people alive at the time of the Framing thought or intended the Constitution's words to mean (and in so doing must decide what evidence is relevant, which collection of people is appropriate, and what understandings or beliefs or other mental states of those people matter). She must then determine whether some of the relevant mental states of some of the people in question are in conflict and, if so, what to do about it. And she must, finally, figure out how to apply those mental states—which were formed with reference to facts as they existed in the late eighteenth or mid-nineteenth centuries—to the very different and unforeseen facts as they exist today.

It is implausible to think that this process will very often be easy, or that it will very often generate anything like a clear and noncontroversial result. We might be forgiven, in fact, for accusing Justice Scalia of understatement when he admits that originalist methodology "is always difficult and sometimes inconclusive" (Scalia 1989, 84). And we are unlikely to take any comfort in the track record of originalism as actually employed by judges or other interpreters. Consider, for example, the Court's recent Second Amendment case *District of Columbia v. Heller*, in which Justice Scalia writing for the Court used originalist methodology to discover an individual right to bear arms, while Justices Stevens and Breyer in dissent each employed originalist interpretation to reject such a right.[14]

Or consider the controversy over whether *Brown v. Board of Education*, an explicitly nonoriginalist decision,[15] can be defended on originalist grounds.

[14] See District of Columbia v. Heller, 554 U.S. 570, 572–636 (2008) (Scalia, J., for the Court); 554 U.S. at 636–80 (Stevens, J., dissenting); 554 U.S. at 681–723 (Breyer, J., dissenting).

[15] After an initial argument in *Brown*, 341 U.S. 141 (1953), the Court requested rebriefing and reargument regarding "the understanding of the framers of [the Fourteenth] Amendment" on the question of school segregation. See Urofsky and Finkelman (2011b), 859–60. In its unanimous decision, however, the Court declared that the evidence of original intent was "inconclusive," Brown v. Board of Education, 347 U.S. 483, 489 (1954), and elected to resolve the question "in light of [the] full development [of public education] and its present place in American life" rather

Although a number of prominent originalists believe that it can (see McGinnis and Rappaport 2009b, 842; Barnett 2006, 260), all of them rely primarily on a single article by law professor (and one-time federal judge) Michael McConnell (1995) that makes this case.[16] That article swims upstream against a strong consensus of historical and legal scholarly opinion (see Klarman 1995; Berger 1977; Avins 1967; Bickel 1955) and, revealingly, it appears to employ the now out-of-vogue "original intent" approach rather than the "original meaning" methodology favored by the current originalists who cite it. In any event, as David Strauss (2005, 304–05) notes, whether McConnell is right or wrong is beside the point: The very existence of the controversy affirms the *Brown* Court's finding that the originalist evidence is "inconclusive" and thus undermines any claim that originalism is an especially determinate methodology.

10.2.2 Originalism and the Costs of Stare Decisis

On the benefits side, then, it is quite unlikely that originalism renders stare decisis superfluous. But what about its costs? Perhaps the costs of obedience to erroneous precedent are, from an originalist perspective, exceptionally high.

As with benefits, any supposed correspondence between the methodology that tells us a precedent is erroneous and the costs of obeying that precedent appears tenuous at best. (On this point I disagree somewhat with Kozel.)[17] If an originalist uses her approach to determine that, say, *Plessy v. Ferguson*[18] was wrongly decided, and a nonoriginalist uses his approach to reach the same conclusion, both interpreters will have identified an incorrectly decided constitutional precedent, with whatever attendant harms (substantive injustice, political illegitimacy, distortion of constitutional doctrine) follow from continued obedience to that incorrect decision. The nature and degree of these harms does not seem contingent on *why* the precedent was incorrect. If originalism were an especially determinate methodology, we might worry about a special cost to judicial integrity from obedience to incorrect precedent: A Court seen as following a clearly erroneous precedent might, for that reason, lose the respect of the public and the other branches of government. But originalism, as I've argued, cannot make things nearly this clear.

than by "turn[ing] the clock back to 1868 when the Amendment was adopted," 347 U.S. at 492–93.

[16] McConnell also wrote several shorter articles echoing the same arguments, which originalists often cite in addition to the principal article. Some pro-*Brown* originalists also cite as support an article by Akhil Amar (2000), but as David Strauss (2005, 304 note 10) notes, Amar relies primarily "on the text of the Constitution, rather than the original understandings."

[17] See his discussion in Chap. 9, Sect. 9.4; see also my treatment of that discussion in the Introduction to this volume.

[18] 163 U.S. 537 (1896). The Court in *Plessy* held that the Fourteenth Amendment did not prohibit legally enforced segregation according to race. *Plessy* was overruled *de facto* by *Brown* and its progeny.

Of course, different interpretive methodologies often will produce different conclusions about whether a given precedent is erroneous. Originalists almost universally disagree with the Court's recognition of an abortion right in *Roe v. Wade*,[19] for example, while many nonoriginalists think *Roe* was correctly decided. This raises the possibility that originalism will identify *more* erroneous precedents than nonoriginalism will. And indeed originalists sometimes allude to the fact that their approach, if followed, "would seemingly lead to the rejection of many of the landmark cases most treasured by constitutional law professors, and even by the general public" (Barnett 2006, 259–60). Many of these cases, after all, were decided on nonoriginalist grounds, *Brown* and *Roe* being leading examples. If these decisions can't be justified by originalist methods, then originalists will see them as incorrect constitutional interpretations with all their associated harms, even if nonoriginalists would not.

The potential for originalism to upset much settled precedent may well explain both the typical originalist distrust of stare decisis and the angst that distrust sometimes causes among originalists. Contemporary originalism gained steam in the late 1970s and 1980s as a politically conservative device to critique progressive Warren Court and early Burger Court decisions[20] like *Roe*, *Griswold v. Connecticut*,[21] and *Miranda v. Arizona*.[22] As conservatives have gained power on the Court over the past 30 years—first under William Rehnquist (appointed Chief Justice by Ronald Reagan, a Republican, along with three new Associate Justices), then under Rehnquist's former clerk John Roberts (appointed Chief by the Republican George W. Bush)—originalism has ascended along with them. And stare decisis has begun to look inconvenient—an obstacle to overruling the nonoriginalist, progressive decisions of an earlier era.

But not all nonoriginalist precedents are anathema to originalists. *Brown v. Board of Education* is Exhibit A for this phenomenon; as Barnett (2006, 260) puts it, "if one had to choose between original meaning and *Brown*, most"—including most originalists—"would choose *Brown*." As I've mentioned, some originalists try (unpersuasively) to avoid this particular conflict by concluding that *Brown* actually can be defended on originalist grounds. But *Brown* is only the most salient manifestation of the difficulty. I doubt many originalists would be comfortable with an Equal Protection Clause that did not protect gender equality, for example, or with a Free Speech Clause that did not protect commercial speech, or with an Establishment Clause that forbade only official state churches supported with tax dollars; yet even the most creative originalists would be hard-pressed to reconcile their discomfort with the original understandings of these provisions. So originalists typically cannot be content simply to reject stare decisis out of hand; they must at least grapple with

---

[19] 410 U.S. 113 (1973).

[20] Classic uses of originalism in this critical vein include Bork (1990), Meese (1985), and Berger (1977).

[21] 381 U.S. 479 (1965). In *Griswold*, the Court held that married couples have a constitutional right to use contraceptives, thus setting the stage for later "right of privacy" decisions including *Roe*.

[22] 384 U.S. 436 (1966). The Court in *Miranda* applied the Fifth Amendment to hold that confessions by criminal defendants can be admitted as evidence only if certain warnings were administered prior to interrogation.

the question whether erroneous constitutional decisions might nonetheless bind subsequent Courts.[23]

Perhaps, then, originalism has a "special difficulty" with precedent because originalism is driven by a desire for politically conservative results. Many progressive constitutional decisions were decided on nonoriginalist grounds; this explains the (politically conservative) move toward originalism. Overruling those decisions requires evading or rejecting stare decisis; this explains the originalist skepticism of precedent. The originalist problem with stare decisis is, on this view, a product of its politically conservative underpinnings.

Of course, the notion that a theory of interpretive methodology, or a theory of stare decisis, can be justified only by the pursuit of particular substantive results is likely to seem intuitively problematic. In the next two sections, I will articulate a normative foundation for this intuition. For present purposes, the important point is that there is nothing in the methodology of originalism *itself* that creates a unique or exceptional conflict with stare decisis. As Randy Kozel argues in Chap. 9, a satisfactory account of the relationship between an interpretive methodology (like originalism) and the question of constitutional stare decisis requires looking beneath the methodology to its normative groundings. An interpretive methodology can tell us whether a constitutional precedent was wrongly decided, but it cannot, without more, tell us whether we nonetheless should obey that decision.

In what follows, I want to suggest that an understanding of constitutional stare decisis—of whether, and why, the Court should obey prior constitutional decisions it believes to be wrong—requires an understanding of whether, and why, the Constitution deserves obedience in the first place. It requires, that is, an answer to the question of constitutional authority. Answering that question, I will contend, can generate (or at least support) answers to the questions of interpretive methodology and stare decisis as well.

10.3 Interpretive Methodology and Constitutional Authority

In the previous section, I raised the possibility that originalism's "special difficulty" with constitutional stare decisis is a function of its conservative political underpinnings. Suppose this is true. Would there be anything wrong with it?

It is worth noting that originalists rarely defend their methodology, or their distrust of stare decisis, as means of imposing certain substantive political or moral values. Instead, originalists typically advert to more abstract, relatively value-neutral goals—judicial constraint (see Scalia 1989, 1997a; Bork 1990), promotion of the "public interest" (McGinnis and Rappaport 2007, 2010) or of the "common good" (Strang 2006), preservation of "popular sovereignty" (Lash 2007; Whittington 1999). This apparent taboo hints at a recognition that tying originalism to particular substantive values is

[23] It is revealing, I think, that most attempts by originalist theorists to accommodate stare decisis would have the effect of upholding *Brown* (even assuming *Brown* was wrongly decided) while overturning *Roe*. E.g., McGinnis and Rappaport (2009b), Lash (2007), and Strang (2006).

somehow illegitimate. I will argue in the next section that such a recognition is supported by a sound understanding of constitutional authority. First, however, it may be useful to examine a prominent exception to the rule of value-neutral arguments for originalism. That exception is the originalist theory of Randy Barnett.

Barnett (2004, 9) defends originalism as an implication of his account of constitutional authority. "The Constitution … is a piece of parchment under glass in Washington, D.C.," he notes. "Why should we pay any attention to it"? Barnett agrees that, as I will argue in Sect. 10.5, this question cannot satisfactorily be answered with the notion that we have *consented* to be bound by the Constitution. Instead, he contends, legitimate constitutional authority ultimately depends on whether the system of laws established by the Constitution is substantively *just*, or at least "not unjust." And he asserts that substantive justice consists of certain "natural rights" that promote liberty (4, 52–86). "[I]f a constitution contains adequate procedures to protect these natural rights, it can be legitimate," he says (4). As it happens, Barnett argues, the Framers also believed in these libertarian natural rights and "incorporated effective procedural protections of these rights into the Constitution" (53). The Constitution as created by the Framers, then, is legitimately authoritative, according to Barnett. And so to determine the meaning of that Constitution, we ought to be bound by what it was that the Framers actually created. This requires interpreting the Constitution, in the first instance, by looking for "the meaning [its words] had at the time they were enacted" (90).[24]

Barnett's approach thus justifies originalism as a means of promoting particular substantive values, in the form of libertarian "natural rights." I will have more to say in the next section about this feature of his theory. For the moment, however, I am interested in the fact that Barnett defends an originalist methodology as an implication of his justification of constitutional authority. Is this connection inevitable? That is, must the normative underpinnings of originalism, or of any interpretive methodology, ultimately reside in some account of why the Constitution is authoritative in the first place?

As a conceptual matter, I think the answer is no; but as a practical matter the answer is yes. One way in which the normative grounding of an interpretive methodology might be disconnected from the normative grounding of the law being interpreted is if that law *has* no normative grounding—if it lacks legitimate authority altogether. Imagine, for example, a theory of the least-offensive way to interpret the illegitimate diktats of an all-powerful despot. Where the law is illegitimate but also unchangeable and unavoidable, the best we can do might be to come up with the least-harmful way to interpret and apply that illegitimate law. We might then say that the interpretive methodology is normatively legitimate even though the law being interpreted is not.

But it seems unlikely that the interpretation of the American Constitution fits this model. This is not (merely) because the Constitution seems more legitimate than the commands of a despot. It is due, rather, to the fact that we could, if we (as a society)

---

[24] "In the first instance," because Barnett recognizes that there will be no identifiable, determinate original meaning with respect to many constitutional questions (2004, 118–21). Where a determinate original meaning cannot be identified, Barnett supports constitutional "construction": the judicial creation of a constitutional meaning "that is consistent with its original meaning but not deducible from it" (121).

chose, replace the Constitution through means that are peaceful and democratic, even if they happen to be technically illegal (though they need not be). The Framers, after all, substituted the Constitution for the Articles of Confederation in this way.[25] Even if the Constitution is not legitimate, its illegitimacy therefore is avoidable. And it would be difficult to justify pursuing the least-harmful method for interpreting the Constitution if we thought the Constitution itself was illegitimate and thus not worth interpreting. If we thought the Constitution was illegitimate, the normatively justifiable thing to do would be to replace it altogether, not to attempt triage by devising a relatively inoffensive way to interpret it.

Thus it would make little sense to attempt a legitimate theory of interpreting an illegitimate Constitution. As a practical matter, we must believe the Constitution itself is legitimately authoritative before considering how best to interpret it. But is it possible that our reasons for thinking the Constitution is legitimate can be entirely independent of our reasons for preferring one or the other method of interpreting it?

I very much doubt it. Suppose we believe, as Barnett does, that the Constitution is legitimately authoritative because obeying it tends to protect certain libertarian natural rights. It would then make little sense to discern the meaning of the Constitution in a way that is not designed to further this purpose. The likely result of doing so would be to apply the Constitution in many situations in which its authority is not justified.

For example, suppose we adopt Barnett's natural-rights grounding of constitutional authority; but suppose we then choose a method of interpreting the Constitution that has a different grounding altogether (say, that it is the best way to constrain judges). It will only be happenstance that these diverse rationales—protecting natural rights and constraining judges—converge to produce the same result in any particular case. In some cases, perhaps in many, the goal of constraining judges will conflict with the goal of protecting natural rights. A constrained judge, for instance, might fail to strike down a piece of legislation that impairs a natural right the Constitution was designed to protect. It would make much better sense to tailor our interpretive methodology to our reason for having and obeying the Constitution in the first place.

Here is a somewhat more theoretical way to make the point, with a debt to the work of Ronald Dworkin. Constitutional law is a conscious human practice with moral implications. We as a society have (and to some extent each of us as individuals has) a choice whether to engage in it or not, and our choice to engage in it implies a determination that the practice is morally worthwhile on the whole. In

[25] The possibilities of replacing the Constitution through peaceful democratic means are not limited to those delineated by Article V of the Constitution itself, which provides for amendments according to certain procedures. We might, using non-Article V democratic procedures, decide to discard the Constitution and (using non-Article V democratic procedures) draft and ratify an entirely new one. This is precisely what the Framers did with respect to the Articles of Confederation. Article XIII of the Articles required the approval of Congress and the unanimous approval of each of the state legislatures for amendments. The procedure specified in Article VII of the new Constitution proposed by the Convention of 1787, however, contemplated ratification by special conventions (not the legislatures) in nine of the thirteen existing states (not unanimously), and it did not require the approval of Congress. This is in fact the procedure that was followed, albeit with the eventual endorsement of the Confederation Congress (see Urofsky and Finkelman 2011a, 12).

determining how the practice operates—how best to interpret the Constitution's commands, for instance—we ought to consider the practice in its morally best light and perform it in a way that is consistent with this moral vision.[26] Constitutional law purports to bind us in important ways, and if it is a morally justifiable practice, that binding authority has a justifiable moral grounding. The way we perform a core aspect of the practice—interpreting the Constitution, that is, determining how it binds us in particular instances—therefore must reflect, indeed promote, that moral grounding. Constitutional interpretation must further constitutional authority.[27]

It would be difficult to justify an interpretive approach designed to identify the meaning of an unjustifiable Constitution, or to identify its meaning without reference to the reason the Constitution is justifiable. To put the matter concisely: A persuasive answer to the question of interpretive methodology must follow from a persuasive answer to the question of constitutional authority.

10.4 Constitutional Authority and Values Imposition

Which brings us to the issue of whether Barnett's account of constitutional authority is in fact persuasive. The answer, I'm afraid, is no. The problem is that Barnett's account is not really an account of constitutional *authority* at all.

10.4.1 The Concept of Legal Authority

The concept of authority is among the most elusive in legal philosophy.[28] For present purposes, we can think of authority as the capacity to impose a moral obligation of

---

[26] This is essentially Dworkin's understanding of the project of "interpretation" writ large. See his lengthy discussion in Dworkin (1986), 45–86.

[27] This is not to say that every feature of a practice like constitutional law must be justifiable by reference to the moral grounding of the practice as a whole. Some features of a practice might serve to effect side constraints rather than to promote the underlying purpose of the practice. Consider the rule in ice hockey requiring players to wear helmets. Wearing helmets probably cannot be justified by reference to the overall purposes of the practice of ice hockey (athletic competition, entertainment, physical exercise). Some even think wearing helmets impedes some of these purposes. The helmet rule, rather, is justified by the side constraint of preventing serious injury while playing hockey.

There may be aspects of the American practice of constitutional law that resemble the helmet rule in ice hockey in this respect, though I am at a loss to identify one. In any event, interpretive methodology almost certainly does not qualify. How we interpret the Constitution is far too central to our practice of constitutional law itself to be justifiable solely or primarily by reference to a side constraint. Constitutional interpretation is our means of determining how constitutional law binds us, and binding us is simply what constitutional law does. It seems impossible to understand how the Constitution binds without also understanding why it does so.

[28] For a thorough exploration of its problematics, see Shapiro (2002).

obedience. If constitutional law possesses authority, then those subject to it (legislators, executive-branch officials, judges, citizens) have a moral obligation to obey it. If it lacks authority, those subject to it may have *reason* to obey it—the fear of punishment for disobedience, for example—but they lack a moral *obligation* of obedience.

There are three key operative distinctions underlying the concept of authority. The first is between authority and mere coercion. If we attribute real authority to law, we recognize an obligation to obey it even absent a meaningful threat of sanctions for disobedience. As H.L.A. Hart (1994, 82–91) observed, our attitude toward valid legal commands differs from our attitude toward the orders of an armed gunman. We view the former as authoritative, as legitimately binding, and thus as imposing an obligation to obey even without the teeth of sanctions. We view the latter as illegitimate and thus as merely coercive, not authoritative.

The second key distinction is between the kind of obligation imposed by authoritative law on the one hand, and a garden-variety *reason* to act on the other. If we recognize a law as valid, we treat it as more than just another factor relevant to our process of deciding how to act. The facts that it is dark and rainy outside are *reasons* to drive slowly; the fact that the law sets a speed limit imposes an *obligation* to drive slowly. While it is implausible that this obligation is absolute and indefeasible,[29] it must at least have greater normative force than most other relevant reasons for action.

A closely related third distinction, and the one most relevant for present purposes, is between a reason or obligation to act that is content-*dependent* and one that is content-*independent*.[30] A content-dependent reason is a reason to attribute a certain moral status to an action—to conclude, for example, that the action is morally obligatory on the one hand or morally prohibited on the other. The facts that it is dark and rainy outside are content-dependent reasons to drive slowly; they are reasons to attribute a certain moral status (moral desirability, perhaps even moral necessity) to the act of driving slowly. A content-independent reason, in contrast, is a reason to take or refrain from a certain action regardless of one's beliefs about the moral status of that action. The fact that the law imposes a speed limit is a content-independent reason to drive slowly; it is a reason to take that action without regard to whether we believe the action is morally desirable or morally necessary.

As this example suggests, legal authority requires content-independence. The obligation to act that the law imposes on us must be independent of the moral status we attribute to that action; the law must be capable of obligating us to take actions we (otherwise would) think morally incorrect or suboptimal or wrong, that is, actions we otherwise would conclude we should not take. If we have an obligation to obey the law only when it tells us to do the morally right thing, then the supposed authority of the law is illusory: Our obligation is to obey the requirements of morality, not those of the law. Only if we have an obligation to obey the law *even when it is wrong*—even when it requires us to do something other than what morality dictates—does the law really possess authority over us.

[29] On this point, see Peters (2011), 33–36, 44–47.

[30] For a clear explanation of content-independence, see Shapiro (2002), 389.

This requirement of content-independence may seem rather abstract, but it has real-world significance for the effectiveness of law. To see how, imagine that the Constitution tells us to do something other than what we think morality requires. Perhaps, for example, it commands us to afford due process to a terrorism suspect, even though we think national security creates a moral imperative to imprison the suspect without trial. If our obligation to obey the Constitution depends entirely on the moral status of its content—of what it is telling us to do—then we will recognize no obligation of obedience in this case, or in any case in which we disagree with its requirements. We will simply do what we think morally best in such cases—and the Constitution will fail to function as law.

A Constitution that fails to motivate obedience in cases of disagreement with its commands would be a disaster. This is particularly true because constitutional law is less susceptible than ordinary law to obedience through coercion. Legal subjects might often obey *sub*-constitutional norms simply to avoid the consequences of being caught disobeying them. (I need not recognize the legitimate authority of the tax code in order to fear criminal prosecution for tax avoidance.) In the constitutional context, however, it is very often unrealistic to think that disobedient subjects will be punished for their disobedience. The contested nature of many constitutional norms frequently makes it difficult to say with any confidence whether someone has obeyed them or not. Enforcement mechanisms, moreover, are clumsy: In the United States, constitutional disobedience by government officials typically can be "punished" only by the blunt instrument of voting them out at the next election or by the extreme and rare measure of impeachment and removal from office. And the entity that is the ultimate subject of the Constitution's constraints—the democratic majority itself—is immune even to these sanctions.

Effective constitutional law therefore depends largely on people's willingness to obey it in circumstances in which they disagree with its commands but face no meaningful threat of sanctions for disobedience. Indeed, we can think of a constitution as an attempt to coordinate behavior in the face of disagreement. The people subject to constitutional law will of course disagree on matters of substance—on whether terrorism suspects deserve due process, whether reproductive freedom deserves protection, whether Congress may require the purchase of health insurance, and so on. The purpose of constitutional law is to resolve, or at least to manage, these substantive disagreements so that we can function with reasonable coordination as a society. Constitutional law can succeed in this function only if those subject to it will accept and obey its results—even when they disagree with them in substance. Constitutional law, then, must provide reasons to obey its results that are not dependent on their substance. As Jeremy Waldron (2006, 1371) puts it, "the point is as old as Hobbes":

> We must set up a decision-procedure whose operation will settle, not reignite, the controversies whose existence called for a decision-procedure in the first place. This means that even though the members of … society … disagree about [matters of substance], they need to share a theory of legitimacy for the decision-procedure that is to settle their disagreements. So, in thinking about the reasons for setting up such a procedure, we should think about reasons that can be subscribed to by people on both sides of any one of these disagreements.

10.4.2 The Content-Dependence of Values Imposition

We can now begin to see why Barnett's theory fails as an account of the authority of the Constitution. Barnett grounds constitutional authority—our obligation to obey the Constitution's commands—in the desirability of certain substantive results or values (his list of libertarian "natural rights"). On the relatively abstract level of morality, such a theory cannot support the obligation of obedience it promises. One's obligation, on Barnett's theory, is to obey natural rights, not the Constitution itself. One then should do as the Constitution commands only insofar as this will foster the protection of these natural rights. If obeying the Constitution fails to protect natural rights, one has no obligation (on Barnett's account) to obey it.

On a more practical, sociological level, Barnett's theory cannot motivate obedience to constitutional law. If one agrees with Barnett's list of natural rights, then one has a reason to do as the Constitution commands whenever doing so would promote those rights. But if one disagrees with the rights on Barnett's list, or with the entire concept of natural rights; or if one agrees with Barnett's list of rights but disagrees, in any given case, that obeying the Constitution would promote them; then one will perceive no obligation to obey the Constitution. Barnett's approach provides no reasons for obedience that, in Waldron's words, "can be subscribed to by people on both sides" of a disagreement about natural rights. And thus it fails to justify constitutional law as "a decision-procedure whose operation will settle, not reignite, the controversies whose existence called for a decision-procedure in the first place."

Barnett's theory is an example—rare in its honesty—of what I will call a *Values Imposition* account of constitutional authority. Such an account attempts to ground the authority of the Constitution in its supposed capacity to promote particular substantive values or results. As I've argued, the attempt inevitably fails, because it is content-dependent, not content-independent. Values Imposition accounts attribute authority, not to the Constitution itself, but to the desired values or results. In so doing, such accounts fail to motivate obedience by those who disagree with these values or results.

Values Imposition accounts are rare; while Barnett's is not the only example, it is probably the least apologetic.[31] And with all respect to Barnett himself, who is one of our most resourceful constitutional theorists, the analysis in this section suggests the reason for their scarcity. Values Imposition accounts cannot plausibly support constitutional authority. And thus they cannot plausibly entail particular

[31] The account offered by Hadley Arkes (1990, 1994) might be Barnett's only rival in this respect. Unlike Barnett, however, Arkes does not directly address the question of the Constitution's authority, and unlike Barnett, Arkes is not an originalist: He advocates direct resort to natural-law principles in constitutional adjudication. Other accounts that might be read to ground originalism in Values Imposition are those of Richard Kay (1998) and Lee Strang (2006). Kay, at least, joins Barnett in adopting a relatively libertarian understanding of the values the Constitution is designed to implement; Strang is less committal on this point, identifying the Constitution with what he terms the "Aristotelian tradition" of pursuing "the common good."

methodologies of interpreting a (nonauthoritative) Constitution, or particular reasons to obey or not to obey erroneous judicial interpretations of the (nonauthoritative) Constitution.

10.5 Consent

Originalists sometimes point to the normative force of *consent* as a grounding for their approach. And at first glance, justifying constitutional authority based on consent seems more promising than a Values Imposition account. Consent might be capable of providing a content-independent reason, perhaps even an obligation, to act. Our consent is an exercise of our autonomy; by consenting to something, we are asserting our capacity to plan our own lives. The power of consent to impose moral obligations can apply even when what we are consenting to is the subjugation of our own judgment or wishes to those of others. If I agree to allow my spouse to choose the paint color in our kitchen, for example, I am consenting to be bound by her decision, even if I dislike its substance. Less trivially, perhaps, by purchasing a home subject to a covenant that allows a homeowner's association to make rules governing various issues, from the color of our siding to the content of our garden to the amount of the maintenance fees we must pay, my spouse and I are consenting to be bound by those rules, even if we think them burdensome or unwise. There are of course many similar examples great and small.

So, if Americans as a people have given our consent to be bound by the Constitution, we might be bound even when we disagree with what the Constitution requires. In fact, we might be bound even if what the Constitution requires would (otherwise) be morally wrong or suboptimal. The moral obligation created by our consent conceivably might outweigh or alter the preexisting demands of morality, just as my consenting (for example) to adopt a child imposes moral duties to that child that would not exist without my consent.

Some prominent originalists have suggested that their methodology can be justified by this normative power of consent. Edwin Meese (1986, 102), who served as Ronald Reagan's second Attorney General and was an influential catalyst of the burgeoning originalist movement in the 1980s, described the Constitution as "the instrument by which the consent of the governed—the fundamental requirement of any legitimate government—is transformed into a government."[32] Following Meese, law professor Steven Calabresi (2007b, 21) argues that the consensual authority of

[32] Meese's attribution of constitutional authority to "the consent of the governed" has a distinguished pedigree. Alexander Hamilton and John Marshall, two titans of the founding generation, both famously described the Constitution as the consensual act of "the people." See Hamilton, *Federalist No. 78* (1826), and *Marbury v. Madison*, 5 U.S. 137 (1803). Quoting the Declaration of Independence, Lincoln (1946, 304) described "the sheet anchor of American republicanism" as the principle "that no man is good enough to govern another man, *without that other's consent*" (emphasis in original).

the Constitution implies both the necessity of originalist interpretation and the illegitimacy of stare decisis:

> [I]t is only the text of the written Constitution to which we the people of the United States have given our consent. The people have never consented to be governed in a formal way by the five hundred volumes of the *U.S. Reports* [which contain the text of Supreme Court decisions]. We know from the Declaration of Independence that a fundamental precept of our constitutional order is that governments are instituted and dissolved by the people and that legitimate government requires the consent of the governed. The American people have consented to be governed by the Constitution, but they have not consented to be governed by the Supreme Court's decisional case law.

To similar effect are theories, like those of Keith Whittington (1999) and Kurt Lash (2007), that ground originalism in the consensualist notion of "popular sovereignty." "By construing the Constitution in terms of the intent of its creators," Whittington (1999, 111) writes, "originalism … enforces the authoritative decision of the people acting as sovereign."

Because it purports to identify a content-independent obligation to act, what I will call a *Consent* account avoids the conceptual failure of a Values Imposition account as a justification of constitutional authority. But a Consent account fails for another reason: Its descriptive precondition—the existence of actual consent—has not plausibly been met in contemporary America, and probably cannot plausibly be met in any reasonably complex modern society.

To see why, we can start with the observation that the first three words of the Constitution, "We the People," are a fiction.[33] Even in 1789, when the original Constitution took effect by its own terms, the electorate eligible to participate in the ratification process was only a subset of "the People" as a whole, that is, of the population that would be bound by the document. Slaves of course could not vote; neither could women in any state, or those without property in many states, or free blacks in some. And even among those who could participate in the ratification process, approval of the new Constitution was far from unanimous. A substantial percentage of the American people at the time of the Framing therefore cannot be said to have consented to the Constitution in any affirmative sense.

This consent gap is only compounded by what is sometimes called the "dead hand" problem: the chronological distance between our own time and the crucial Framing periods. No American alive today was alive when the original Constitution was ratified in 1788, or when the Bill of Rights was added in 1791, or when the Reconstruction Amendments were added between 1865 and 1870; so none of us could have given our consent to those actions when they occurred. And our failure to amend the Constitution pursuant to the procedures specified in Article V cannot amount to consent, because we did not consent to Article V either.[34]

It is true that some living Americans have expressly consented to be bound by the Constitution. Naturalized citizens do so when they take their citizenship oaths, and government officials are required by Article VI to swear or affirm that they will

[33] I owe this admittedly provocative but quite accurate phrasing to Randy Barnett (2004, 14).

[34] On this point, see Siegel (2009), 1404–05.

"support this Constitution."[35] But this is a very small percentage of the citizenry. The vast majority of us have not given our express consent to the Constitution's authority.

Of course, there are theories of *tacit* consent, like those of Rousseau (1954, 168), who located consent to be bound by law in the act of "residing within the state after its … establishment", and Locke (1963, 392), who found consent in the "Possession, or Enjoyment, of any part of the Dominions of … government." But these theories are unconvincing because they suppose a choice that, for most people, does not exist. Most of us cannot simply pick up and leave our homes, our families, and our jobs to emigrate elsewhere; the costs of doing so would be prohibitive, or at least considerably higher than the costs of living under a Constitution to which we would not consent if given a meaningful choice. And where would we go if we could leave? Except perhaps for billionaires who can purchase remote private islands, most of us could move only to other extant societies with their own existing systems of government, which may or may not be preferable on the whole to the one we are considering leaving. Valid consent requires the option to *withhold* consent, to say "no" (see Barnett 2004, 16–17); but for very few (if any) of us is this a realistic alternative.

The idea that we have an obligation to obey the Constitution by virtue of our consent, then, is implausible; "government by consent," in the conditions of contemporary America, is simply loose talk. And it is worth noting that even if constitutional authority by consent were descriptively plausible, it would not provide the strong support for adopting originalism and rejecting stare decisis that originalists like Calabresi (2007b) claim for it. To imagine that we have consented to the Constitution is not to imagine that we have consented to an exclusively originalist method of interpreting the Constitution. The system of government under which we now live and from which we benefit (contra Calabresi 2007b) does in fact include the Court decisions reproduced in the *U.S. Reports*, and has since almost the beginning of the Republic. And if we read through those decisions, we will find examples of many different methodologies for interpreting the constitutional text employed by the Court over the years, including but hardly limited to originalism. (Indeed, the "original public meaning" version of originalism now popular is a relatively recent innovation, having supplanted the older "original intention" variant only in the last quarter century or so.) It is difficult to see how we can be said to have implicitly consented to one of these methodologies but not to any of the others. As Reva Siegel (2009, 1405) writes, "[I]f we are to construe the living as having implicitly consented to any constitutional understanding or arrangement, it is to the Constitution as it is *currently* interpreted, with its many pathways of change."

[35] On its most natural reading, the oath required by Article VI compels officials only to support the Constitution while carrying out their official duties, not to obey it in other capacities. And keep in mind that if an official has no duty to obey the Constitution generally, she has no duty to obey Article VI's oath requirement in particular. It is at least debatable whether an official who has taken the required oath, believing that she is under no obligation to obey the Constitution, would be subject to such an obligation simply by virtue of having taken the oath.

Consent cannot plausibly underwrite the authority of the Constitution, and so it cannot underwrite a particular methodology for interpreting it or a theory of whether and when erroneous interpretations are binding. And even if it could, originalism unadulterated by stare decisis would not be the result. If we are looking for a way to justify originalism, to condemn stare decisis, or both, we will have to look elsewhere.

10.6 Moral Guidance

Many influential theories of constitutional law and judicial review, including some originalist theories, imply a justification of constitutional authority that I will call a *Moral Guidance* account. According to a Moral Guidance account, the authority of constitutional law rests in its capacity to promote morally correct action, not in a specific sense (as defined by particular moral values or outcomes), but rather in a general sense—as an increased likelihood of acting correctly, whatever correct action may entail in any given case.

As we've seen, constitutional authority cannot be built on the desire to achieve particular (controversial) values or other outcomes; those who disagree with the desired values would have no reason to acknowledge the Constitution's authority. But as Jeremy Waldron (2006, 1373–74) notes, we might be able to attribute authority to procedures we think are likely to generate good outcomes, even if we can't agree ahead of time on what those outcomes are:

> Instead of saying (in a question-begging way) that we should choose those political procedures that are most likely to yield a particular controversial set of rights [or moral values or other outcomes], we might say instead that we should choose political procedures that are most likely to get at the truth about rights [or values, or outcomes, etc.], whatever that truth turns out to be.

If we can agree that constitutional procedures are, generally speaking, more likely to generate morally good outcomes (with respect to certain matters, at least) than are ordinary democratic procedures, we might then attribute authority to constitutional law even if we disagree with some of the particular results it produces. A useful analogy is the policy of subjecting children to their parents' control until they turn 18. We may not agree with every decision a given parent makes, but we think parents are, as a general matter, more likely to make good decisions regarding the child's welfare than is the child herself (or, for that matter, other potential decisionmakers, such as the state). So we generally cede decisionmaking authority to parents, knowing that we will not agree with how they exercise that authority in every instance.

Grounding constitutional authority in the general capacity for moral guidance, not in particular moral values or outcomes, can skirt the content-dependence problem that dooms Values Imposition accounts. Of course, Moral Guidance accounts cannot provide a reason to obey constitutional commands one *knows* to be morally erroneous; they cannot provide a reason to do the wrong thing. But they can leverage the ubiquitous fact of uncertainty about morality to create a reason to obey commands one *thinks* are erroneous. The premise of Moral Guidance accounts is that the constitutional process is more likely to generate morally good outcomes than the alternatives.[36] If one accepts this premise, then one has a reason to obey even a constitutional outcome with which one disagrees. That reason is that the constitutional process is more likely to have gotten it right, morally speaking, than the alternative decisionmaking procedures—including the exercise of one's own judgment. This reason for obedience stems from one's own uncertainty about what morality requires, and from one's willingness to defer to the constitutional process in cases of uncertainty. Again, parental authority is a good analogy: Even if we disagree with a particular decision a parent makes about her child, our general confidence in the comparative superiority of parental decisionmaking gives us reason to defer to that decision anyway.

Some influential constitutional theories can be read to attribute this sort of Moral Guidance authority to the act (or acts) of constitutional Framing. Alexander Hamilton, for example, suggested such an approach in *Federalist No. 78* when he elevated the "solemn and authoritative act" of creating a constitution above whatever might result from the "ill humors" and "momentary inclination[s]" of ordinary politics (Hamilton 1826). Much more recently, Bruce Ackerman's (1998) notion of "dualist democracy" invokes a Moral Guidance approach in distinguishing between the extraordinary participation and deliberation characteristic of "constitutional moments" and the rough-and-tumble of "normal politics." These approaches seem to have in common a belief that something special about the Framing process—its broadly participatory scope, its deeply deliberative nature—generates special moral wisdom that justifies our obedience to its results.

---

[36] One can imagine a Moral Guidance account that depends, not on the superior quality of the outcomes generated by the constitutional process itself, but rather on the quality of the outcomes likely to be generated by a legal subject's *interaction* with the constitutional process. The idea would be that even if there is no reason to think the constitutional process is morally wiser (more accurate) than the alternatives, a decisionmaker's need to take account of constitutional commands promotes moral wisdom (and thus morally correct outcomes) by forcing her to question the judgment she would reach were it not for those commands. This strikes me as a sort of Burkean notion—an argument for a presumption against changing the status quo without some strong, articulable reason to do so.

And indeed we need not stretch our imagination too far to conceive of such an account, as Deborah Hellman's "epistemic" justification of precedent-following in Chap. 4 of this volume appears to be one, albeit in modest form. It is important to note, however, that Hellman's account is intended to justify only the presumptive force of constitutional stare decisis, not the authority of constitutional law writ large. Her account is appealing as a justification (again, Burkean in its character) of a default rule in favor of following precedent absent a good reason not to. But constitutional law writ large, unlike constitutional stare decisis (on Hellman's reasonable understanding in any event), presents itself as an absolute requirement, not as a default rule. Our purported obligation to constitutional law is to obey it, full stop, not simply to follow it unless we can think of a good reason to do otherwise. So this Burkean version of Moral Guidance is less viable as an account of constitutional authority in general than as a justification of presumptive precedent-following in particular. And I am not aware of any advocate of originalism who has attempted to ground that methodology in this kind of Burkean argument.

It is not difficult to see how this type of Moral Guidance account might underwrite originalism. If our reason for obeying the Constitution stems from the special moral wisdom of the Framing, then we ought to identify those judgments actually made by the Framers and apply them, so far as we can, to current problems. It is the Framers' judgments that contain the comparative moral wisdom that justifies obedience; the farther away we move from actual judgments of the Framers, the more attenuated our reason for obeying the Constitution becomes. Nonoriginalist constitutional law therefore is not (authoritative) *law* at all; it has no claim to our obedience. If we want constitutional law to be law, we have to interpret and apply it using an originalist methodology.

And in fact some originalists expressly ground their methodology in versions of the Moral Guidance account. The most prominent example is the work of John McGinnis and Michael Rappaport (2007, 2010), who argue that requirements of supermajoritarian approval, like those used to adopt the original Constitution and those that apply to subsequent amendments, tend to produce rules that are conducive to the public good. This is so, McGinnis and Rappaport contend, because supermajoritarian requirements necessitate broad consensus and, given the difficulty of amending the rules they generate, impose a sort of Rawlsian "veil of ignorance" that discourages narrowly self-interested rulemaking. Obtaining the benefits of the supermajoritarian procedures of the Framing requires implementing rules actually approved by those procedures—that is, it requires originalist methodology.[37]

A Moral Guidance justification of originalism might deflect the content-dependence problem of a Values Imposition account, as I've explained. And Moral Guidance seems more plausible than a Consent account, at least as an initial matter, because it does not depend on the problematic notion that most or all Americans today have somehow consented to be bound by what the Framers decided generations ago. Moral Guidance accounts depend, rather, on whether the *process* of constitutional Framing is the procedure that is "most likely to get at the truth" about rights or other moral matters, in Waldron's (2006, 1374) phrase. If the answer to this question is yes, then arguably we would be justified in imposing the results of that process even on those who have not consented to be bound by them.

Versions of Moral Guidance accounts that focus on the special capacities of the Framing process, moreover, like that of McGinnis and Rappaport, seem capable of underwriting the typical originalist distrust of constitutional stare decisis while also

[37] Note that the particulars of the Moral Guidance account in question seem likely to determine the type of originalist methodology that should be used. If we attribute the special moral wisdom of the Framing to characteristics of the overall process, as Hamilton, Ackerman, and McGinnis and Rappaport seem to do—to its participatory and deliberative nature, for example, or to the supermajority requirement—then we ought to prefer the sort of "original public meaning" approach favored by most current originalists. That approach, after all, seems most likely to capture the superior wisdom in question, which flows (on this view) from the broadly public nature of the Framing. On the other hand, if we attribute special wisdom to something about the Framers themselves— to their extraordinary erudition or foresight or abilities as statesmen, say—then we should look more specifically for actual intentions or judgments of those particular people (an "original intentions" approach that is currently out of fashion).

potentially tempering that skepticism in certain contexts. If the authority of constitutional law resides in decisions made by the (comparatively wise) Framing process, then any departure from those decisions undermines that authority. A precedent that resolves a constitutional question without invoking the special wisdom of the Framing would lack legitimate authority, on a Moral Guidance account, and thus a subsequent decision following that precedent would lack authority as well. To follow erroneous precedent is to obey nonauthoritative law, and to require that others (those subject to the Court's rulings) obey it.

McGinnis and Rappaport (2009b) identify three possible exceptions to this principle, however. The first is simply a case in which the costs of disregarding precedent, measured in the familiar rule-of-law terms I described in Sect. 10.2.1, would be disastrously high (834, 836–37). The second and third exceptions are derived directly from the particulars of McGinnis and Rappaport's Moral Guidance account and as such are more interesting. A precedent that was decided erroneously by originalist standards might nonetheless become so entrenched, McGinnis and Rappaport acknowledge, that the precedent itself attains the equivalent of supermajoritarian approval, giving it a moral status roughly equal to rules generated at the Framing (837–41). Even more intriguingly, McGinnis and Rappaport (842) contend that some erroneous (i.e., nonoriginalist) precedents should be followed because they "operat[e] to correct imperfections in the supermajoritarian [Framing] process" itself. As I explain in Sect. 10.7.1 below, the processes of framing the original Constitution, the Bill of Rights, and the Reconstruction Amendments were saliently flawed in their exclusion of slaves and many free blacks, not to mention women and some non-propertied citizens. McGinnis and Rappaport suggest that if *Brown v. Board of Education* was incorrect on originalist grounds,[38] it might still have precedential value as an "attempt to correct" one of these "defects" (the exclusion of slaves and other blacks) "by interpreting the Constitution so that it has the content that appropriate supermajority rules would have produced" (841–43).[39]

[38] McGinnis and Rappaport (2009b, 842–43) do not believe *Brown* was incorrect on originalist grounds; but they assume it was incorrect for purposes of demonstrating their notion of "corrective" precedent.

[39] While I mostly want to avoid critiquing particular justificatory theories of originalism, I can't resist noting that McGinnis and Rappaport's maneuver here—validating nonoriginalist precedents that "interpre[t] the Constitution so that it has the content that appropriate supermajority rules would have produced"—operates as a sort of bait-and-switch. McGinnis and Rappaport justify constitutional authority on the ground that supermajoritarian requirements for making constitutional law generally produce good outcomes; the idea is that there is something special about the supermajoritarian process that generates wise decisions. For the Court to give the Constitution "the content that *appropriate* supermajority rules *would have produced*," however, is to substitute the Court's own (normative) judgment—a judgment about what *appropriate* supermajority processes *would* decide—for the (descriptive) decisions actually generated by supermajoritarian means. The distinction is analogous to that between *actual* consent (a matter of descriptive fact) and *hypothetical* or "constructive" consent of the Rawlsian sort (necessarily the result of normative judgment). (On this distinction between actual and constructive consent, see Peters (2011), 53–54.) Once the Court starts playing the normatively laden game of determining what an "appropriate" process "would have" decided, it is hard to see why the Court should accept *any* decision actually

10.7 Moral Guidance and Plausibility

Moral Guidance accounts avoid the salient objections that apply to Values Imposition and Consent accounts. But they come with their own baggage. The claims they make about the superior moral wisdom of the Framing as a general matter are subject to reasonable doubt, to say the least. In particular cases, moreover, those claims will be especially vulnerable, for two related reasons. First, particular cases often will involve issues that the Framing generation could not have anticipated and therefore could not have used its supposedly superior wisdom to resolve. Second, the fact that a person subject to a constitutional command disagrees with the substance of that command will serve, for that person, as a reason to doubt the moral wisdom of the process that generated it, and thus to reject the command's authority in that case.

I will address each of these problems in turn, using the example of a hypothetical member of Congress, Cato, who must decide whether to obey the Constitution despite his disagreement with its content in his case. Suppose Cato is asked to vote for a bill that would allow suspected terrorists to be detained indefinitely without trial. Cato thinks the bill is good policy, perhaps even necessary for national security. But he also believes the bill would violate the Constitution's guarantee of due process of law. What reason does Cato have to obey the Constitution despite his substantive disagreement with the outcome of doing so?

10.7.1 The Salient Defects of the Framing

On a Moral Guidance account, Cato's reason to obey the Constitution is that the Framing process was morally wiser than the ordinary democratic process of which he is a part. Thus Cato is more likely to do the right thing, morally speaking, by obeying the Constitution than by acting on his own judgment. But Cato will have good cause to doubt the underlying premise of this account.

The generation that framed the original Constitution (ratified in 1788) and the Bill of Rights (1791) tolerated slavery, and indeed affirmatively protected it in the document.[40] It excluded women, many people of color, and most non-propertied people from the vote. It viewed Native Americans as uncivilized savages and barred

---

produced by supermajoritarian procedures if the Court finds that decision disagreeable. The disagreeable nature of such a decision, after all, would serve as evidence that the procedure that generated it was in some way not "appropriate."

[40] Article I, § 9, cl. 1 prohibited Congress from banning the importation of slaves until 1808. Article IV, § 2, cl. 3 prohibited free states from emancipating or harboring escaped slaves. In addition, Article I, § 2, cl. 3 counted slaves as three-fifths of a person for purposes of congressional representation (and therefore also representation in the Electoral College, see art. II, § 1, cl. 2) and direct taxation.

most of them from citizenship altogether.[41] Whatever decisional advantages might have flowed from the unusually participatory and deliberative nature of the Framing probably will seem, to Cato, to have been compromised, if not entirely negated, by these salient exclusions from the process. And the supposed moral wisdom of those who did participate will appear suspect in light of their tolerance (often their endorsement) of slavery, colonial genocide, racism, gender hierarchy, and property-based oligarchy.

Now it may seem that a requirement that the Framing process *generally* be morally wiser than ordinary politics sets the bar too high. A Moral Guidance account demands only that the Framing process be relatively wise with respect to certain issues—namely those governed by the Constitution. But in fact this demand is more ambitious than it may at first appear. The Framing process, after all, determined both what to include in the Constitution and what to leave out of it. If Cato and the rest of us are bound by the Constitution, we are bound both by what the Constitution contains—by rules like the Due Process Clause and the Commerce Clause—and also by what the Constitution does *not* contain, in the sense that we are not free to give constitutional status to rules the Framers did not in fact include in the Constitution. So, for example, when originalists criticize decisions like *Roe v. Wade* for illegitimately "creating" or "expanding" constitutional rights, they are claiming that the judges who decided those cases were disobeying the Constitution, not by failing to implement rules it includes, but rather by implementing rules it does not include.

If Cato is to defer to the judgments of the Framing generation with respect to the rules they included in the Constitution, then he also must defer to their judgments with respect to the rules they left out of it. Cato must defer to the Framing, for instance, on questions involving the rights to life, liberty, and property—subjects unquestionably included within the scope of the Due Process Clauses—and also on questions involving claimed rights to, say, education or health care, subjects (arguably) not included within the scope of those Clauses. Cato must treat life, liberty, and property as constitutionally protected, and he must *not* treat education or health care as constitutionally protected.[42] On a Moral Guidance account, this means Cato must attribute to the Framing a moral wisdom that is quite broad—extending not only to the rules included in the Constitution, but also to the choice of which rules to include and which rules to omit. It will not be enough, on a Moral Guidance account, for Cato to believe that the Framing possessed superior moral wisdom on issues clearly covered by constitutional rules, like the protection of life, liberty, and

[41] Article I, § 2, cl. 3 entirely excludes "Indians not taxed" from the population to be counted for representation purposes.

[42] The fact that Cato and others subject to constitutional law are prohibited from treating these entitlements as constitutional in stature does not, of course, prevent Congress or other sub-constitutional lawmakers from protecting them through statutes or other sub-constitutional means. And I should make it clear that I am not assuming that rights to education or to health care cannot in fact legitimately be found in the Constitution. These seem like plausible examples of subjects "left out" of the Constitution, but there may be reasonable arguments to the contrary. I use them here only by way of example.

property, or the freedom of speech and religion, or equality, or the regulation of interstate commerce. Cato also will have to believe that the Framing was comparatively wise with respect to issues not covered by constitutional rules, like education and health care.

Moral Guidance accounts thus make bold claims about the relative moral wisdom of the Framing. It is quite unlikely that the Framing can live up to these claims, given its salient substantive misjudgments (the protection of slavery, for example) and its troubling procedural defects (the exclusion of women, of many people of color, and of most nonpropertied citizens). So it will take a very big leap of faith for Cato to buy into the Moral Guidance account in the first place.[43]

10.7.2 The Problem of Unforeseen Circumstances

But suppose Cato does accept the Moral Guidance premise that the Framing process, as a general matter, is morally wiser than he is (as a participant in ordinary democratic politics). Cato still might reasonably reject that premise as applied to his particular case.

In creating the rule embodied in the Due Process Clause—"No person shall … be deprived of life, liberty, or property, without due process of law"—the Framing generation, after all, could not have had the facts of his case in mind. Americans in the late eighteenth century had no experience of worldwide terrorist movements, the threat of nuclear or biological terrorism, the hijacking of jetliners for use as passenger-laden missiles, or for that matter of a society anywhere near as ideologically, racially, ethnically, and religiously diverse as our own. Indeed they could not have anticipated these developments with even the remotest degree of accuracy. In requiring due process for the deprivation of liberty, then, the Framing generation was not bringing its (by-hypothesis) superior moral wisdom to bear on anything like the actual problem Cato now faces.

So even if Cato is inclined to defer to the judgments of the Framing as a general matter, he has no reason to defer to the judgment of the Framing as applied to his particular case—simply because there is no such judgment to defer to. The rule embodied in the Due Process Clause does not include a specific judgment about how the facts of Cato's case, unforeseen and unforeseeable by the Framers, should be resolved.

[43] In presenting the foregoing argument to various audiences, I often am confronted with objections along the lines of "But the Framers were extraordinarily wise, tolerant, cosmopolitan, etc. in comparison to most people of their time." While I'm not ready to accept the historical accuracy of this proposition on its face, I have no trouble granting it for the sake of argument. Even if we assume that the Framers were comparatively morally wise for their time, that is beside the point. The Moral Guidance account rests on the notion that the Framing process is comparatively wise as compared to the alternative *present-day* decisionmaking procedures, including most relevantly the procedures of majoritarian representative democracy. Even if the Framers were wise by the standards of their day, this fact does not establish (and in my view does not even serve as evidence) that the Framing process is more likely to generate morally correct answers to the relevant questions than is contemporary democracy.

To be clear, the problem here is not that there is no constitutional *law* on the issue Cato faces. Cato, remember, has interpreted the Due Process Clause to prohibit the bill he is considering. So we are putting to one side the indeterminacy issues that might hinder the identification of "original meaning" in any given case. The problem at hand, rather, is that the (by-hypothesis) applicable legal rule does not reflect (cannot reflect) an actual judgment by the rulemaker—the Framing process—with respect to the particular circumstances confronting Cato. In enacting a rule that covers Cato's case, the Framers did not specifically consider Cato's case itself. In this respect, the Due Process Clause is no different from most general normative rules: It applies in cases that its enactors could not have foreseen.[44]

Nor is the problem here the worry that the Framing process, had it actually considered these circumstances, would not or might not have resolved them wisely. The problem is that the Framing process *did* not consider (*could* not have considered) these circumstances and thus did not resolve (*could* not have resolved) them at all. So Cato cannot know *how* the Framing would have resolved his case if it had considered it. And he cannot defer to a nonexistent judgment.[45]

Note, too, that this problem cuts in two directions: It afflicts both cases where a constitutional rule applies and cases where no constitutional rule applies. In Cato's case, his obedience to an applicable constitutional rule ("No person shall … be deprived of life, liberty, or property, without due process of law") would not be justified by the premise of the Moral Guidance account, because there is no specific judgment of the Framing to defer to in his case. But imagine a case in which no constitutional rule applies.

Suppose, for example, that an originalist judge in 1954—call him Gaius—must decide whether enforced racial segregation in public schools should be declared unconstitutional; and suppose that Gaius believes that the original meaning of the applicable constitutional provision, which provides that "No State shall … deny to any person within its jurisdiction the equal protection of the laws," allows school segregation. By Gaius's lights, there is no constitutional rule on the issue of segregation: The Constitution neither prohibits it nor requires it.[46]

---

[44] This is one cause of the phenomenon noted by Aristotle in Book V of the *Nicomachean Ethics*: that "all law is universal but about some things it is not possible to make a universal statement which shall be correct." General normative rules often produce "incorrect" results in particular cases because those cases involve circumstances the rulemakers did not anticipate.

[45] Of course, Cato might attempt to construct a specific judgment that the Framers *might* have rendered had they considered the particular circumstances he faces. But now—as with McGinnis and Rappaport's (2009b) notion of "corrective" constitutional precedents (see the discussion in note 39)—Cato has left the realm of descriptive identifications of judgments actually made by the Framers, and entered the very different sphere of normatively infused imaginings of what the Framers would or could or should have decided. Whatever comparative moral wisdom resides in the judgments of the Framers has become attenuated and perhaps has been completely abandoned.

[46] Or we might say, without affecting the substance of the argument, that there is a constitutional rule *allowing* (but not prohibiting or requiring) school segregation.

Nonetheless, Gaius reasonably might conclude that because the process of framing the Fourteenth Amendment, which includes the equal-protection rule, did not consider (*could* not have considered) “public education in the light of its full development and its present place in American life throughout the Nation”[47] in 1954, there is no actual judgment of the Framing to defer to. And thus Gaius might decide to, in effect, disobey the Constitution by ruling that the Constitution prohibits school segregation, on the ground that the Moral Guidance account offers no reason to defer to a nonexistent judgment of the Framing. Gaius’s disobedience would take the form, not of disobeying an existing constitutional rule, but rather of enforcing a nonexistent one.[48]

We can begin to see now the serious plausibility problems that afflict Moral Guidance accounts. Those accounts make ambitious claims about the general moral wisdom of the Framing process, claims that are substantially undermined by the salient moral errors and procedural deficiencies of the Framing. And they require a relatively specific judgment of the Framing in any given case, a judgment that is increasingly unlikely to exist as we move farther away from the world the Framing generation knew.

10.7.3 The Problem of Disagreement

Cutting across these two considerable difficulties is a third: A person subject to constitutional law, like Cato or Gaius, will disagree with the substance of the Constitution in most cases that matter. A subject who agrees with what the Constitution requires in her case will of course simply do whatever that thing is; she will not need to ask whether to obey the Constitution at all. Constitutional authority (like all legal authority) makes a real difference only when a legal subject disagrees with the content of a constitutional command.[49]

---

[47] This language is of course taken from the Supreme Court’s actual decision in *Brown v. Board of Education*, 387 U.S. 483, 492–93 (1954), in which the Court held that enforced racial segregation in public schools violates the Equal Protection Clause. One way to read *Brown* (not the only way, and probably not the best way) is as an act of justified disobedience of the original meaning of the Equal Protection Clause—disobedience, because the original meaning of the Clause allowed school segregation; justified, because the Moral Guidance account offers no reason to obey the Constitution absent a specific judgment of the Framing.

[48] Or (again) we might say that Gaius has disobeyed an existing constitutional rule to the effect that school segregation is allowed (but not prohibited or required).

[49] The existence of a constitutional command also might make a difference where a legal subject is uncertain about how to act: She might default to the action commanded by the Constitution. Whether legal obedience as a default rule is an instantiation of legal authority depends on the reason why the subject defaults to obedience. If she defaults to obedience for fear of sanctions for disobedience, she is not treating the law as truly authoritative, as I explained in Sect. 10.4.1. The same holds true if she defaults to obedience because the existence of the legal command serves as evidence for her that the action commanded is the morally correct or best one; now she is acting based on content-dependent reasons (reasons to attribute a certain moral status to her action) rather

The problem for Moral Guidance accounts, however, is that a subject's disagreement with a constitutional command also serves as a reason to reject that command's authority. This is because substantive disagreement constitutes evidence that the basis of that authority—the superior moral wisdom of the Framing process—does not in fact exist.

Consider Cato's belief that the terrorist-detention bill is morally good policy. The Moral Guidance account tells Cato that, despite this belief, he should obey the Due Process Clause and vote against the bill, because the process of Framing that Clause was morally wiser than he (as part of the democratic process) is. But Cato's moral approval of the bill is evidence, for Cato, that the Clause's prohibition of the bill is morally incorrect; and this in turn is evidence that the Framing process that authored the Clause was not so morally wise after all. Cato's disagreement with the content of constitutional law thus gives Cato reason to question the authority of constitutional law. And the requirement of content-independence—that legal authority be based on something other than the moral status of what the law requires—is undermined.

I said in Sect. 10.6 that a Moral Guidance account cannot provide a reason to obey constitutional commands one *knows* to be erroneous; Moral Guidance accounts require uncertainty about the content of morality. We can assume for purposes of the argument that Cato is afflicted by this uncertainty, and that most actual subjects of constitutional law share this affliction. This is not the same thing, however, as assuming that subjects of constitutional law like Cato typically lack strong beliefs about the content of morality. It seems likely that most people in a position to decide whether to obey the Constitution will, most of the time, have their own views about what morality requires; indeed we should hope this is the case, as a world in which legislators, government officials, and for that matter ordinary citizens typically are entirely at sea about what they ought to do would be a very scary place in which to live. So we can assume that many or most decisionmakers like Cato, while recognizing their own *uncertainty* about what morality requires, will at the same time have *beliefs* about what morality requires, beliefs upon which they would feel comfortable acting absent a constitutional command to the contrary.

To believe that morality requires some action (*X*) is to believe that a command to do *not-X* is morally wrong. If Cato believes, then, that morality requires *X*—say, the detention without trial of suspected terrorists—then Cato believes that a command to the contrary—say, the constitutional requirement of due process of law—is morally wrong. Now this belief by itself need not convince Cato to disobey the constitutional command. Cato, we are assuming, accepts the premise of the Moral Guidance account that the Constitution, in essence, is more likely to be morally correct than he is. Cato's acceptance of this premise might convince him to disregard his (inconsistent) belief that the Constitution is, in this instance, morally incorrect.

than content-independent reasons as legal authority requires. (Again, see the discussion in Sect. 10.4.1.) Only if she defaults to obedience for some content-independent reason—a reason to act that is unrelated to the moral status of the action—is she treating the law as authoritative.

But Cato's belief that the Constitution is morally incorrect in this instance will serve as *evidence*, for Cato, against the proposition that the Constitution is more likely to be morally correct than he is. Consider again the analogy of parental authority. We can accept the premise that parents, generally speaking, are the best decisionmakers about their children's welfare while simultaneously believing that a particular parental decision is incorrect. But our belief that a particular decision is wrong will undermine our acceptance of the general premise of parental authority. If we perceive a particular parental judgment—say, the decision not to inoculate one's children—as especially foolish, our confidence in the general principle of superior parental decisionmaking capacity will be called into doubt.

And note that—crucially—we need not reject the premise of parental authority as a general matter in order to determine that it fails *in this particular case*. We may believe that parents are the best decisionmakers for their children in many more cases than not, and even that *these* particular parents are the best decisionmakers in many more cases than not, while still concluding, based on this one (by our lights) extraordinarily foolish decision, that these parents are *not* the best decisionmakers *in this case*. Our belief that a particular decision is wrong, in other words, may convince us that this case is an *exception* to the general rule of parental authority.

The same possibility obtains with respect to Cato. Cato's belief that the requirement of due process is morally erroneous in his case might lead him to question the underlying Moral Guidance premise of constitutional authority, namely the supposedly superior wisdom of the Framing process. Or, less dramatically and therefore more probably, it might cause him to reject the application of that premise to his particular case, even as he continues to accept it more generally. Cato might conclude that because the Constitution (by his lights) is morally wrong in his case, the premise of superior constitutional wisdom therefore does not apply in his case. And so Cato might conclude that the Constitution simply does not possess authority in his case; he has no obligation to obey its command.

Note, too, that the persuasiveness of this skepticism is enhanced to the extent there are independent grounds to question the wisdom of the Constitution. And we have already seen that at least two independent grounds are likely to exist in any given case. The first is the set of reasons to question the plausibility of Moral Guidance accounts as a general matter: the arbitrarily exclusionary nature of the Framing and the saliently erroneous moral judgments made by the Framers. The second is the unlikelihood that the Framers considered any given set of circumstances like Cato's when they framed their constitutional rules. These grounds, in combination with the evidentiary force of disagreement, spell trouble for a Moral Guidance account. For the account to work, legal subjects like Cato will have to accept its rather questionable premise of generally superior moral wisdom; they will have to agree that this premise applies specifically to a given case the Framers could not have foreseen; and they will have to do so in spite of their substantive disagreement with the constitutional law in that case and their consequent doubt about the basis for the law's authority.

At bottom, then, the Moral Guidance approach is not a very persuasive grounding for constitutional authority. Part of the problem is context-sensitive: The salient moral failings of the American Framing are not inevitable features of any constitutional framing process. Nonetheless, they are features of the system we have. And the other components of the problem seem more universal. No process of constitution-making can envision every circumstance in which its rules will apply; as a constitution gets older and older, this shortcoming will grow more and more apparent. And every constitution must be capable of motivating obedience even by those who strongly disagree with the substance of its commands. If the only ground for obedience is Moral Guidance, then, constitutional authority often will fail, in our system or in any other.

If a Moral Guidance account cannot persuasively justify constitutional authority itself, then it cannot persuasively dictate methods of constitutional interpretation or determine the propriety of constitutional stare decisis. Like Values Imposition and Consent accounts, it can explain neither a preference for originalism nor a distrust of precedent.

10.8 Dispute Resolution

Where, then, can originalists turn? In theory, the three accounts of constitutionality I've canvassed to this point—Values Imposition, Consent, and Moral Guidance—all might support originalism and reject, or at least cast doubt on, constitutional stare decisis. But none of them works as a plausible account of authority.

There is a fourth type of account available, which I will call a *Dispute Resolution* account. A Dispute Resolution account locates constitutional authority in the capacity of constitutional processes to resolve, avoid, or mitigate certain kinds of disagreements. Our reason to obey constitutional commands on this account is not that we think the constitutional process is wiser than we are, but rather that deferring to that process will avoid some of the costs of disputes that ordinary democracy cannot resolve.

Dispute Resolution accounts seem more promising than their rivals as justifications of constitutional authority, for reasons I will briefly explain below. As I also will explain, however, they can support only a selective, modest form of originalism, and they are likely to favor rather than distrust constitutional stare decisis.

10.8.1 Footnote Four

The most prominent example of a Dispute Resolution account in American constitutional theory is what we might call the *Footnote Four* account, so named for its origin in the well-known footnote of that number in the Supreme Court's 1938 *Carolene Products* decision.[50] As later expounded by John Hart Ely (1980), the

[50] United States v. Carolene Products Co., 304 U.S. 144, 152 at n.4 (1938).

Footnote Four account holds that aggressive constitutional review of legislation is justified in two types of circumstance where the democratic process cannot be trusted to decide issues fairly. First, those holding democratic power might have a strong interest in consolidating that power by restricting the political process (by, e.g., gerrymandering voting rules or penalizing criticism of the government). Second, democratic decisionmaking might be distorted by irrational bias against "discrete and insular minorities" defined by traits like race or religion (as with laws, e.g., requiring racial segregation in public schools).

Footnote Four justifies constitutional judicial review as a means of preventing or remediating these democratic dysfunctions. Well-constructed constitutional rules might prevent dysfunction from occurring in the first place, by prohibiting unjustified restrictions on political speech, for example, or barring unequal treatment based on race without a demonstrably compelling reason. And politically insular constitutional courts, protected by life tenure, might impartially resolve disputes over the application of these rules, determining whether a particular speech restriction or a given racial classification is justified. Citizens will be more likely to accept constitutional resolutions of these issues than resolutions through ordinary democratic procedures, because they will see the constitutional process as relatively fair and impartial.

Footnote Four thus implies a Dispute Resolution account of constitutional authority. It holds that establishing, obeying, and applying certain constitutional rules will resolve some disputes better than ordinary democracy could resolve them. A person's reason to obey a constitutional command with which she disagrees, on this account, is that doing so will resolve (or avoid, or mitigate) some costly disagreement that otherwise would not be so well resolved (or avoided or mitigated).

As proffered by the *Carolene Products* Court and elucidated by Ely, the Footnote Four account emphasizes the impartiality of the judicial process relative to ordinary democratic politics. But the focus of the account might be enlarged somewhat, to encompass not just constitutional adjudication but the process of constitutional framing as well. Just as federal judges in the United States are buffered from the self-interests and biases of ordinary politics by the device of life tenure, so the Framers are shielded from those influences by the passage of time. Because the Framers of most key constitutional provisions have been dead for one or two centuries, they could not possibly have had a stake in the particular political controversies of our own era. Deferring to decisions made by the Framers, then, might enhance the perceived impartiality of the constitutional process. The "dead hand" problem that haunts Consent and Moral Guidance accounts is not a problem at all on the Footnote Four account, but rather an advantage.

Thus enlarged, Footnote Four might be thought to imply some version of originalism. I will have more to say on this point below. Allow me to note first, however, that a Dispute Resolution account like Footnote Four seems capable of avoiding the fatal flaws in the other justifications of constitutional authority I've canvassed. Unlike Values Imposition accounts, Footnote Four offers a content-independent reason to obey the Constitution, namely that doing so will resolve certain disputes more effectively than ordinary democracy could. Unlike Consent accounts, Footnote

Four need not pretend that Americans today have consented to be bound by everything the Framers decided; it requires only that most contemporary Americans accept constitutional law as a relatively fair means of dispute resolution. And unlike Moral Guidance accounts, Footnote Four is not undermined by the obvious moral fallibility of the Framers, by their inability to predict how their rules would apply, or by inevitable substantive disagreement with what the Constitution commands. Whether the Framers were morally wise or prescient is not important on the Footnote Four account; what is important is that the rules they devised, as interpreted and applied by politically insular courts, are more impartial than ordinary democratic politics with respect to the issues they resolve.

So there is some cause to believe that Footnote Four is a more robust platform for constitutional authority than the other approaches I've discussed.[51] But what might the Footnote Four account tell us about constitutional interpretation and stare decisis?

First, it might support originalism—but only selectively, and far from exclusively. Where the Framers can be seen as relatively impartial with respect to current controversies, Footnote Four suggests deferring to their judgments. If there is a danger of power-entrenchment by a current democratic majority, for example—laws restricting political speech, say—it might make sense to obey decisions made by the Framers, who had no interest in consolidating the political power of a majority that would exist many generations later. On some constitutional issues, however—race relations, for instance, or gender hierarchy, or religious tolerance—the Framers' relative impartiality will be far less evident, to say the least. Deference to the Framers' judgments in these areas would not be justified by Footnote Four.

Footnote Four, moreover, allows for nonoriginalist techniques where on-point judgments of the Framers do not exist or cannot be found. This is because Footnote Four attributes relative impartiality not just (or even primarily) to the Framing, but also (and perhaps more importantly) to the adjudicative process. The eighteenth-century Framers could not have considered the problems of international terrorism and weapons of mass destruction when they authored the Due Process Clause, but twenty-first-century constitutional judges can take account of those phenomena in applying the Clause. If, as Alexander Hamilton (1826) suggested in *Federalist No. 78*, "the independence of the judges" insulates them from the political self-interest that afflicts ordinary politics, then judges can apply the Due Process Clause with authority, even if what they are applying is something other than the particular judgments made by the Framers. The authority of their decisions flows not from the Framers' supposed moral expertise, but from the comparatively impartial posture of the judges themselves.

So Footnote Four seems likely to reject originalism altogether in some circumstances, and to allow for nonoriginalist techniques where originalism is indeterminate. What about constitutional stare decisis? Footnote Four will be far more receptive to stare decisis than, say, the Moral Guidance account, and in fact it may

[51] Elsewhere I have described and defended at length a justification of constitutional authority that might be considered an expanded version of the Footnote Four account (Peters 2011, 246–348).

see stare decisis as a benefit. The Moral Guidance account derives the entirety of the Constitution's authority from the supposed wisdom of the Framers, and so if the Court gets the Framers' judgment wrong, the resulting decision lacks authority. In contrast, Footnote Four attributes some constitutional authority to the adjudicative process itself. Getting the Framers' judgment wrong therefore is not necessarily fatal to the authority of a constitutional decision on the Footnote Four approach. Indeed, "getting it wrong" according to whatever interpretive methodology the Court uses need not deprive the Court of its authority—so long as the general perception of the Court's relative impartiality remains intact. Adherence to an "incorrect" precedent, then, need not be anathema on the Footnote Four account.

Indeed, adherence to precedent might actually bolster the Court's perceived impartiality (and thus its authority) on that account. Stare decisis can promote the perception of impartiality by visibly preventing the Court from reaching its preferred result; this is the essence of the most-controversial argument in defense of stare decisis offered by the plurality in the *Planned Parenthood v. Casey* decision,[52] much discussed elsewhere in this volume. A Court that is seen to be following precedent is a Court that is seen as impartial to that extent. In this sense, stare decisis might be an element of constitutional authority on the Footnote Four approach rather than an obstacle to it.

10.8.2 The Rule of Law

Footnote Four is not the only variety of Dispute Resolution account that might be thought to support originalism. Originalists sometimes defend their methodology as a way to promote the familiar rule-of-law values of predictability, consistency, protection of reliance interests, and the like (see Solum 2008, 129). The notion is that tethering constitutional interpretation to original intent or original meaning prevents courts from reaching unanticipated or widely divergent results.

The rule-of-law values might be thought to justify constitutional authority on Dispute Resolution grounds. The existence of clear, determinate constitutional rules, as I suggested in Sect. 10.2.1, would avoid most legal disputes about the issues covered by constitutional law[53] and would make those disputes that do arise relatively easy to resolve. The dispute-avoiding benefits of clear constitutional rules would, on this account, serve as a content-independent reason to obey them, thus potentially justifying their authority. The familiar insight here is that sometimes it is better for things to be (clearly) decided then for them to be decided correctly.

As an initial matter, however, it is doubtful that the rule-of-law values by themselves can justify any but the most bare-bones version of constitutional law. On some constitutional issues, it may indeed be more important that the rules be clear

[52] 505 U.S. 833, 861–64 (1992).

[53] Of course, clear, determinate rules would not avoid *factual* disputes about whether a constitutional rule with agreed content has been violated in any given case.

than that they be correct; the basic structural features of democratic government (who makes the laws, who enforces them, who interprets them) come to mind. Democratic government, or government in general, could not exist without these literally *constitutive* constitutional rules. And indeed most of the foundational constitutive rules of American constitutional law are expressed with relative determinacy in the text—rules like the qualifications to serve in Congress or as President,[54] for example, or the means of electing those officials,[55] or the procedures for enacting legislation.[56] Once a basic governmental framework is in place, however, the government created by that framework is likely to be capable of fulfilling the rule-of-law values reasonably well through ordinary legislation. Those values themselves cannot explain why constitutional law should constrain that government beyond what is necessary to constitute it.

Even where these rule-of-law values seem capable of justifying constitutional authority, they are unlikely to support either strong originalism or an outright rejection of constitutional precedent. This is because, as I noted in Sect. 10.2.1, originalism is endemically underdeterminate; rarely can it provide a clear, noncontroversial answer to a constitutional question. And while originalism might be no worse (and in some cases might be better) than other interpretive approaches in this regard, the best way to enhance the determinacy of constitutional law is likely to be the very system of stare decisis that many originalists distrust. Thomas Merrill (2007, 226) identifies three reasons to think this is so. First, "the legal norms that we apply in resolving disputed questions of law are much thicker if we look at the universe of precedent than if we look at originalist materials"; it is much more likely that the Court has addressed a particular issue, or a closely analogous issue, than that the historical materials will reveal a clear originalist answer to that issue. Second, precedent is more accessible to the relevant decisionmakers than is evidence of original understanding; Court decisions are published in publicly available, indexed, searchable reporter volumes, while "[t]he materials that bear on original understanding are vast, are frequently inaccessible, and in some cases are only now being discovered." Third, "the style of reasoning from precedent is much more congenial with the skill set of the typical American judge or justice, than is reasoning from originalist materials"; judges are trained as lawyers, not as historians.

Originalism's "special difficulty with precedent" therefore cannot be explained by reference to the rule-of-law values. More generally, a Dispute Resolution account of constitutional law lends only tepid support for originalism and cannot justify a thoroughgoing distrust of constitutional stare decisis.

---

[54] See, e.g., U.S. Const. art. I, § 1, cls. 1–2 (stating the qualifications of members of the House of Representatives); art. I, § 2, cl. 3 (stating the qualifications of members of the Senate); art. II, § 1, cl. 5 (stating the qualifications of the President).

[55] See, e.g., U.S. Const. art. I, § 2, cl. 3, & amend. XIV, § 2 (stating the election procedures for members of the House); art. I, § 3, cls. 1–2, & amend. XVII (stating the appointment (and later the election) procedures for members of the Senate); art. II, § 1, cls. 1–4, and amend. XII (stating the election procedures for the President).

[56] See U.S. Const. art. I, § 7.

10.9 The Centrality of Authority

So where does the "special difficulty" come from? The accounts of constitutional authority that answer this question are not plausible accounts. The accounts that are plausible can't answer the question.

The most honest answer might be the one given by Randy Barnett. Barnett frankly defends originalism as a means of promoting the libertarian natural rights he believes the Framers intended to protect. And he admits to ambivalence about constitutional stare decisis, rejecting those precedents that fail to protect natural rights but grudgingly accepting those that, like *Brown*, seem to correct the Framers' rare moral mistakes.

While Barnett's theory has the advantage of honesty, it suffers from the considerable drawback of failing altogether as an account of constitutional authority. Barnett offers no reason to obey the Constitution to someone who disagrees with his (or the Framers') views on natural rights. But his theory is useful nonetheless, because it casts in stark relief a fundamental truth about constitutional methodology. We cannot answer methodological questions without first deciding why the Constitution binds us at all. Originalism and stare decisis are defensible only insofar as they reflect a defensible theory of constitutional authority.

References

Ackerman B (1991) We the people: foundations. Cambridge University Press, Cambridge/London

Amar AR (2000) Foreword: the document and the doctrine. Harv Law Rev 114(1):26–134

Arkes H (1990) Beyond the Constitution. Princeton University Press, Princeton

Arkes H (1994) The return of George Sutherland: restoring a jurisprudence of natural rights. Princeton University Press, Princeton

Avins A (1967) De facto and de jure school segregation: some reflected light on the Fourteenth Amendment from the Civil Rights Act of 1875. Miss Law J 38(2):179–247

Barnett R (2004) Restoring the lost Constitution: the presumption of liberty. Princeton University Press, Princeton/Oxford

Barnett R (2006) Trumping precedent with original meaning: not as radical as it sounds. Constitutional Comment 22(2):257–270

Berger R (1977) Government by judiciary: the transformation of the Fourteenth Amendment. Harvard University Press, Cambridge, MA

Bickel AM (1955) The original understanding and the segregation decision. Harv Law Rev 69(1):1–65

Bork RH (1990) The tempting of America: the political seduction of the law. Touchstone, New York

Calabresi SG (ed) (2007a) Originalism: a quarter-century of debate. Regnery Publishing, Washington, DC

Calabresi SG (2007b) A critical introduction to the originalism debate. In: Calabresi SG (ed) Originalism: a quarter-century of debate. Regnery Publishing, Washington, DC, pp 1–40

Dworkin R (1986) Law's empire. Harvard University Press, Cambridge, MA

Ely JH (1980) Democracy and distrust: a theory of judicial review. Harvard University Press, Cambridge, MA/London

Grey TC (1975) Do we have an unwritten Constitution? Stanford Law Rev 27(3):703–718
Hamilton A (1826) Federalist no.78. In: Federalist, on the new constitution. Glazier & Company, Hallowell, pp 432–439
Hart HLA (1994) The concept of law, 2nd edn. Oxford University Press, Oxford/New York
Kay RS (1998) American constitutionalism. In: Alexander L (ed) Constitutionalism: philosophical foundations. Cambridge University Press, Cambridge, pp 16–63
Klarman MJ (1995) *Brown*, originalism, and constitutional theory: a response to Professor McConnell. Va Law Rev 81(7):1881–1936
Lash KT (2007) Originalism, popular sovereignty, and reverse stare decisis. Va Law Rev 93(6):1437–1481
Lawson G (1994) The constitutional case against precedent. Harv J Law Publ Policy 17(1):23–33
Lawson G (2007) Mostly unconstitutional: the case against precedent revisited. Ave Maria Law Rev 5(1):1–22
Lincoln A (1946) In: Basler RP (ed) His speeches and writings. World Publishing Co, Cleveland
Locke J (1963) In: Laslett P (ed) Two treatises of government. Cambridge University Press, New York
McConnell MW (1995) Originalism and the desegregation decisions. Va Law Rev 81(4): 947–1140
McGinnis JO, Rappaport MB (2007) A pragmatic defense of originalism. Northwest Univ Law Rev 101(1):383–397
McGinnis JO, Rappaport MB (2009a) Original methods originalism: a new theory of interpretation and the case against construction. Northwest Univ Law Rev 103(2):751–802
McGinnis JO, Rappaport MB (2009b) Reconciling originalism and precedent. Northwest Univ Law Rev 103(2):803–855
McGinnis JO, Rappaport MB (2010) Originalism and the good Constitution. Georgetown Law J 98(6):1693–1768
Meese E III (1985) Speech before the American Bar Association. In: Calabresi SG (ed) Originalism: a quarter-century of debate. Regnery Publishing, Washington, DC, pp 47–54
Meese E III (1986) The law of the Constitution: speech at Tulane University. In: Calabresi SG (ed) Originalism: a quarter-century of debate. Regnery Publishing, Washington, DC, pp 99–109
Merrill TW (2007) Remarks, panel on originalism and precedent. In: Calabresi SG (ed) Originalism: a quarter-century of debate. Regnery Publishing, Washington, DC, pp 199, 223–227
Paulsen MS (2003) The irrepressible myth of *Marbury*. Mich Law Rev 101(8):2706–2743
Paulsen MS (2005) The intrinsically corrupting influence of precedent. Constitutional Comment 22(2):289–298
Peters CJ (2011) A matter of dispute: morality, democracy, and law. Oxford University Press, New York
Posner RA (2003) Law, pragmatism, and democracy. Harvard University Press, Cambridge, MA
Rousseau JJ (1954) In: Kendall W (ed) The social contract. Regnery Gateway, Chicago
Scalia A (1989) Originalism: the lesser evil. Univ Cincinnati Law Rev 57(3):849–865
Scalia A (1997a) Common-law courts in a civil-law system: the role of United States federal courts in interpreting the Constitution and laws. In: Gutmann A (ed) A matter of interpretation: federal courts and the law. Princeton University Press, Princeton, pp 3–47
Scalia A (1997b) Response. In: Gutmann A (ed) A matter of interpretation: federal courts and the law. Princeton University Press, Princeton, pp 129–149
Shapiro SJ (2002) Authority. In: Coleman J, Shapiro S (eds) The oxford handbook of jurisprudence & philosophy of law. Oxford University Press, Oxford/New York, pp 382–439
Siegel RB (2009) *Heller* & originalism's dead hand—in theory and in practice. UCLA Law Rev 56(5):1399–1424
Solum LB (2008) Semantic originalism. Illinois public law and legal theory research papers series no. 07-24, Available at http://papers.ssrn.com/abstract=1120244
Strang LJ (2006) An originalist theory of precedent: originalism, nonoriginalist precedent, and the common good. N M Law Rev 36(2):419–486
Strauss DA (2005) Originalism, precedent, and candor. Constitutional Comment 22(2):299–309

Strauss DA (2007) Remarks, panel on originalism and precedent. In: Calabresi SG (ed) Originalism: a quarter-century of debate. Regnery Publishing, Washington, DC, pp 199, 217–222
Strauss DA (2010) The living Constitution. Oxford University Press, New York
Urofsky MI, Finkelman P (2011a) A march of liberty: a constitutional history of the United States, volume I, 3rd edn. Oxford University Press, New York
Urofsky MI, Finkelman P (2011b) A march of liberty: a constitutional history of the United States, volume II, 3rd edn. Oxford University Press, New York
Waldron J (2006) The core of the case against judicial review. Yale Law J 115(6):1346–1406
Whittington KE (1999) Constitutional interpretation: textual meaning, original intent, & judicial review. University Press of Kansas, Lawrence

Index

C.J. Peters (ed.), *Precedent in the United States Supreme Court*, Ius Gentium: Comparative Perspectives on Law and Justice 33, DOI 10.1007/978-94-007-7951-8,

MIX
Papier aus verantwortungsvollen Quellen
Paper from responsible sources
FSC® C105338

If you have any concerns about our products,
you can contact us on
ProductSafety@springernature.com

In case Publisher is established outside the EU,
the EU authorized representative is:
Springer Nature Customer Service Center GmbH
Europaplatz 3, 69115 Heidelberg, Germany

Printed by Libri Plureos GmbH
in Hamburg, Germany